Marijuana
The Law and You

Marijuana

The Law and You

A Guide to Minimizing Legal Consequences

Ed Rosenthal
William Logan
Jeffrey Steinborn

Published by Quick American Archives, a division of Quick Trading Company

Distributed by: Quick Trading Company
P.O. Box 429477
San Francisco, CA 94142-9477
(510) 533-0605

Publishers Group West

Printed in the United States of America

Dedicated to legalizers who would make this book irrelevant.

"Got two reasons why I cry
away each lonely night
First one's named sweet Anne Marie
and she's my hearts delight
Second one is prison, baby
the sheriff's on my trail
And if he catches up with me
I'll spend my life in jail"

Special thanks to Beverly Potter, who inspired us to publish this book.

Table of Contents

1 Growers Beware

2 How the Police Bust People

3 What to Do If the Cops Come

4 The Search

5 The Arrest

6 Choosing a Lawyer

7 The Courts

8 Basic Steps to Defend a Drug Case

9 The Theories of the Case

10 Beating the Warrant

11 Handling the Government Informant

12 Guerrilla Trial Tactics

13 Filing A Civil Rights Action As Part of an Aggressive Criminal Defense

14 Demonstrative Evidence

15 Forfeiture

A Appendices

Table of Authors

Chapter 8. Basic Steps to Defend a Drug Case
William Logan

Chapter 9. The Theories of the Case
Ed Rosenthal – Sections A and B3
William Logan – remainder

Chapter 10. Beating the Warrant
Jeffrey Steinborn

Chapter 11. Handling the Government Informant
Kent Schaffer

Chapter 12. Guerrilla Trial Tactics
Mary A. Kane

Chapter 13. Filing a Civil Rights Action as Part of an Aggressive Criminal Defense
Bobby Lee Cook and James F. Wyatt, III

Chapter 14. Demonstrative Evidence
Marvin D. Miller

Chapter 15. Forfeiture
Jeffrey Steinborn

Alphabetical Listing

Preface

by Tony Serra

Marijuana, The Law and You is a guidebook for self-defense against harsh, punitive and unfair marijuana laws. It is at once manual of legal techniques and strategies, and a manifesto to overcome the oppressive American War on Drugs.

This is a book of multiple dimensions: a reference book, a book of marijuana law, and most importantly, a book on techniques to avoid martyrdom for marijuana use. It provides the knowledge we need to protect ourselves from the authoritarian policies of the U.S. government.

This is a political book. Every marijuana user must have a copy in this era to help remain free.

Marijuana, The Law and You should first be scanned and the subject matter absorbed. Next, it should be read in depth for insight and overview. Each of us will see that it touches our needs and concerns at several levels.

The parts of the book we find pertinant should be underlined, noted, thought about and discussed with friends. We should solicit further legal opinions about them, too. This book should be used then, as both a reservoir of knowledge and a springboard for further research.

We must always be ready and vigilant. Knowing the law is one of our weapons against injustice. Understanding how the law affects us lessens our chance of becoming victims of injustice; political prisoners captured in the War on Drugs.

This book is for the realist, for the true believer and for those who wish to preserve their freedom and the Constitution.

—*Tony Serra*

Foreword

by Robert Fogelnest

Criminal. Felon. Convict. Prisoner. These are just some of the terms applied to the hundreds of thousands of otherwise law abiding people incarcerated in American jails and prisons for violations of the current marijuana prohibition. Expanded police powers, reduced personal liberty, enormous social and financial costs are some of the consequences of that prohibition.

In a recent Harris Poll, 88% of Americans responding said that they believed that drug and alcohol addiction call for medical treatment, 63% said that they thought that the federal government should spend more money on treatment, and 87% expressed the belief that some of the costs of treatment should be included in health care benefits.

A twenty-fifth year reunion survey of the Harvard/Radcliffe Class of 1969 (Al Gore's graduating class) disclosed that 80% of the Harvard graduates, and 76% of the Radcliffe graduates, had consumed marijuana at least once, and that a majority of those graduates support the legalized use of marijuana.

In June of 1994 the Special Committee on Drugs and the Law of the Association of the Bar of the City of New York issued a report, entitled "A Wiser Course: Ending Drug Prohibition," which opposed the current prohibitionist system. In September of the same year a reader call-in survey conducted by the Boston Globe disclosed

that 97% of the callers favored the legalization of marijuana for medical use.

Throughout the nation, courageous bar associations, judges, and prosecutors have called for decriminalization of marijuana. Over fifty senior judges refuse to accept drug cases as a protest against government policy.

The primary focus of current government policy with respect to drug use continues to be arrest and incarceration. The United States has, in 1994, reached an all time high of more than one million people held behind bars, one third for drug violations. This makes the U.S. the country with the highest rate of incarceration in tyhe industrialized world. Not surprisingly, a disproportionate number of those in jails and prisons are members of minority groups.

According to *High Times* magazine, in October of 1984 an ounce of marijuana could be had for as little as fifty dollars. Ten years later, the price might be ten times that amount, or more. Despite its increased cost and the incarceration of record numbers of people, marijuana has not been eliminated from society. In 1937, when marijuana was criminalized federally, there were an estimated 50,000 users. Now between twenty five and fifty million people use it, an increase of 5,000-10,000 percent.

Recent polls indicate that marijuana use is increasing again. The conclusion is clear: current government policies will not reduce the use of marijuana and continued law enforcement will result in the criminalization of many otherwise law abiding citizens at great social and financial costs to society. It is not likely to change for the better in the foreseeable future.

Unlike crimes against people or property, a new set of techniques must be employed to successfully prosecute victimless crimes. These include entrapment, purchased testimony and perjurious law enforcement officers. Every day, in courtrooms throughout America, criminal defense lawyers fight tirelessly to minimize the damage done to our citizens, and our nation, by laws which damage individuals, their friends and relatives and society as a whole more than the substances they were designed to eliminate from the scene.

Only the knowledgeable, committed criminal defense lawyer stands between an individual caught in the web of a failed government policy and the destruction of that persons life. Current laws have two arms which threaten people: imprisonment and the loss of property. Even without a conviction, current laws permit the seizure of property. Competent defense lawyers protect people from both of these injustices.

The criminal defense team defends the accused against the imposition of mandatory minimum prison sentences. These laws deprive judges of the authority to exercise their wisdom and discretion in making the sentence fit the crime, and place that power, instead, in the hands of the prosecution, composed of ambitious government bureaucrats.

Far too few jurists have the courage of Los Angeles Superior Court Judge Carol J. Fieldhouse who has stated "I refuse to dispense injustice. I wasn't put here to annihilate people because some politically hungry morons wanted to."

The criminal defense team challenges the truth of claims made by admitted criminals who have contracted with the government to provide testimony in exchange for escaping punishment themselves and often for substantial monetary incentives. The team exposes perjury by corrupt law enforcement officers who break the law in their zeal to obtain convictions, and further their careers. By protecting the individual the criminal defense team preserves and defends the Constitution. As expressed in the motto of the National Association of Criminal Defense Lawyers, it is these attorneys who serve as "Liberty's Last Champions."

This book, written by some of the most skilled, most experienced, respected criminal defense lawyers in America. These champions of liberty explain how to defend people accused of marijuana offenses. They discuss the issues and the techniques used to address them.

Using *Marijuana, The Law and You* you will learn how to confront the issues. The authors explain in detail the techniques they use to ferret out the truth and to bring reason to the court.

This book is especially important. Most people accused in marijuana cases have no experience with the criminal system and frankly, are not prepared for the bruising battle ahead of them. *Marijuana, The Law and You* describes the proceedure, and gives people an idea of what to expect, but it goes much deeper. First, the book tells people how to stay out of trouble. This may be as helpful to readers as other sections. The saying, "No one wins in a lawsuit" is doubly true for criminal defendants. They have nothing to gain, and even when they win, and are found "not guilty," it is at great personal cost.

One section of the book shows how a layman goes about choosing an attorney. Any licensed lawyer is permitted to defend the accused in a criminal case. However, only a specialist, a competent criminal attorney familiar with drug law can provide the expertise needed to win a case.

Other sections describe how the defendent can help the defense team develop a strategy, and help in investigation of the case. The attorney will find sections on cross examination of experts, courtroom techniques and winning strategies very useful.

This volume is of value to anyone who wishes to better understand how the lives and property of otherwise lawabiding people are attacked in the War on Drugs, but also to other attorneys who can study the techniques of the masters.

When he asked me to write this introduction, Ed mentioned that he had visited libraries and bookstores and had seen hundreds of books on civil law, but not one book for the public on the nuts and bolts of defending a criminal case. This book will empower people wrongly accused of criminal activity or accused of "lifestyle" crimes to help in their defense.

Editor Ed Rosenthal knows a lot about marijuana. He has studied it for more than 25 years.

He also knows more about marijuana law as any layman (and most lawyers). Through his work as an expert witness in marijuana cases, and years as an author and journalist in the field, Ed has worked with, and observed, some of the best criminal defense lawyers in the country. He understands the issues involved, the atmosphere in which those issues are litigated, and the consequences when those issues are decided adversely to the person under attack by the government. In many ways he can be looked upon as front line war correspondent.

Ed has solicited and selected materials from the top lawyers in marijuana law. He has integrated them with his additional contributions to make a cohesive, knowledgeable book about the real world of criminal defense. This book will take you into the world of marijuana and the law. Be very careful — it is a war zone.

—*Robert Fogelnest*

Introduction

by Ed Rosenthal

Marijuana, The Law and You is published to help keep you out or get you out of trouble. It was designed to show the basic concepts of the legal process as well as the nuts and bolts of trying a case. It is a guidebook and reference for both laypeople and lawyers on how to conduct a successful defense of a marijuana case. *Marijuana, The Law and You* provides the information anyone connected with cannabis needs in order to fight to stay free.

There are about 400,000 marijuana arrests each year. People are faced with hard choices which will affect them the rest of their lives. Unfortunately, there is little information for people on how to stay out of this predicament. This book describes the information police use to make arrests, how they conduct searches and what they consider suspicious.

Most marijuana offenders have little contact with the law before their arrest. They need to learn how to protect themselves and their loved ones from government interference with their liberty. These decisions should be based on a firm grasp of the situation. *Marijuana, The Law and You* tells you the secrets of some of the best criminal lawyers.

Most attorneys who try marijuana cases do not do it as a specialty. Although they may know the "law" in general, they are amateurs as compared with the narcs and prosecutors who do these cases on a daily basis. By providing literally hundreds of years of experience of some of the brightest, winningest attorneys, this book fills some of the gap.

In 1976 an acquaintance of mine was arrested for growing a few plants. He said not to worry, he had hired a lawyer. At the proceedings the private attorney, who had little experience with drug cases, was unprepared to cross examine the prosecution witnesses, who were blatant liars. He had no witnesses ready, and in fact, my acquaintance implicated himself on the stand. He was sliced and diced by the state's attorney, who even then was an old pro at drug cases. My surprised friend, who had believed he was in the safe hands of an attorney, was led out in handcuffs to serve over a year in jail. His dream of going back to school for his law degree was shattered by his felony conviction. It took him years to put his life back together. He paid a heavy price for his small garden and several sales of tiny amounts.

For a few years I solicited and edited articles for a monthly legal column which appeared in *High Times Magazine*. This assignment gave me insight into the special kind of person which makes a good lawyer. Foremost s/he has to be smart, and his/her brain must be exercised, honed and well oiled. The ones that I talked with do not suffer fools gladly, They were a challenge to work with.

The other thing that an attorney must have is fire. A burning desire to vindicate him/herself in battle by winning the case. I thought I had understood that, and had experienced it as an expert witness when it was clearly my testimony which was decisive in the case. However skipping ahead for just a moment, it was in 1995 that I truly experienced the satori, the state of ecstasy to the point of dysfunction, from helping to win a case. I couldn't work for days, but could only glow in a state of extreme pleasure. This occurred as a result of just two words repeated three times: Not guilty! (see my favorite case, following.)

One lawyer, William Logan, who is an author in this book, came to my office in 1984 to try to induce me to be an expert witness. He was the defense attorney in a marijuana case and intended to cross examine the cop. He had to show the court that the cop knew little about pot, and was not qualified to render an expert opinion. He also asked me to appear for the defense, but since I could not, he needed enough information to do it himself. I thought, this was one dedicated lawyer. He had passion and would settle for nothing less than the best he could do.

A couple of years later, I happened to attend a lecture by Tony Serra. In his intense speech, he talked about the attorney as a Viking Warrior. When he goes to Valhalla he can fight all day. In the evening his wounds are healed so that he is ready for the next day's battle. He also spoke of the attorney as a defender of liberty and justice who is the final protector of the individual against the onslaught of the government.

A few months after that, I served as an expert in my first case. Since that time, I have had the opportunity to watch some of the best attorneys do their work. I have seen the way they develop the case, their strategies and their courtroom techniques. I learned from each case. Editing this book was an accelerated version of that learning experience

The attorneys who wrote this book told me that as they read each other's work, they learned useful information that will enable them to better defend victims of marijuana laws. My hope is that by disseminating essential information this book saves a lot of time for all of its readers.

Ed's Favorite Case

The case was U.S. v Nancy and Pete[1]. The defendants were caught in an outdoor garden with 172 plants on three foot centers. The prosecution claimed the yield at ripening would be 172 lbs., one pound per plant. The federal charges were cultivation, intent to sell, and conspiracy with a total minimum 12 year sentence. Three state police testified for the prosecution.

I was the only witness for the defense. Based on the 1992 DEA Yield Data, (which is in the appendix) I showed that the plants would yield 9.5 lbs., which is consistant with personal use for two people over several years or less. Rather than concentrating on my testimony, the prosecutor tried to impugn me personally and then in a brilliant error handed the jury several legal papers I had written thinking that they would be prejudiced by them.

Obviously, he had not read the material, because they outlined our strategy (included in the Strategy and Theory sections and throughout the book) and showed that our intention in questioning their cops was to show what jerks they were (actual questions included). The arrogant prosecutor had not even showed the sample cross to his witnesses and they were were unprepared for a vigorous cross examination. They withered on the stand. For instance, they insisted that they saw sin-semilla plants and then described male flowers.

Since the prosecutor had never read the material, he did not notice that he had presented the jury with the actual sentencing guidelines. Usually the government wants to hide the sentence from the jurors because they would think it too harsh.

The jurors composed of Nancy and Pete's peers decided that they did not believe the police. They would not send these people, who had already been traumatized by the arrest and its aftermath, to federal prison. The pair were found guilty only of misdemeanor possession, with a sentencing range of 0-6 months.

I was already back home when the jury verdict came in. I could not believe it. As its meaning permeated my totality I glided into an ecstatic state which lasted for several days. I imagine that a good attorney could be driven just by the desire to achieve that near orgasmic state often.

The attorneys for the two defendants, William Rork and the team of Irigonegaray and Eye were excellent. They were able to integrate into the defense the techniques described throughout this book and to develop a cohesive strategy. At the end of the trial and with a verdict better than we hope for, we were one happy team.

Growers Beware

A. ABROGATION OF THE BILL OF RIGHTS

Since the 1970s, the United States government has been creating a new set of crimes, based on hearsay and intent rather than actual perpetration. The RICO and CCE laws allow the government to prove a case against an individual with no hard evidence. (RICO stands for "Racketeering-Inspired and Corrupt Organizations;" CCE stands for "Continuing Criminal Enterprise.")

To enforce these laws, the government has developed new ways of interpreting the Bill of Rights. For instance, "use immunity" has been used to gut the Fifth Amendment's protection against self-incrimination. Under the 1987 crime bill's provisions, which have been upheld by the Supreme Court, your testimony under oath provides you with immunity from prosecution for the crimes described in your testimony. However, the state is allowed to prosecute you if it can build a case without using your testimony to gather the information that proves your crime.

The "good faith exception" to the Fourth Amendment's protection from search and seizure without probable cause has made a mockery of that provision's intent. Warrants are routinely issued without probable cause, allowing informers to use public information to bolster credibility. (The suspects have two kids named X and Y and a white four-door 1968 Falcon. They live in the white house on Extecey Street. They have an unusual electric box on the outside, left side of the house.) Just to tip the scales in favor of police misconduct, the courts have held that even if the warrant is bad, the prosecution can use the illegally gathered evidence as long as the officers acted "in good faith."

In the 1970s, the government instituted a revolutionary new set of laws, worse than any seen in this country since the infamous Alien and Sedition Acts, which were enacted under John Adams's administration and repealed soon after.

First the conspiracy laws were revamped so that any planning for a criminal act could be considered a conspiracy, and the planners could be prosecuted for that conspiracy. (Two people conspiring to commit a misdemeanor are committing a felony.) The RICO and CCE acts have also been used to make mountains out of molehills.

When these laws were under consideration, their proponents claimed that they would be used to clean up the Mafia, or Cosa Nostra. However, since their enactment, they have been used to fill federal prisons with unfortunate schnooks. All that is required for you to fall victim to these statutes is that the prosecution prove you were involved in two related criminal acts. (Two sales of dime bags?) The conspiracy, RICO, and CCE laws have created a whole new class of criminal: someone the government just wanted to nail.

Originally, the idea that there must be a reason to deny a citizen his/her liberty led to the concept that to prove a crime you must present a body of evidence. If there is no evidence, there is no crime.

B. THE BILL OF RIGHTS

The provisions of the English Magna Carta were written into the Bill of Rights, which comprises the first ten amendments to the United States Constitution. They are as follows:

Amendment I. Congress shall make no law respecting an establishment of religion, or prohibiting the free exercise thereof; or abridging the freedom of speech, or of the press; or the right of the people to peaceably assemble, and to petition the Government for a redress of grievances.

Amendment II. A well regulated Militia, being necessary to the security of a free State, the right of the people to keep and bear Arms, shall not be infringed.

Amendment III. No Soldier shall, in time of peace, be quartered in any house, without the consent of the Owner, nor in time of war, but in a manner to be prescribed by law.

Amendment IV. The right of the people to be secure in their persons, houses, papers, and effects, against unreasonable searches and seizures, shall not be violated, and no Warrants shall issue, but upon probable cause, supported by Oath or affirmation, and particularly describing the place to be searched, and the persons or things to be seized.

Amendment V. No person shall be held to answer for a capital, or otherwise infamous crime, unless on a presentment or indictment of a Grand Jury, except in cases arising in the land or naval forces, or in the Militia, when in actual service in time of War or public danger; nor shall any person be subject for the same offense to be twice put in jeopardy of life or limb; nor shall be compelled in any criminal case to be a witness against himself, nor be deprived of life, liberty, or property without due process of law; nor shall private property be taken for public use, without just compensation.

Amendment VI. In all criminal prosecutions, the accused shall enjoy the right to a speedy and public trial, by an impartial jury of the State and district wherein the crime shall have been committed, which district shall have been previously ascertained by law, and to be informed of the nature and cause of the accusation; to be confronted with the witnesses against him; to have compulsory process for obtaining witnesses in his favor, and to have the Assistance of Counsel for his defense.

Amendment VII. In Suits at common law, where the value in controversy shall exceed twenty dollars, the right of trial by jury shall be preserved, and no fact tried by jury, shall otherwise be reexamined in any Court in the United States, than according to the rules of common law.

Amendment VIII. Excessive bail shall not be required, nor excessive fines imposed, nor cruel and unusual punishments inflicted.

Amendment IX. The enumeration in the Constitution, of certain rights, shall not be construed to deny or disparage others retained by the people.

Amendment X. The powers not delegated to the United States by the Constitution, nor prohibited by it to the States, are reserved to the States respectively, or to the people.

As a result of the experiences of the Civil War, and the realization that all citizens had certain rights, the Fourteenth Amendment was ratified in 1868. Since the early 20th century it has been considered by Constitutional scholars to be a part of the Bill of Rights. The first section reads, "All persons born or naturalized in the United States and subject to the jurisdiction thereof are citizens of the United States and the state in which they reside. No State shall make or enforce any law which shall abridge the privileges or immunities of citizens of the United States; nor shall any State deprive any person of life, liberty or property, without due process of law; nor deny to any person within its jurisdiction the equal protection of laws."

C. HERE COME THE FEDS

Each state has its own rules and laws regarding the amount of marijuana you can possess or grow and still not be a major criminal. Marijuana is illegal everywhere. Familiarizing yourself with how bad it could be will help you make an informed decision as to how bad you want to be. The most pathetic case is the defendant who says, "I didn't think it was so bad to possess/grow that much."

The federal law applies to everyone, all the time, in every state. There are supposed to be rules, criteria, guidelines that federal prosecutors follow in deciding whether or not to prosecute your case. The truth is that the Feds prosecute you if they want to. No reason is required.

Growing or possessing on federal land is usually prosecuted in federal court. Cases are passed off to the state only if the operation is small and the prosecutors have a busy schedule. Federal border busts in San Diego, California, can be resolved as a misdemeanor on the right day, in the right court, with the right defendant and good legal moves.

Cultivation projects on BLM (Bureau of Land Management) land usually wind up in federal court unless they are very small. The federal 100-plant-minimum mandatory sentencing seems to influence the cops.

ENGLISH COMMON LAW

English common law, a system that was imported to America, evolved over a period of a thousand years. One of the main protections offered by the law is the requirement of a writ (legal order) of habeas corpus.

Habeas Corpus

Habeas corpus became part of English law as a result of a peace treaty signed by King Edward the Elder in 906. In 904, Aethelwold, his cousin, led the Danes (Viking colonists) in East Anglia and Northumbria to revolt over unjust treatment. In order to keep the barons' loyalty, Edward agreed to a legal code known as the Laws of Edward and Guthrum. Among the concerns of the Danish barons that were addressed was the king's habit of imprisonment without cause.

The code was generally adopted as English common law and was reaffirmed by various kings during their reigns, most notably Henry I (who reigned from 1100 to 1135), who promulgated the Leges Henrici, whose goal was to maintain the Laws of Edward and Guthrum.

The Magna Carta

The concept of limitations on the rights of the crown (read "government") was even more clearly delineated in the Magna Carta, signed by King John. King John increased taxes to pay for two disastrous wars in which he unsuccessfully attempted to reclaim lost territories in Normandy. To ensure the barons' compliance, he forced them to put up hostages. The entire population had grievances. The government was accused of corruption, nepotism, strong-arm tactics, discounting the people's wishes, and generally lowering the standard of living. King John alienated the church by temporarily placing its finances in lay hands and appropriating the money to the royal treasury.

Finally, tired of the corruption and abuses resulting from absentee management, the barons formed a council. First they had all the local sheriffs swear allegiance to it, rather than to the king. John, realizing that he had no choice, agreed to meet with the barons. On June 15, 1215, the barons they presented him with their demands, known as the Articles of the Barons, which became the basis for further discussions. A more elaborate charter was signed later in the year.

Article 36 of the Magna Carta states, "Nothing shall henceforth be given for a writ of enquiry touching life or limb, but it shall be granted freely and not denied." This reaffirmed the common-law rule that a person cannot be placed in custody except for a criminal charge, conviction, or civil debt. *Habeas corpus*, literally translated, means "produce the body." It commands the custodian to present the prisoner to the court and to show cause why s/he is imprisoned.

The Shaftesbury Act

In spite of the promises of earlier kings, later monarchs continually eroded their subjects' rights. The situation came to a head in 1679 after a few celebrated cases in which King Charles II refused to act on writs by petitioners. Parliament passed the Habeas Corpus Act, sometimes called the Shaftesbury Act (after its chief supporter). Upon presentation of a writ, it called for the following: (1) The custodian has to bring the prisoner to court and show why s/he is being held. (2) The prisoner must be allowed to post bail. (3) There can be no reimprisonment once a prisoner is set free on a writ. (4) There must be a speedy trial or discharge from indictment. (5) There can be no imprisonment in distant or overseas territories.

Growing or distribution efforts that seem to be interstate or international in scope are often seen by the Feds as fair game. Shipping some bud back East may be a righteous thing to do, but the Feds will be alerted if the U.S. Postal Service, UPS, or Federal Express gets suspicious and busts the load. They are also likely to prosecute if the bust occurred at a federal or state border, if the suspects were obviously out-of-town talent, or even if the stay-at-home, purely local crime is just "too big" for the local courts to adequately punish.

The last and most disgusting use of federal (versus state) prosecutorial power is when the search warrant is illegal under state law and the evidence is, or probably would be, suppressed by the state court. Since state courts follow state rules and precedents, and federal courts look to federal law and precedents, it's quite possible that your state gives you (or would if it could) more protection from a cop's illegal actions than do the Feds. The Feds, remember, allow the "good faith" acceptance of a bad warrant, which has all but nullified the protections of the Fourth Amendment.

The law allows state and federal prosecutors to decide who to prosecute, and for what. Even if the state prosecutes and you're found not guilty, you can still be prosecuted by the Feds. Federal rules apply to state busts and state cops when these come to federal court.

If you've been prosecuted by the state court and a jury has brought in a verdict of not guilty, it may be more difficult for you to be prosecuted in federal court for the same crime, but it's not impossible.

The Feds also have a series of creative "crimes" they can charge you with. Conspiracy is considered a separate crime. There is always some inventive prosecutor who can think up a (slightly) different crime to hit you with. You'd think that if you were not guilty of hitting someone, you wouldn't be guilty of violating their civil rights by hitting them. Courts have ruled otherwise.

E. SENTENCING GUIDELINE COMMISSION

The Federal Sentencing Guideline Commission, was set up to devise uniform sentencing guidelines. The purpose was to give the courts less discretion in handing out sentences. The Commission has been a prosecutor's dream. Regular Joes are regularly slapped with 5- to 10-year sentences as their property is confiscated and their dependents thrown out on the street.

In 1989, the Commission announced guidelines for implementing the laws of the Omnibus Crime Control Act. These guidelines determine the sentences for various crimes. In marijuana cases, the sentencing level is determined by the quantity of marijuana seized by the government.

F. SENTENCING GUIDELINE LEVELS

Though few people would seriously object to a long sentence for a violent repeat offender, long mandatory sentences for marijuana crimes seem cruel and unusual. There may be over 100,000 people in state and federal jails for pot crimes. The Feds won't release the figures because they know the public would react adversely if the truth were known.

If you're busted or prosecuted by the Feds, your relevant offense conduct (defined below) and your offense level, which is calculated from it, are extremely important. "Relevant offense conduct" refers to anything that you've done that has relation to what you're charged with. The judge decides on the relevant offense conduct and, thereby, on the offense level. These are terms used for the purpose of defining, for sentencing purposes, how serious your criminal activities were. The crime you were charged with or were convicted of does not matter. The jury and prosecutor are not the final deciders of the amount of product you must stand trial for.

Once you have been convicted and a date has been set for sentencing, the judge will order you to report to the probation office for an interview with a probation officer. If you are held in custody until sentencing, then s/he will visit you. The probation officer investigates you by reading the police reports and talking to the cops and the prosecutor. You get an hour or less to tell your side of the story. The probation officer creates a Presentence Investigation Report, which is presented to the court. If you disagree with the opinions voiced in the report, you can try to show the judge at sentencing that the numbers in the report are bogus. For instance, an independent report can be prepared by a specialist hired by you. The judge decides the relevant offense conduct, and thereby the offense level. S/he then goes to the charts, and the drug quantity table shows where you fit into the great scheme of crimes and criminals in America.

You can be given additional time for many individual factors that are or are not present. Accepting responsibility for your crime is good, having a leadership role is bad—that sort of thing.

Your mouth can send you away for a long time, as can your coconspirators. The rules are simple because they are so uniformly, unflinchingly hard: If the federal probation officer knows about some deal you did, thought of, or talked about, involving a certain amount of marijuana, you'll probably be facing that weight at sentencing.

The general rule is: *more dope, more time.* The cops, the federal probation officer, and the Assistant United States Attorney seem often to be working to find and/or create scenes and deals just to raise the weight and your time. The poor Placerville, California, marijuana grower with 55 plants never thought it would be so bad until the two cops each counted 55 and then they added them together. The 100-plant magic number appeared and the fun began.

1. Basic Levels for Marijuana

SENTENCING GUIDELINE LEVELS

Level	Pot Weight	Hash Weight	Hash Oil Weight
42	300 kg	60,000 kg	6,000 kg
40	60,000-299,000 kg	20,000-60,000 kg	20,000-6,000 kg
38	30,000-<50,000 kg	6,000-20,000 kg	600-2000 kg
36	10,000-<30,000 kg	2,000-6,000 kg	200-600 kg
34	3,000-<10,000 kg	600-2,000 kg	60-200 kg
32	1,000-3,000 kg	200-600 kg	20-60 kg
30	700-1,000 kg	140-200 kg	14-20 kg
28	400-700 kg	80-140 kg	8-14 kg
26	100-400 kg	20-80 kg	2-8 kg
24	80-100 kg	16-20 kg	1.6-2 kg
22	60-80 kg	12-16 kg	1.2-1.6 kg
20	40-60 kg	8-12 kg	800 g-1.2 kg
18	20-40 kg	5-8 kg	500-800 g
16	10-20 kg	2-5 kg	200-500 g
14	5-10 kg	1-2 kg	100-200 g
12	2.5-5 kg	500·g-1 kg	50-100 g
10	1-2.5 kg	200-500 g	20-50 g
8	250 g-999 g	50-200 g	5-20 g
6	Less than 250 g	Less than 50 g	Less than 5 g

2. Enhancements

Besides the basic levels for possession, extra points are given for growing on federal property, using booby traps, carrying firearms, leadership of an organized group, and a myriad of other violations.

The federal laws regarding possession and cultivation of marijuana were last amended in 1989. They are based on the weight of dried processed marijuana or the number of plants involved in a cultivation.

The way the statute is written, if the grower has 49 or fewer plants, for sentencing purposes each plant is considered to weigh 100 grams—a little more than 3½ ounces. However, if the grower is responsible for 50 or more plants, for sentencing purposes each plant is considered to weigh 1,000 grams, or 2.2 pounds. A grower with 51 seedlings or rooted clones is sentenced for 51 kilograms.

For this reason, growers should never cultivate more than 49 plants.

G. SENTENCING TABLE

Once the sentencing guideline level is determined, the court follows another chart, which considers the criminal history of the convicted person. The points are calculated as follows:

3 points: Each prior sentence of more than 13 months.

2 points: Each prior sentence of more than 60 days.

If the crime was committed while the person was on probation or parole, was under supervision by the court, was imprisoned, or escaped.

If the crime was committed less than 2 years after release from imprisonment.

1 point: For each prior sentence of less than 60 days (up to 4 points).

Once the level is determined, the judge refers to the sentencing chart. For each level, there are six different sentencing tables. The most lenient table, Table 1, is for the victim with a previously clean slate, including a job and stability, who would otherwise be considered a credit to the community. Table 6, the harshest, is for the "unredeemable," who have had previous bouts with the law and are considered scum by the courts. Most drug convicts fall somewhere in the middle.

NUMBER OF MONTHS IN FEDERAL PRISON

Level	Table 1	Table 2	Table 3	Table 4	Table 5	Table 6
6	0-6	1-7	2-8	6-12	9-15	12-19
8	2-8	4-10	6-12	10-15	15-21	18-24
10	6-12	8-14	10-16	15-21	21-27	24-30
12	10-16	12-18	15-21	21-27	27-33	30-37
14	15-21	18-24	21-27	27-33	33-41	37-46
16	21-27	24-30	27-33	33-41	41-51	46-57
18	27-33	30-37	33-41	41-51	51-63	57-71
20	33-41	37-46	41-51	51-60	63-70	70-87
22	41-51	46-57	51-63	63-70	77-96	84-110
24	51-63	57-71	63-78	77-96	92-115	100-137
26	63-78	70-87	78-97	92-115	110-137	120-162
28	78-97	87-108	97-121	110-137	130-162	140-152
30	97-121	108-135	121-151	135-168	151-188	168-210
32	121-151	135-168	151-188	168-210	188-235	210-232
34	151-188	168-210	188-235	210-282	235-293	262-327
36	188-235	210-262	235-290	262-327	292-365	324-405
38	235-283	262-327	282-365	324-405	360-life	360-life
40	292-385	324-405	360-life	360-death	360-death	360-death

H. SENTENCING REGULATIONS

1. Cultivation Kicker

This is how the law calculates the weight of a grower's plants: In the case of an offense involving marijuana plants, if there are 50 or more plants, treat each plant as equivalent to 1 kilogram of marijuana; if there are fewer than 50 plants, treat each plant as equivalent to 100 grams of marijuana. However, if the actual weight of the marijuana is greater, use the actual weight of the marijuana.

This means someone convicted of cultivating a garden of 140 mature plants and 100 cuttings is considered to be growing 240 kilograms of marijuana—Level 26—and is sentenced to between 63 and 150 months, depending on his/her prior legal history. Although the evidence might weigh less than 3 kilograms, s/he is sentenced as if s/he were a large-scale grower. A true case of blind justice—with a thumb on the scale.

This is a direct violation of the rule of habeas corpus, that the crime with which the defendant is charged must fit the body of evidence. By ascribing an arbitrary set weight to the evidence regardless of its actual weight, the government is discarding one of the major concepts on which our laws have been built and evolved for the past thousand years.

> Judges have very little discretion regarding sentencing or humanizing the law. In a case in the Pacific Northwest, some small-time growers were convicted under the 1988 guidelines, which defined each plant as 100 grams no matter what the actual quantity. They were caught with a garden of mature plants that weighed only 10 grams each. In spite of the evidence, the judge declared the law constitutional and sentenced the drug offenders according to the guidelines.

2. One Thousand Plants

Another section of the law, Section 841 1A, states:

"Except as otherwise provided in Section 845, 845a or 845b any person who violates subsection (a) shall be sentenced as follows:

"1000 kilograms or more of a mixture or substance containing a detectable amount of marijuana, or 1000 or more marijuana plants regardless of weight:

"Such person shall be sentenced to a term of imprisonment which may not be less than 10 years or more than life and if death or serious bodily injury results from the use of such substance the term shall not be less than 20 years or more than life, and a fine not to exceed $4,000,000. If a person commits such a violation after a prior conviction of a felony drug offense has become final, the person shall be sentenced to a minimum of 20 years and not more than life and if death or serious bodily injury results from the use of the substance, shall be sentenced to life imprisonment."

3. One Hundred Plants

"100 kilograms or more of a mixture containing marijuana or 100 or more marijuana plants regardless of weight. Such a person shall be sentenced to a term of imprisonment not less than 5 years or more than 40. 20 years if death or serious bodily injury occurs, and a fine of up to $2,000,000. With a single prior drug felony: 10 years."

4. Ninety-nine Plants

"In the case of less than 50 kilograms of marijuana, except in the case of 50 or more marijuana plants regardless of weight or 10 kilograms of hashish or one kilogram of hash oil, such person shall be sentenced to imprisonment for no more than 5 years and a fine of no more than $250,000. If the person has a prior drug conviction, the term of imprisonment shall be no more than 10 years."

5. Life Imprisonment

"If a person commits an offense after two or more prior convictions for felony drug offenses have become final, the person shall be sentenced to mandatory life imprisonment."

I. TIME OFF

Under the federal system, only 15% of the sentence can be subtracted for good behavior. A person sentenced to 10 years in prison serves a minimum of 8½ years.

How the Police Bust People

A. INFORMERS

Everyone who has read a whodunit or seen a detective movie has a good idea of how sleuths work. They examine all the evidence; they use tips, hunches, and psychology to find the perpetrator. Narcs use these techniques too. They also use lies, extortion, and blackmail to bust and convict people.

> In one case, an attorney was charged with cultivation. He and his girlfriend had gotten into a verbal fight and he had ordered her out of his house. She dialed 911. When the police arrived, she said, "The marijuana plants are in the other room."
>
> * * *
>
> Another grower got into a disagreement with a customer, who called in the police.
>
> * * *
>
> A student in San Diego had 51 very small plants in his backyard. Unbeknownst to him, his neighbor could see the plants and, on the basis of his religious beliefs, condemned the use of God's herbs. He turned in his neighbor, and got a small financial reward too.
>
> * * *
>
> A group of workers were at a bar. A few of them went outside to smoke a joint. A coworker took note of who went outside and reported the stoners to his company because he resented working with "drug abusers."
>
> * * *
>
> A grower split up with his flaky partner and they divided the plants and equipment. Flake's plants died and he was very envious of his successful former partner, so he turned him in.
>
> * * *
>
> One of two best friends, C, started growing. The other, D, couldn't because of his housing situation. At first C gave his friend D free pot. After a few months, he offered to sell stash to D at a nominal price. D became angry as C prospered. C was fronting D stash, but had not been paid. D asked for more pot. C refused and asked his friend to pay the money he owed. D turned C in.

There are some things you can do to minimize contact with police, and to reduce the impact if such contact does occur. Most busts result from the information provided by an informer, from an accident, or from suspicious activity. Investigations also account for some busts. Many of them can be avoided with a little care and common sense.

1. The Snitch Mentality

People become snitches for a variety of reasons. Anger, self-righteousness, and envy are the three most common.

The number of people turned in by snitches for personal reasons pales by comparison to the number of people who are snitched on by arrestees who seek to reduce the number of counts for themselves. This is the cops' favorite way of busting people because it takes little time, effort, or intelligence on their part to get a good scorecard.

Charges are often reduced if a defendant "cooperates" by turning in friends or associates. Under federal sentencing guidelines, a defendant's sentence is reduced if s/he turns in other people. These are potent weapons used by the state to induce people to snitch. They have caused family members and best friends to betray each other. These laws and policies have turned American morality on its head. Nobody respects a tattletale, yet American courts are turning citizens into snitches. Rather than teaching responsibility for one's actions, the government is now teaching its citizens that the honorable path is to unload your time onto someone else.

> K was growing in the hills and lived in a house in the nearby town where he kept his equipment. He invited an underage girl over. She was later picked up for shoplifting and snitched on him in exchange for leniency.
>
> * * *
>
> L was sentenced to 6½ years for cultivation. After 4 months in prison, he squealed to reduce his sentence by 18 months.

Obviously, smart growers keep their activities as secret as possible and on a need-to-know basis. They never discuss their garden, show it to anyone, or even tell people that they own one. A good way to arouse suspicion is to "imply" a garden: Talking about it, or about how plants grow, or about how you used to grow them, is sure to bring an inquiring mind closer to the garden.

> Grower E met two women in a bar in August and, later, the boyfriend of one of them. He offered to smoke a joint with them. The boyfriend was a former ripoff artist turned informer for profit. He figured this guy's leaf joint meant ownership of a garden. He "befriended" E and, a month later, after gaining E's confidence and inducing E to front him most of the harvested crop, turned him in.

2. Recognizing Snitches

How do you recognize a snitch?

Does someone you know seem not to need legal advice from a lawyer after a serious bust? Perhaps s/he is getting it from the cops or the prosecutor.

Does s/he want to talk about "old times"—including dates, names, and amounts—over the phone? Does s/he want to discuss where the money went? Does s/he suddenly begin to address friends by the names their mothers gave them, instead of "Smokehole" or "Stinky"?

Is there a big change in the drug-use habits of a recently busted friend? Did s/he really "reform" or did s/he agree with the cops not to use while s/he busted others? S/he always used to come and smoke a doobie. Now s/he just wants to score and split.

If the person who has sold ounces for years suddenly has a great deal on drugs, or offers to buy or sell them in quantities out of proportion to his/her usual amounts, or in partnership with a money or drug man who is "backing" the deal—something may be fishy.

Cops—and especially snitches—smoke and snort to "protect themselves" in an undercover situation. That can mess up their credibility in court. Generally they don't do it, and they almost always deny having done it, irrespective of the truth. The defendant's word against theirs is a dicey proposition at any time. If the defendant is saying s/he supplied and also did the drugs that the cops did, how does that help? How does s/he establish the cops' misbehavior without testifying to his/her own and blowing the rest of the case?

> One case was resolved because a credible underage witness testified that the cop and the informant did drugs and offered them to her. The phone records verified her calls with them, which helped show she was telling the truth. This kind of evidence is always important for impeachment, but only rarely can it be used to muscle the prosecution into a deal or a dismissal.

THE UNINVOLVED-CITIZEN INFORMANT

The uninvolved citizen is considered the most reliable type of informant. The police need no corroboration of his/her report of crime for them to act upon it. Usually the citizen informant is a person who is a victim of or a witness to a crime. Obviously, if someone sees a bank robbery and says "That's the man," the police don't have to do much verification in order to detain and probably arrest the suspect. The same holds if a hunter, fisherman, backpacker, or other tourist sees a back-country project, or if the meter man sees the Jesus Light beaming from under the garage door. Their information is probably good enough for the police to get a warrant and make a visit.

If somebody at the electric company notices that a meter is showing the consumption of a lot of juice, they may suspect the existence of a grow room and call the cops. They're sometimes rewarded with money for this tip ($1,000 per bust in my area), so assume they're looking diligently. This information may bring the cops to the house, where they'll try to see the project, or they may fly over with Forward-Looking Infrared Radar (FLIR) to see if it's hot. They check trash cans (perfectly legal), ask a compliant UPS for delivery records, and gather information from cooperating grow-supply stores. All this goes into an affidavit to support a search warrant; it's usually issued, and the garden is usually busted.

Burglars and robbers sometimes become citizen informants. It might seem, on a moral and ethical basis, that the person who comes with larceny in his/her heart and a weapon on his/her hip is more deserving of prosecution than the person who is growing a weed for his/her own use. It is unusual, however, for police and district attorneys to be sympathetic to marijuana growers to any extent whatsoever. There was an almost-forgotten time when marijuana growers were given a reasonable disposition of the case (and, though rarely, a dismissal) in return for their testimony against the people who were there to rob them.

Growing marijuana and possessing it for sale carries a maximum sentence of 3 years in jail in California. Assault with a deadly weapon and kidnapping with bodily injury can add up to life in prison. The law does not recognize a right to protect

A worst-case scenario (which, fortunately, ended well) occurred when a grower discovered two young pirates in the patch, armed with pruning shears and knives, carrying burlap bags in which they meant to haul the take, and wearing rubber Richard Nixon masks. Upon confrontation, the young culprits fled. After a brief chase, one of them fell over a bank on the edge of the road they were traversing and broke his leg. The pursuers caught him and ordered him to crawl back up to the trailer near the garden. Realizing he was truly injured, they took him to the hospital to receive medical attention; at the same time, they took his brother to a highway intersection to hitchhike home. In the ultimate act of charity, they gave him money for food during the journey.

After two days in the hospital, the young thief decided that the growers were responsible for his situation and told the police the location of the marijuana garden. He related some of the details of the episode to the police (omitting the fact that he was there to steal the pot). They arrested husband, wife, niece, and nephew on charges ranging from kidnapping with bodily injury to possession for sale and cultivation of marijuana. Some of the charges carried a prescribed penalty of life in prison without possibility of parole.

As the objects of a successful investigation and a skillful interrogation, the alleged victims of the crime—the pirates—realized that the truth would be extracted under cross-examination and that pursuing the case this was not in their best interest. They declined to testify against the pot growers. The four adult pot smokers were growing 24 small plants. The court ordered them to participate in a program of treatment, education, and rehabilitation (drug diversion). The case was eventually dismissed. The moral of this story is "Threatening pot pirates with guns increases your potential liability a hundredfold."

pot crops. Don't think that the police will have any sympathy for you under these circumstances.

Before a prospective deal, the buyer might consider why a dealer who has the ability and desire to move a large quantity of product would give a small-timer such a good deal, or why such a dealer would even deal with him/her in the first place. After all, most people in the illegitimate business of dealing dope have all the connections they want or need. The middle ground of buyers who sell and sellers who broker for others is well filled.

Sometimes the cop or the informant buys small quantities several times, then asks to do a bigger deal (buying or selling). Usually there is an unnamed person behind the scenes who wants to "okay the product" or "see your money" before the deal goes through. Police sometimes ask to see a sample, then come back with a search warrant for the rest of it.

Remember the four elements of any drug bust: cops, crooks, drugs, and money. If cops and two of the other three are in the same room at the same time, there's trouble in paradise. All four together are really a problem.

4. Undercover Cops

Police and their agents don't have to admit they're cops if they're asked directly. Being undercover means you never have to say you're sorry. The whole modus operandi of undercover cops is to lie to you well enough to make you believe they're not what they are. Their lives may depend on their ability to fool you, a veteran crook. They seldom have much trouble. An average judge or jury member doesn't stand a chance of being able to tell when an undercover cop is lying. These guys are professional liars and they love doing it!

The mentality of the undercover cop is too strange for the average person to grasp. Why would someone be your friend, pay your bills, eat your food, stay in your house, occasionally sleep with you or your daughter (or son), and then bust you and everyone around you? I think these Judas-goat/informant/undercover narcs are sick people. The few honest ones I've met got out of the work as quickly as they could. Two years is about as long as anyone of real substance and moral character can successfully live the convoluted lies that the undercover lifestyle demands.

Statistics show that many narcotics enforcement officers are not honorable men and women. The rate of ripoffs, drug thefts, payoffs, and general sleaze in the drug law world is frightening. My clients don't all lie about the sleazy things cops or informants did to and with them, and if a tenth of what they say is true, then the system is in grave danger and we're living in a truly Orwellian situation. Who do you call if the cops are crooked? A hippie? The Guardian Angels? Parents Against Pot?

B. ACCIDENTS

1. The Accident

Accidents occur at the most inopportune times.

Grower G was growing in a commercial space above a gallery. The day before the gallery was to open a new show, the grow room sprang a leak.

* * *

A rented car stalled and its trunk popped open while it was being towed.

* * *

There was a fire next door and the fire department broke in to reach the other apartment.

* * *

Grower H bypassed the meter and circuit breaker to power his system. First there was a small fire, then the electric company investigated.

Although a person can't always stop accidents from happening, many of them can be prevented or ameliorated. For instance, a passive watering system is less likely to leak than an active one. Smoking a joint in a car while transporting grass could create a disaster. Using an unlicensed car, or one that stands out or has mechanical problems, is asking for trouble.

2. Loose Talk

Loose talk is a major category of being stupid in public. People don't talk to strangers about their medical or sexual problems. Growing projects are at least that important! Telling anyone who doesn't need to know is taking a huge risk. Once you've told your secret, no one can predict or control who will hear it, what fact or fantasy they'll hear added to the repeated story, or where it will ultimately be told.

In small towns, everyone gets the local gossip: what you do for a living, who you sleep with, what habits you have. No one can control this, but you can be careful. It's necessary to have some "legitimate" work or source of income. You must be doing something to pass the time. Having inherited money is not uncommon, and removes the need to "work" for a living. Getting welfare assistance in the off season and passing as wealthy when the crop comes in is not good form.

Conspicuous consumption in a small town may verge on stupid in public. Except for those who have a publicized inheritance, smart growers do not exceed reasonable expectations of visible income or lifestyle. Instead they go on vacation in the city, where $100 bills are commonplace, and where, without raising any eyebrows, they can be the people their neighbors never see.

If you party excessively at harvest time, and flash cash, you'll be identified as a grower. The garden's location will become a matter of speculation. If it is at or near your house, it will be found.

If you attract the attention of the wrong sort of people, you and your family could be in serious danger. There are armed thieves out there who will kill.

Successful growers resist the temptation to talk to strangers who seem to have an interest in growing. Even if the stranger doesn't know who you are, s/he can bring unwanted attention. Undercover cops often say they're growers, and seem to know a lot, and don't hesitate to talk about their projects. Smart growers won't take this as a sign that these are "real" or friendly people. Shouldn't these friendly people be more careful? Would you want to put your life in the hands of such fools?

People who act outrageous in public often are busted and cause official inquiries into their lives. This causes problems, especially if they're not prepared to answer questions about their money sources (the car, the land payment, and the food must come from somewhere).

> One grower successfully harvested his crop, but got rowdy in the development where he lived. The cops came, smelled the pot, and arrested him.

3. The Automobile

Many busts result from an auto stop. This is a fertile area for law enforcement because people lose some rights when they enter a private or public vehicle.

a. A Clean Body

The most obvious, and most often overlooked, cause of a bust is a vehicle that has mechanical defects. Broken lights, brakes, turn signals, tail lights, headlights, and even the lowly license plate light provide ironclad probable cause for any cop, anywhere, any time, to stop a vehicle.

After the stop, the vehicle is likely to be subjected to at least a cursory search. It could be more intensive. At worst, it's a thorough poke-around and smell, sometimes with a dog, looking for things "in plain sight."

To avoid suspicion and hassle, careful drivers also wash the car, clean the windows, and have a working horn and windshield wipers.

The second major cause of mobile inconvenience is the traffic cop. Unless you obey all traffic laws, especially those small-town speed limits, you may have to talk with a cop. You should have your valid license and car registration with you. Even though some states don't require car insurance, many drivers have found it safest to carry it and have proof of it with them. Noncitizens should have a valid visa or green card ready.

It is a false economy to avoid any of this preparation. Not having the car in good and legal shape, or not having proper documentation, can mean years in jail. The time you spend in preparation to protect yourself and your freedom pays off a thousandfold.

b. A Clean Interior

A nosy cop can bust a suspect after seeing a roach or recognizing stash. If the suspect is carrying a stash of less than 1 ounce, perhaps an opaque container is enough to keep it private. Some non-see-through types of plastic kitchenware are popular in my area *[or were until this book was published—Ed.]*, and stash boxes (especially road boxes) come in all types, sizes, and materials.

Less favored are containers that advertise or display their contents. I have a metal tin whose bold print announces that it contains "One Ounce of Grass" and also specifies "a lid" of grass. The original contents were tea bags of Lemon Grass Tea (a decidedly non-controlled substance). However, the canister begs for police inspection, and is far too cute for use outside the home. Clear plastic bags, or clear plastic-wrapped packages,

are also bad choices, because the contents can come into "plain view" much too easily.

One of the most ingenious road boxes I've seen is an oil can or auto-products can that has been converted to a safe. These inexpensive, easily obtainable devices have saved many people a lot of trouble by being so obviously a "regular thing" that they were not even inspected. The cops know about these cans, so they might look into them. Some of them have reverse threads on the bottom; some have "real stuff" in part of the can, so that it sprays or pours a little of the advertised contents if tested.

If the police must open or, even better, if they must break open a package to see and recognize its contents, the law affords the victim of this break-in more protection from police intrusion and invasion of privacy. The stash package should be closed and sealed.

You should never consent to any search. However, you should not deny that the package is yours or disclaim any interest in it, because the law protects only those things that you choose to keep private. Of course, you must take some minimal, reasonable precautions so that a cop standing where s/he has a right to be (such as giving you a ticket or at a sobriety checkpoint) can't see or smell contraband.

Smart travelers don't smoke pot, use alcohol, or ingest any other drugs while they are driving. It's both illegal and stupid. People who can't control their habits are placing themselves in a more dangerous situation. They could suffer from their abuse of drugs.

c. The Package in the Trunk

If the police can't prove your fingerprints are on the inside of the container holding the pot, and you say nothing, the prosecutor and the cops must show somehow that you knew the dope was there. Possession of the container might not be enough to show you knew of the contents. Who put that in the car? When? Who else drives the car? All these questions, if left unanswered at the scene, can convince a jury that you're not guilty.

Larger packages are subject to the same rules. If the package is wrapped, sealed with tape, and not associated with the people in the vehicle (for instance, if it has been put in the trunk), the cops must have some evidence to show that people in the vehicle knew the package was there, and that they knew what was in it.

In one case, the packages were addressed ("That's not my handwriting!") to Joe Zingo, with Stan Smith's return address. At trial, the defendant has an open field run with the questions of who these people were, why they had the package, and what they were going to do with it. A courtesy extended to an acquaintance, such as taking the package to the post office, is not evidence that you committed a crime.

Let the police look for Joe and Stan, the owners of the package. Can the defendant describe them? Why must the defendant know where they live? How did s/he meet them and get their package? When will s/he see them again? A bit of mental preparation will enable you to answer the questions easily and consistently, at the proper time and place—which is not to the cops at the scene.

It amazes me that travelers rarely develop a cover story and rarely have lawyers and bail arranged. This lack of preparation looms much larger if they're arrested.

The single most important rule for travelers is to invoke their constitutional right to remain silent and to have a lawyer present while talking to the cops. In all cases, the traveler should be polite, identify him/herself, ask if s/he is under arrest ("Am I free to go?"), and refuse to consent to a search.

It may be that the cop stopped the person for a bad tail light, saw a wrapped and sealed box, and said, "What's in the box, kid?" or some local variation thereof. Ideally, the proper response is to

politely ask, not answer, questions. This is an absolute right, and you should always protect your rights, because they protect you from unreasonable police intrusion into your life.

The perfect answer to the "What's in the box, kid?" question is to ignore it. Miss Manners says that difficult social situations are handled by politeness, so we don't have to be rude or lie to anyone. If we're asked a rude or indelicate question, ranging from "Can I search your car?" to "Are these kids yours or adopted?" the polite thing to do is not to answer the question, but rather to respond with a question of our own, which we follow up relentlessly until the original question is forgotten or abandoned.

A good response to the "What's in the box, kid?" question is to ask why you were stopped, or to offer the paperwork to the cop while talking about the license, the car registration, the weather, or your cousin Bill. Given the physical distractions of handling the papers and listening to your ramblings, the questions may fade.

If the cop persists in his inquiry as to whose package that is, what's in it, and why it's in the car, you should ask him why he wants to know, what the problem is, what he thinks it is. Does he have a tip, or is he just curious, or what? If it's just idle curiosity, he has no need to know. You need no reason whatsoever to say "No" to cops who just want to poke their noses where they shouldn't be. Just be careful to be polite to them.

The cops may say that a suspect's refusal of consent to search can be used as evidence of guilt and of knowledge of what the suspect (and now the cop) knows is in the box. That's a lie. Assertion of constitutional rights can never be held to be evidence of guilt of anything. If that weren't the rule, we'd be forced to choose between the rights guaranteed to us, and suffer for making the choice.

If you don't consent to a search of the box, and don't say it's not yours, there are very few legal ways a cop can get inside the box, and almost all of them require a search warrant issued by a judge. If you haven't done anything else to get yourself arrested, the judge won't issue a search warrant based on your refusal to consent to a search, and unless the cop lies and says you consented to the search, the evidence will be suppressed.

d. Who Controls the Box?

There's no harm in saying that the box is in your custody and under your control. This is not admitting any knowledge of its contents.

If you say the box is *not* yours, you'll later find that you goofed. The law protects only owners and others with a legitimate expectation of privacy in an area searched or a thing seized. If the box is not yours and you don't assert the natural, logical right to control it and exclude others, you don't have legal standing (discussed below) to suppress any evidence uncovered by the search.

People usually do this because they feel that asserting some association or control over a package with drugs in it will incriminate them. "Hey, man, it ain't my package," in all its more or less eloquent forms, regularly appears in police reports. If the box is in the car you're in, whether it's yours or not, the jury will want to hear some explanation of the W's — Who, What, When, Where, Why. The time to give that explanation is at trial, not at the scene. Absent some other explanation, the jury normally believes that people own items found in their cars.

When the subject of a stop tells the police that the box is in his/her custody and under his/her control, s/he is not necessarily admitting that s/he knows the circumstances surrounding the contents. S/he must be able to explain coherently how s/he got the box, from whom, and what his/her intent was with regard to it (apart from the contents, of which s/he has no knowledge).

Some items in a car make cops less suspicious. A babyseat and some kids' items such as a doll, teddy, or book make cops less nervous. Legal papers, kept neat in a file box but clearly marked (not your case) makes them less inquisitive. Cars marked as company vehicles are less interesting to cops. A box of books in the backseat makes them more respectful.

If you give an explanation like this at the scene of the encounter with the police, you'll find that the cops immediately begin to try to discredit the story. You'd be best off waiting for the attorney to arrive before you try to give any detailed explanation.

If you take someone else's package to the store or post office for him/her, you have the possessory right to control the box, and to keep other people from taking it or opening it. If you say, "The box is in my custody [or control] now and I cannot give you permission to open it," you've asserted enough of your rights to challenge the search later, and you can still go to trial saying "Prove it!" about the contents of the box.

If you say you have control over the box, this doesn't mean you know what's in it, or have any possessory or ownership (or even use) rights in the contents. Opening a package prepared and ready for mailing, without a warrant, is a fairly serious thing. On the other hand, mailing drugs is a major crime.

If things are sticky, you won't talk yourself out of an arrest. The cop will just take your statements and twist them or remember the bad parts. If you say nothing, there will be no debate about what was or was not said. Any statement that helps will help more with a lawyer present. Any statement given without a lawyer will be used to screw you later.

It is a truly rare person who is adequately prepared and able to tell the story to the cops at the scene and to have it told to his/her benefit later in court.

C. GROWERS BEWARE!

The federal government wants to put growers in prison. To accomplish this goal, a Draconian series of laws have been enacted that have little relation to justice and make a mockery of the tradition of law that has developed over the past thousand years.

1. Suspicious Activity

The United States is the most violent industrialized country. As a result, it has one of the most paranoid populations in the world. Americans are suspicious of people who simply look or act differently than they do. This has serious implications for the grower of marijuana.

> Grower I lived in a suburb in South Dakota. Other houses in the tract had crew-cut lawns and looked neat. I's house had a lawn overgrown with weeds and messy drapes showed through the windows. J lived in a quiet apartment development, most of whose tenants were young families. There was constant traffic to and from his apartment.
>
>   * * *
>
> M was an oil maker. One spring day, he went to his town's fair, where he got into a conversation with a narc who was in uniform that day. The cop told me later that he smelled pot on M. Several weeks later, M went to City Hall to apply for a permit. The same cop noticed him and, obviously, learned his name and address. Later that day, while M was out, a 911 hang-up call was mysteriously made from his house. The police answered the call and found some oil.

2. Respect Mother Nature

Disrespect for Mother Nature can invite a bust. I've visited gardens where the ground was littered with trash—discarded grow supplies, empty fertilizer boxes, broken pipe fittings, and other junk.

> In one case, the forest itself seemed to be offended and an eerie sequence of events "accidentally" led to the bust. Trash carried out by the growers, and small animals who raided it, were spotted quite far away, arousing curiosity. An observer took a short walk to a nearby ridge overlooking it all and made a call to the cops, who easily followed the trash dispersal pattern and located the garden and the growers. The man who called the cops said he could see the litter, not the plants; in the remote back country, that was enough to bring it all down.

Cut branches and uprooted vegetation are a giveaway. Smart growers treat the garden as a part of the natural landscape. The aerial overflight has ended the clean-cut methods of the '70s. The cut end of a branch may stand out because its color or shape is not natural-looking. A 3-inch-diameter branch cut can be visible for a quarter mile. It is easily, if accidentally, spotted from any airplane or helicopter that happens by, cops or not.

Any disruption of nature stands out. Nonnatural shapes and colors stand out dramatically. From an airplane, the circular shape of the piled brush enclosure, or of the DoughBoy pool used for water storage, is eye-catching.

Paths are also quite noticeable from the air; if they lead to anything of interest, a bust will follow. Established animal trails to and from gardens are often used. Obvious paths, from anywhere people might be expected to come from, should be avoided. Rocks can be used as stepping stones, tree limbs as bridges; other "trailless trails" can be devised to break the line from any well-traveled path to the private one.

One project was compromised by the removal of one limb of a tree. The people on the main path had never considered fighting their way through the live oak brush covering a well-constructed and almost invisible path. The location was blown after four years because one of the laborers decided to make it easier to get to the garden. He removed one branch. The path stood out and begged to be walked on. It led to the water spring and the garden site. No bust, but only because the grower immediately knew it was over and moved the garden.

Unbusted growers' paths are tended like Zen gardens. A person who "sees" the environment can "read" which creatures have been visiting. There are usually areas of clean, bare dirt where one would ordinarily leave a trail. To conceal activity, these are swept clean coming and going, leaving no tracks to be seen.

One successful grower always left her shoes at the garden and took care not to leave tracks as she came and went. She knew immediately when a person had been on her path, but by carefully following the tracks, she was able to tell the project had not been compromised. She was brave, and took many extra precautions until harvest.

3. Notes from Underground

Almost everyone knows that a clearing in the woods with neat rows of plants in it is easily spotted during a flyover or a walk-by. Any investigator who saw something so obviously the work of human hands, in such a remote area, would instantly be suspicious.

Fences erected to keep deer or cows out of the patch can disturb the landscape sufficiently to appear from the air as geometric and regular—not natural—features. Another argument against fencing is that any person who happens by knows that something is going on behind the fence. Cops in airplanes and helicopters look for the color and shape of the plants and the shapes of garden areas.

There is some truth in the idea that marijuana has a particular color. Some studies have indicated that a particular wavelength of light is specific to marijuana plants. The Feds have used super-sophisticated, computer-controlled, color-differentiated spectroscopic analysis from satellites and spy planes to determine the extent of coca and cannabis cultivation worldwide. The usual "color bust" comes because the plants are well fed and well watered, unlike the struggling native vegetation. One grower's solution was dinner for all the plants in the neighborhood.

In a number of cases, I've gone up in a small plane, checking to see whether cops actually could have seen the garden as they said they had. The bottom line, most of the time, is that the judge agrees with the cops that they saw what they said they saw. It's very difficult to prove they didn't see what was, in fact, there. In my experience, cops can identify cannabis from 400 yards.

Water lines are responsible for some seizures. If the line is not buried at least 6 inches deep, it has a very distinctive infrared signature (worm lines on the hillside), easily identified by the cop with an infrared video camera. If a hiker or deer hunter sees water lines or an in-stream pickup system, either a bust or a ripoff may soon follow. A garden using a stationary reservoir as a water source is an easy bust. One grower claimed he was never busted because he used a water-bag reservoir, mounted in his pickup, to irrigate his plants. He buried the lines.

Paths to and from the water and the project are clearly visible from the air, and often direct attention to the garden. It is likely that animals have made trails near the project. These trails can be used gently, but not cut and pruned and worn down to a wide swath.

Careful growers want to know before they get to the project if someone has been there. One grower told me she developed several spots along the path where she could check for strange footprints. She found that both sandy and muddy areas can serve this purpose. Native Americans used tall grass. They could see where it had been trampled.

Likewise, footprints (shoe tracks) are just like fingerprints. Wise growers avoid taking home the shoes they wear in the garden. Even a particular kind of mud found on shoes, or particular vegetation stuck to clothing, can be used in court.

Usually man-made things, not the plants themselves, attract attention. I've gone into the bush with cops and fishermen and stood 10 feet from a garden, expecting some notice and comment. They didn't see it, I didn't mention it, and we walked away. I took a picture in Jamaica when our tour bus stopped so we could enjoy the scenery. Only later did I see the 50 or so 8-foot-tall marijuana plants about 30 feet from the bus.

Good fences around the property, posted with lots of "No Trespassing" signs, can help—or can hurt if they stick out as an overly emphatic assertion of privacy.

Growers are sometimes trapped by their tools. Cops try to match equipment from the project with material from the house. If the grower has garden tools at home, do they match those at the garden? Did s/he buy the pump they found? Are the suspect's fingerprints on the hoses, timers, books, food, and other items at the site? Most growers leave prints around because it's almost impossible to work on a garden and always wear gloves.

The smart grower keeps his/her stash well hidden. S/he expects that if cops bust a garden and connect it to him/her, the cops will search his/her house and sift through his/her life history.

Paper trails of money and drug sales are hard to hide and easy for the cops to get. The prophet Bob Dylan said, "To live outside the law you must be honest." Or at least appear so, say I.

Someone else might put a different spin on a person's irresistible urge to save every roach and empty bag. The prosecution could claim that it is "prepackaged marijuana for sale" and "packaging material."

Violence in the trade has increased as the per-ounce price of marijuana has rocketed past the per-ounce value of gold. If a small bag or a plant is worth thousands of dollars, there are reasons to be fearful as well as careful. However, guns always imply violence, and the cops and courts take them very seriously. The cops and the system consider any gun or other weapon a big threat. People face years in prison for having a gun available for offensive or defensive use when growing or dealing marijuana. I advise all growers to get rid of their guns.

4. Photos

Many people photograph gardens they've worked on. Some photos may be from this year or last year; some might be from 10 or 20 years ago. Photos are very strong evidence against you. Inventive federal prosecutors have seen CCE (Continuing Criminal Enterprise) charges lurking in a proud grower's photographs.

Occasionally the photo processor is the rat. The lab technician may look at your roll of film to pass the time or for quality control. If s/he notices a garden, s/he may report the photos. Rewards are regularly given for information that leads to a bust, especially one with a property seizure attached to it.

5. Phone Taps

After a bust (or even before), outlaws sometimes notice clicks and pops and wheezes on the phone line. Is somebody listening in on your conversations, or is it just a flaw in the phone company's service? The technology available to any major law enforcement group enables it to tap phones without your being able to tell. They merely have to put something near the wires that eventually lead into your house in order to pick up what's going over those wires.

On the other hand, it's extremely difficult to obtain a legal wiretap warrant. A federal judge must review the circumstances and issue that warrant. These warrants are usually issued only in the largest, most involved drug investigations. The decision as to what constitutes a "big" drug dealer or investigation is entirely dependent on how much the cops have to do and who else they're hassling this week.

A final observation: Very few policemen would be willing to risk their careers by conducting an illegal wiretap. If one were discovered, it would cost the cop not only the case but probably also his job and pension, and might even lead to prosecution and a prison sentence. I think most police officers are too concerned for their own welfare to commit this violation of the law.

Car phones, or any other cordless instruments, have no privacy. The cops can, and do, listen to the radio waves legally without a warrant. A simple scanner will let them, or anyone, listen to you. There are so few exceptions to this the that smart dealers take this slogan as gospel: "Use a cordless, go to jail."

6. Stealth

Careful growers remove nails and strings used for drying racks after use. All leaf parts, stems, pots, and equipment are removed and disposed of.

All unused growing supplies are placed in or near the vegetable garden, or off the property. Supplies such as manure, hoses, or anything like that are not stockpiled.

> Cop photos showed a 30-bag stash of worm casting, a soil supplement, next to a shack in the woods with no landscaping. It was visible from the front driveway of the house, a place where the cops have an arguable right to be, even on pretty slim grounds.

Starter plants in a greenhouse are an invitation to trouble when seen by a neighbor kid poking around the yard.

I am repeatedly amazed by the number of otherwise sensible growers who think nobody notices what they're doing.

> A real estate agent in California was busted and convicted of conspiracy to grow because of an empty shipping box that had previously held grow lights. The box was addressed to another person (according to the label), but lights of the same kind were found in the starter room at the project house, and the realtor had sold the land three times to growers, all of whom had been busted. The last time, the cops were angered by the agent and decided to look carefully at what was at his house and office.
>
> * * *
>
> A major conviction and property seizure were obtained when a cop said that the now-empty room in the barn had been a grow room, and that starter plants there had later been taken out into the country and planted in five separate gardens. The defendant had never been seen in any of the gardens, just "in the area" on his motorcycle, on public roads. In the room in question (according to the cops) was a pattern on the floor indicating big pots that had leaked excess fertilizer. That and one marijuana leaf in a spiderweb in a corner. Guilty.

The United States Supreme Court says you can have no expectations of privacy for trash you place in a can and put out for collection. That means the cops can root around in your trash like true pigs and become amateur garbologists. This esoteric science is used to generate expert (?) opinions about what is going on inside the house, based on what is thrown out. It shows that there is probably no depth to which the cops will not descend in order to bust you for growing. They'll arrange with your trash collectors to receive the trash picked up by the latter. (If you have good trash karma, the trash people may tell you the cops have asked about you.)

BEAT THE HEAT GUIDELINES

1. There is no foolproof test to tell whether you're dealing with law enforcement personnel. It does no good to ask, "Are you a cop?" Cops are allowed to lie about being a cop. Narcs are allowed to do drugs. People you have known and trusted for years may have become informers. Entrapment is extremely hard to prove in court: you have to show that you had absolutely no interest in using/selling drugs, before the police invited you.

2. When dealing with the police, keep your hands in view and don't make sudden moves.

3. If detained or arrested, don't talk to the cops. Just give your name and address; say you're not going to answer any other questions; then ask for a lawyer.

4. Police are only required to read you your rights if both: (a) you're under arrest and (b) they want to ask questions. If the cops ask you questions, but haven't arrested you, and you answer their questions, your statements will be used against you. More importantly, if you are arrested and the cops don't ask questions, but you talk to them, your statements will be used against you. Just because the police did not read you your rights, doesn't mean that you can beat your case.

5. If you've been arrested and accidentally started answering questions, don't panic and give up. As soon as you remember your rights, state, "I want to remain silent now. I'm not going to say anything else without a lawyer."

6. If the cops come to the door with an arrest warrant, step outside and lock the door. Cops can search any room you go into. Don't go back into the house to get your wallet or use the bathroom. If they do have an arrest warrant, hiding in your house isn't likely to help, so you might as well go, without letting them inside to search.

7. Do not let the police into your home if they don't have a search warrant. Don't let them "invite themselves in." Make sure to say, "You do not have my consent to enter this house." If the cops say they do have a search warrant, take it and read it to see whether it's real. Look to see that it's signed, and has your correct address and a recent date. If the warrant is no good, tell them to go get another. The cops may threaten to tear the house apart if you make them get another warrant, but they'll probably do that anyway, even if you let them in immediately.

8. If you're a minor, and one of your relatives or teachers is telling you to make statements to the police without your lawyer there, don't give in. Be respectful but firm. Don't let an authority figure talk you into giving up your rights.

9. Watch out for the Good Cop-Bad Cop routine. Remember that the "good cop" is likely to be someone of your own race or gender. Watch out for other common interrogation techniques, such as insisting that your buddies have snitched you off, so you might as well snitch on them; or claiming that the police have all the evidence they need to convict you, and your best bet is to confess right away. It's easy for cops to play games with you when you're scared and alone.

10. If you're arrested with friends, make an agreement that no one will make statements to the police until everyone's been able to talk to a lawyer and decide what to do. Be aware of the paranoia which tends to set in after you've been separated.

11. In jail, don't talk to your cell mates about what happened to you, who was with you, or even whom you know. Stick to safe topics, such as: movies, music, sports, sex, etc.

E. POLICE INVESTIGATION

1. Techniques

The police rarely initiate an investigation on their own. Usually they're given a tip, information from a snitch, or other leads. Once they start, they have many options.

Legally, they can do quite a few things to check on indoor cultivation. They can go to the electric company and see if there is unusually high use of electricity. They can check around the perimeter for grow light leaks, odors, or unusual activity such as high traffic. They may also observe growing equipment or activities inside the house. Other investigative techniques include questioning neighbors and checking the auto licenses of visitors.

The police can also use thermal imaging, which measures the infrared energy coming from the house. The more heat an object emits, the better it shows up on a thermal image. Electric companies use the technique to show homeowners where they have heat leaks in their homes. Anything emitting heat shows up: warm-blooded animals, heaters, hot water pipes, and electric lights. High-wattage lamps show up brighter and in greater detail than low-energy-emitting objects.

Thermal imaging can be a potent weapon, but it has its limitations. It works best in one- or two-story buildings. An inner room of a third-story apartment, or the inner portion of a basement, is fairly immune to this kind of search.

The police are not allowed to trespass on the property immediately surrounding the home, nor can they use a ladder to peer over a fence. However, they can ask a neighbor to let them look while on his/her property. Though the police are constrained by the Fourth Amendment, private parties are not. For instance, a private party could use a ladder and binoculars to peer into a house or yard, an action police cannot legally take, and then report his/her findings to the police, who could apply for a search warrant based on the report.

To initiate an investigation, police sometimes get a warrant based on an "anonymous" tip or the information of a snitch. Of course, this immediately promotes corruption among the police, who often make the anonymous calls themselves or tell a person in trouble who to snitch off. "We know that you know N. He sold you this dope, right?" Recorder on. "I bought the dope from N."

a. Advanced Computer Sensing

I handled a case that began with a flyover at about 50,000 feet with the U-2 spy plane. The plane was equipped with colored differentiated x-ray spectroscopy, computer-linked to LORAN. Every time the computer thought it saw the particular wavelength of light that is characteristic of marijuana and of no other plant, it noted the location. Later, the local narcs were given calls telling them where to look. The narcs went over the designated areas in fixed-wing aircraft and saw the pot.

When the case came to court, the local narc conveniently omitted any mention of the information he'd previously received. Only after he was thoroughly cross-examined by a team of highly skilled lawyers did that information come to light.

After a brief recess to summon the appropriate officials from the local naval weapons station, questioning resumed. The witness indicated that, in fact, the equipment on board was protected by the National Security Act and that the court could go fly a kite or jump in the lake or some similar euphemism if it thought he (the witness) was going to tell it much of anything.

What he did tell the court was extremely upsetting. He said that the U-2 could look into your backyard from 50,000 feet and tell what you were eating for lunch, as well as probably the dates on the coins lying on the picnic table next to you (and possibly even the mint where each coin originated). It "certainly" could identify marijuana as a specific plant in a specific location from those altitudes. The moral of the story: The helicopter you hear may be the electric company fly-ing high-tension wires, but the spy eye in the sky may be spotting gardens.

b. Cops: Smart or Stupid?

Occasionally outlaws learn through a simple twist of fate that somebody is watching them, knows what's going on, is hip to the situation. Perhaps the police have been told by an informant, seen the garden during a flyover, or discovered by other legal or illegal means that something nasty is going on.

Based on my experience over the years and interviews with many growers, successful and unsuccessful, I think the facts must be analyzed from two points of view:

1. The police are extremely intelligent, devious, conniving, sophisticated, well equipped, and capable.

2. The police really are that dumb. They really do make classic blunders. They really are stu-pid enough to send somebody up to the front door when they'd be better off sneaking around the back.

If you analyze the known facts from both of these bases, you may see that one or the other (or, damn it, sometimes both) explains the conduct of the police.

Outdoor growers have told me that they've heard the whirr of helicopter blades at some point during the project and asked themselves the ques-tion, "Should I stay or should I go?" There is never a clear answer, but I've heard two proverbs on the subject that I appreciate:

•   Discretion is the better part of valor.

•   To live outside the law you must be careful. (Attributed to Lee Doyle, 1970.)

One case exemplifies stupid police tricks. The officers came to a house with a warrant authoriz-ing them to search for drugs. Immediately upon entry, they went to a couch in the front room and put one gram of cocaine under a cushion. Apparently because they thought they were going to find many more drugs of other kinds in the house, no one bothered to write this piece of evidence down as Number 1 on their search war-rant inventory.

After a futile search of the entire house, which turned up no other drugs of any kind (but lots of other bad stuff), the police went back to the couch and "discovered" this one gram of cocaine. It turned out that when they'd entered the basement, they'd taken a piece of plywood that was leaning up against the wall and put it down on the floor so they could scru-tinize the wall surfaces. They didn't realize that they'd covered the floor safe with the plywood. They walked over the plywood and the safe for about 6 hours while they proceeded to disman-tle the house, even removing the wallboard from the upstairs bedroom walls. They never did find the safe.

In another case, the police narcotics agents went out to bust someone named by an informer. On arriving at the scene of the "cov-ered buy," the officer in charge realized that he had busted this particular suspect about a year earlier. Rather than call things off and arrange other personnel for the deal, the officer decided to go ahead with it (apparently deciding to see just how stupid the suspect was).

The defendant confided later that he had thought the officer looked very familiar, but had placed him as a prior satisfied customer, rather than the officer who had arrested him on a pre-vious occasion. Perhaps marijuana does affect your memory. You'd think no officer would be so bold, or so stupid, as to try to pull a scam on the same person twice. You'd also think the vic-tim would recognize the cop who had busted him the preceding year.

2. Blessed Anonymity

In the musical *Fiddler on the Roof*, one character asks, "Is there a blessing for the Czar?" The rabbi answers, "May God bless and keep the Czar—far away from us." This is also the best relationship an outlaw can have with the government. Act inconspicuously, look inconspicuous, and be inconspicuous. Your vehicle should be in good working order and be intelligently camouflaged. It should be neither too new or too old and not too expensive. Your home should be kept neat. The garden and lawn should be typical of the neighborhood. Free growers do not brag, show conspicuous wealth, or make their friends envious.

Neighbors can be an outlaw's best friends or his/her worst enemies, since they often are aware of what is going on before the suspect realizes s/he is in trouble. Smart growers have friendly relations with their neighbors and do not promote suspicion or hostility.

3. Sensitivity and Respect

Busted growers often tell me they knew the bust was coming. They saw the plane; chased away the "hiker;" fired a gun near hunters to scare them. Plainclothes cops sometimes go for a look around and leave footprints, cigarette butts, and other evidence (in one case, an empty doughnut box). If there's a particularly good place (bad for you) from which to observe the garden without being seen, the smart grower checks that place religiously to make sure s/he is not being watched.

Cops like to play cat-and-mouse. If they spot a garden in May, they may wait until October to visit. In a bust, starter plants can be just as big a headache as the monster females. In federal cases, sentencing revolves around plant *count*. Plant size, weight, sex, and yield are not considered. If weight is a consideration in state law, the local cops will probably wait a while to try to catch the grower with some high-weight bud.

Smart growers keep their eyes and ears open. They stay aware of the normal and usual routine at the project (indoors or outdoors, rules are the same!) in case they spot something unusual. Even the most sensitive person may not have an easy time deciding if what s/he has seen/heard/felt was real or imagined, important or merely coincidental. There are very few sure signs you can use to tell if you're being watched. Even when one is faced with almost positive proof, one's inclination is to keep things going.

Many people sit in their attorneys' offices crying the blues about being busted after ignoring clear signs. It is safest to react swiftly and completely to any and all indications that the project has been compromised. If too many people—or *any* of the wrong people—know about the project, there's a very good chance that the grower will get a visit from cops, ripoff artists, or both.

Cops may talk to people who know about a suspect. Will a garden supply store snitch off the customer if asked by government agents? Can the store give your correct address? Credit card information is just like a searchlight pointing to you and your activities. Smart growers are discreet. They buy used items at flea markets, or through the classifieds, or at sympathetic businesses.

The clerks behind the counters at grow supply stores and nurseries may give out customer names to the cops without a whisper or a word to you. If the customer uses a phony name and the cops note and trace the license plate of the vehicle in which the customer came to the store (true story!), it could end up in an Affidavit in Support of a Search Warrant. Delivery is a problem too. UPS cooperates with the cops and assists in busts by having a look around, giving information, and even setting up bogus deliveries complete with cops attached.

4. Record Keeping

People find themselves in deep trouble when police find the paperwork that they've left lying around. It's a police windfall to find records of what was going on, including names of individual plants, yields, characteristics, and, in the more tidy operations, perhaps even the price the product was sold for. Many dealers keep pay/owe data, financial records, and customer/supplier address/telephone books. Few kinds of evidence are more damning and harder to overcome than this type of record keeping.

I've been told that commercial pot growing requires business records. This argument implies that home growers have no reason for keeping garden notebooks around. However, they often do. Many marijuana growers have a close emotional attachment to their plants. In addition, much as with wine growing, in which the grapes and their treatment produce different flavors, each variety and, more subtly, each marijuana plant has a different taste and high. For the most part, this is controlled by genetic factors. Any kind of breeding program entails record keeping for particular plants.

The most devastating records the police can find are those that detail the sales of crops over the years. A dealer may find it necessary to keep some records to determine profit and loss, but I've never understood why they keep old records. Taxes are probably not being paid on sales, so there's no reason to keep them.

In one case, a man was arrested with only 17 mediocre plants, but his records indicated that he had grown and sold $125,000 worth of marijuana 2 years earlier. Because he was keeping these records as a favor to a quadriplegic grower, who wasn't named in the records of sales (Who is "Doc"?) he was found guilty.

In another case, the police sifted through 20 boxes full of records and 600 computer disks and came up with a profile that allowed them to charge three persons (otherwise unknown to them) with conspiracy to cultivate, transport, and sell huge quantities of marijuana over a 6-year period. One of these defendants had to bite the bullet and plead guilty, exposing himself to a state prison term, even though no one had ever seen him smoke a joint and no one had seen him selling, had said he sold, or had caught him with any product whatsoever.

The records that his accomplices kept, coupled with sufficient corroboration of those records by his own accidentally discovered bank records, was sufficient to show the court that he was in fact a coparticipant and coconspirator.

F. DEA OPERATIONS

In November 1989 the DEA served subpoenas on a number of high-tech garden stores. They demanded lists of customers from the stores. In order to give the owners an incentive to cooperate, they seized property and indicted the owners. Most of the establishments that found themselves in legal difficulties were caught in stings, during which the owners or the help admitted that the equipment could be used for marijuana cultivation or discussed the subject at greater length. Once armed with the customer lists and UPS logs, the DEA asked UPS to provide lists of deliveries to specific addresses. Most of the time, agents arrived at these residences without warrants and tried to talk their way in. In some cases they were able to obtain warrants, but most of these appear to have been thrown out by the courts.

In 1991 the DEA set up its own store (since closed) and encouraged its customers to talk about illegal activities. The DEA is still watching the stores. In 1992-93 they tried "administrative subpoenas," which had no legal authority. Still, many stores provided new customer lists. Because of continuing government actions, it's risky to purchase from some stores, and it's hard to know exactly which ones.

To check the bona fides of an establishment, a customer might ask whether the proprietors have ever been hassled and whether they have cooperated with government inquiries. If they say they have, or are unwilling to talk about it, the store is a good place not to shop. If the salesperson implies or talks about illegal activities, it is quite possible a sting operation is in progress or is being attempted.

Smart growers have learned never to purchase goods by mail-order from stores, since stores ship via UPS, which keeps logs of all deliveries. They never make their purchases with credit cards or checks, since these leave paper trails. They don't use their vehicles to transport goods, since their license plates may be recorded at the places they visit. When they go to a garden store, they try to look like typical residents of the area. They purchase all the goods they can from nonsuspect garden shops or, even better, get used goods at flea markets or through classified ads in the newspapers.

RIPOFFS

Suppose you're a grower and this situation occurs: You find thieves in your pot patch, or they find you. Are you prepared to shoot them (or be shot by them)?

Ripoff artists and cops believe the crop is worth a lot of money. Amateur and professional thieves are not uncommon. Almost any grower is a potential target for people who would burgle, rob, and even occasionally kill.

If you're caught with a weapon during the commission of a crime, you're in big trouble. A gun in the house while the pot is in the field might be enough to convict and increase your sentence. A defendant can usually count on the cops' using the guns as evidence of his/her vicious nature and professional status. Sentences are increased by 1 to 10 years—in some cases, even more—just because the defendants possessed guns.

Pulling out and pointing a gun can be charged as a crime ranging from a misdemeanor—brandishing a weapon in a rude, angry, or threatening manner—to felony assault with a deadly weapon. Let's say you pull the gun and then walk the thief out of the area and she/he falls and gets hurt. The charges can escalate to kidnapping with bodily harm: life without possibility of parole. And of course, if you just run them off, will they return? With more people and/or more firepower?

What to Do If the Cops Come

A. WITHOUT A WARRANT

1. General Information

Suppose two cops walk up to a door and say to the person who opens it, "We have reason to believe that you're growing marijuana. We would like to search the place. You can let us in now and we won't take you to jail. Or, if you don't cooperate, when we come back with the warrant, we'll kick the door in." What is that person to do? Tell them to go get a warrant. Here are the reasons: The judge may not grant them a search warrant based on the evidence they present. Even if the police are given one, the courts in later proceedings may find that the warrant wasn't good, because misrepresentations were made in obtaining it or for other reasons. However, if the person waives his/her rights and allows the police to conduct a search without a warrant, there's no chance to fight the search because there's no warrant to be contested.

It will take the police some time to get a warrant. Meanwhile, if things are present that could give the police the wrong impression, these can and should be destroyed. Lists of names that might appear to be pay/owe sheets; stray drugs; packaging material. Even if the warrant is not granted, the visit is still a signal to discontinue suspicious behavior. However, great care must be taken during the shutdown. The police may be curious about moving or similar activities and try to intimidate the suspect who is engaging in them.

If the police knock without a warrant, there is no law stating that you have to open the door or let them in. No matter how they may try to coerce you to open the door, it should not be opened. As soon as it does, one cop is likely to say, "I smell marijuana." This simple statement, some courts may find, gives the police the right to search the premises. Opening the door is a no-win decision.

There is no issue and no hope of having the evidence suppressed if you agree or consent to a search. The police may threaten, promise, and lie, but if you don't consent, you have a chance that the law will later protect you from their excesses.

To insist that the cops must have a warrant is not evidence of your guilt. Your assertion of your rights can never be used as part of their justification for searching you. If you refuse to make their job easier, they may get tough with you, search anyway, and then lie about what was said or done. If you give in and sign a consent form, you have almost no chance of contesting the search. I've never understood why people make it easy for guys who are hassling them. These cops are not your friends, and will use everything they can to screw you later.

2. Consent Searches

If the police have sufficient probable cause to search and/or arrest you, they will do so with or without your consent. If you do consent to a search and they find contraband of any kind (or evidence of any crime), then you know for sure that you'll be arrested, and probably convicted, just because you gave up your constitutional protections against a police search without sufficient cause.

A law enforcement officer can search your home without a warrant if you, or someone who is apparently in control, agrees to it. If you're staying in a hotel room or an apartment, the manager or landlord cannot give permission to search your room, but a maid who sees and tells violates no law. Parents can agree to the search of their children's rooms. They are not supposed to allow the search of the children's personal possessions, although the police and the parents generally ignore this nicety of law.

3. Babysitting the House

You don't have to allow the police to wait at or in your house while one of them goes to get a warrant. Don't give them any opportunity to claim that you consented to their presence at or in your house. If they have legally sufficient grounds for armed occupation, they'll do it. If they can't or don't get a warrant, you win. If you agree to save them the hassle, you lose whether or not they can get the warrant.

> A few years ago, an acquaintance of mine was implicated in an importing operation, but there was no clear evidence linking him to it. The police came; he refused to talk with them or let them in. Because they had no warrant and no probable cause, they never returned.
>
> * * *
>
> A client was visited by four undercover cops, who walked him into his house while neighbors watched. I called the cop shop and told the investigator that the episode had been seen by friendly neighbors. Although evidence was seized, no indictment followed.

4. Exigent Circumstances

Anyone who is being detained or taken from one place to another in police custody, but not necessarily arrested, can be searched for weapons. This is a limited search of the exterior of your clothing. Only if the officer feels some hard object that s/he believes is or could be a weapon can they make you produce the item. If you are arrested, a full search can be done by the police when you're booked into jail.

A law enforcement officer can search your home without your consent and without a warrant in exigent situations (true emergencies). If the police are in hot pursuit of a fleeing felon, the search can't include the dresser drawers, but can include the closet, and anything in plain sight can be seized.

B. WITH A WARRANT

Suppose the police come in with a warrant, arrest a person, and demand cooperation—by which they mean a confession. First they'll ask for a waiver of the suspect's Miranda rights, which are as follows: "You have the right to remain silent. Anything you say can be used against you in a court of law. You have the right to have an attorney present during questioning. If you cannot afford an attorney, you will be provided with one."

If the police do have a warrant, they may knock on the door or break in through it to scare you. In either case, the door should and will open. Even after the door is opened, you have some rights.

C. THE SCOPE OF THE SEARCH

If you're arrested in your home, an officer without a warrant can search only the area immediately around the place where you're arrested. S/he can search only for weapons that could be used offensively or evidence that could be destroyed. An officer can go from room to room to make sure no other people are in the house, but can search no further than that. This is why the officer can't open a desk drawer, but can open a closet door.

If an officer is legally searching for something, anything s/he sees in plain sight (without moving it or something else) that s/he recognizes as contraband, or evidence of a crime, can be seized.

When you're talking to cops, hide any heart-felt bad feelings toward them. Telling the cop who's searching your car that he has canine ancestors may only get you a harsh look, but it also may evolve into a lesson from the Rodney King School of Applied Manners. Always use your best manners when talking to any government official, even a clerk. They have the power of the government behind them. They can wield it to help you or to harm you. The most extreme public servants are cops who occasionally beat, arrest, and shoot people for no apparent reason other than their attitude. Be nice.

D. BAIL

Depending on the seriousness of the crime(s) you're charged with, and, in some cases, the degree of your threat to the public safety, you may be released on bail after being booked.

Bail is money or other securities (such as real property) deposited with the court to make sure that you will appear. Officers at the jail may be able to accept bail for the court. If you can't post (put up) the bail, you'll be kept in custody until a decision is made on your case.

If you're accused of a felony, you must deposit the full amount of bail. The money will be refunded if you make all the necessary court appearances. If you cannot afford to put up the bail, you may be able to get the transaction arranged through a bail bondsperson. They charge 10 percent of the bail amount as a nonrefundable fee. It's just like automobile insurance—you don't get the premium back even if you don't have an accident.

Instead of bail, you may be able to get released on your own recognizance (O.R.). This means you don't have to post bail because the judge believes you'll show up for all your court appearances. Some counties have O.R. projects to assist in the defendant's release without payment of bail, based on the defendant's ties to the community and previous record.

In setting the amount of bail, or deciding whether to release you on O.R., the judge will consider the nature of the crime you're charged with, your past record (if any), and your ties to the community, insofar as these are made known to the judge. Prepare and present affidavits, and bring live people to accompany your statement. Get your lawyer to check out your position and help you present the good points, however few they may be. This is an area where a little work will pay big dividends. Your ability to be assigned a reasonable bail (one you can afford to post) will allow you to be out and preparing to win the case. Make sure your lawyer has all the facts s/he needs at the proper time so you can show the judge that you can be trusted to return.

Anyone growing or possessing pot may get busted. People who are holding should have already thought about that and made plans for the cops' finding what is there, for bail, for the kids, dogs, cats, and fish.

The cops initially set the bail. A Friday arrest coupled with a cop who's really nasty could result in a very long weekend. It could be as late as Wednesday of the following week before you get a chance to convince a judge that $100,000 bail is not appropriate.

The issues at a bail hearing are simple: Will you come back to play the game, and will you be a danger to anyone in the community if released?

Federal courts have a system of pretrial supervision that allows most people to be out of custody on fairly reasonable terms pending trial. The exceptions are frightening. Although the constitutions of the United States and of most states seem by their terms to require and allow bail in noncapital offenses, laws that have been recently enacted allow the court to, in effect, sentence you to jail before you're convicted of any crime—by setting a bail that's impossible for you to post. Only changes made by Congress can stop this Alice-in-Wonderland judicial procedure: "Sentence first, trial later." You're entitled to a hearing on the issue of detention, but if the government goes after you in this way, it's very difficult to get a reasonable bail.

The cops' estimates of $5,000 per pound and 3 pounds of "biomass" per plant sometimes result in newspaper stories indicating millions of dollars in "street value" for your backyard crop. If unchallenged, these absurd estimates can give a judge the impression that you're a real criminal and therefore likely to split if released.

Until the paperwork goes to the local prosecutor for review and filing of the complaint, you are at the cops' mercy. A lot of local prosecutors simply go along with the cops' choice of crimes, and it may be a long time before you have an opportunity to show that the plants in the garden weren't really yours, and certainly aren't worth a million dollars, as the cops told the newspapers.

Bail is important. It takes money, obviously, and usually the title to some real property. Your lawyer can usually suggest a bondsperson. I can usually get my favorite one to immediately write a bond and spring my client, and get the money to her later. I therefore recommend her to my clients, along with a few other choices. If your lawyer doesn't know a local bondsperson, s/he either isn't a local practitioner or doesn't practice much criminal law.

If you post bail and secure it with some assets, such as money or a car, the court and/or the prosecutor may ask rude questions as to where the assets came from. The source of the money or property must be "clean," or it could be forfeited. The property should start and end with a clean paper trail, and come from a person not implicated in any bad business. Parents or friends can loan money they obtained from a legitimate, documented source (such as the sale of something, or a bank or personal loan, or whatever).

When money is borrowed from someone to post bail, the paperwork must be done. Real loans are cemented with a written note, with the date of the loan, the due date (loans are paid back), a face amount, a rate of interest (if there is any), and signatures. If the courts ask, the money must be "clean," with a good paper trail, or the money too will be lost, with no gain of freedom.

> Anyone who was involved with the project should not go to post bail. One sorry character went to the jail to bail out his friends and was recognized by the cop from the photos the arresting officers had taken. He was arrested on the spot, and his efforts to bail out his two friends turned into arranging bail for three.

E. CLEANUP

A good friend who is ready to help in case of legal necessity is a near-necessity. Such people don't need to know about the business in detail, but shouldn't be upset about it. They can help get money and signatures for bail; they can deal with the broken-into house and the terrorized pets.

This good friend should also have instructions to go to the house and make sure it's secure. S/he should close the door (or nail up a board if it's really bad), get the dog if the cops haven't shot it, feed the cats if they haven't been terrorized or shot or both (this is sometimes done "for officer safety"!), and then get a camera and take the "after" photographs A.S.A.P., given that this friend must also deal with the bail, the kids, and so on. The order is: all at once, immediately. It will be appreciated later.

This does not mean your friend goes and removes evidence or cleans your house up. Remember, it was the owner's duty to keep things looking marvelous. When the cops bust an outdoor project, they'll try to determine who is responsible, then try to go to that person's house to search for more evidence of cultivation and sales. They often find exactly what they say they expect to find: dope, scales, money, paperwork, guns, names and addresses of other people. Since the cops do "reasonably expect" to find contraband and/or evidence of the commission of a felony, the law will generally allow them to make a visit to the grower's home.

If there are records of bank accounts at the house, the cops are likely to find them and investigate. Cash deposits are noted and questioned. Crude attempts to launder the proceeds from a dope-growing or sales operation may form the basis for new and intricate felony charges.

F. PHOTOS

Don't clean up until after you take detailed photographs of the scene. Important details may not be apparent at the time, but the photos are a record you may be able to use to your benefit.

> A field investigation video made by a defense expert showed that the defendant had put out a salt lick to attract deer—to a grow site? Get real!—which led to the successful defense contention that someone else had committed the crime. When the "before" photo of an antique handgun was contrasted with an "after" photo showing its clear absence, the jury had serious doubts about the officers' credibility in other, more important matters.

Defendants regularly complain most bitterly about the theft that they believe the cops committed while serving the warrant. The law requires that the police leave a receipt for everything they take. The receipt should be detailed enough to identify each, every, any, and all of those items of "evidence" seized.

When the police raid a house and then things are missing, stolen items should be documented as carefully as possible and a formal complaint should be made. There is a good chance that the prosecutor or head cop will not believe the complaint and/or will not care. S/he may even be in

on the deal, receiving some of the loot. Seized items often are not returned to the owners at the close of the case; instead, they are sold and the proceeds divided between the cops and the prosecutor or used for a party.

G. RETURN OF SEIZED ITEMS

The law allows the cops to seize evidence (things that prove something) or contraband (the drugs, scales, packaging, or containers). Unless a separate civil forfeiture is undertaken, the cops can keep nothing, not even those items purchased with drug proceeds (the TV, stereo, car, whatever) or used to facilitate the commission of the offense. These cannot be legally kept by the authorities after their value as evidence of your crime has been exhausted. This means that when the case is over, most of this stuff can be returned if the defendant requests it.

If the cops take your wallet, credit cards, identification, and so on, their return can be requested. Usually the prosecutor demands a stipulation (agreement) that other secondary evidence (such as a photo or a photocopy) can be used as "evidence." The prosecutor may agree, or the defense attorney can make a motion in court and try to get the judge to order the return of the items.

The other solution when the cops take your license and credit cards is to officially say they've been lost and get replacements. Most of the time this is easier, quicker, and cheaper than trying to wrestle with the cops and the prosecutor.

H. RIGHT TO REMAIN SILENT

You do not have to talk to the police, you have the right to an attorney, and everything you say may be held against you.

The Bill of Rights was created for a reason: to protect people from the power of the state. When people waive their rights, they're giving up precious liberties. You should never agree to talk to the police. They will pervert everything you say, forget to mention or discount any information you give them that might exonerate you. Talking with them gives you no advantage. They're not permitted to make a deal, no matter what they say—"We can't promise anything but we'll put in a good word for you," or "This will make it easier." They may seem sympathetic while they make a bust, but on the stand in court they'll try to make things sound as bad as possible. Why should you talk to your enemy? These guys want to put you in jail. You should have nothing to do with them.

It's true that the police have some options and can give you a hard time if you resist their requests for cooperation. For instance, in California, for some offenses, they can choose between citing you and arresting you, so they might say, "If you cooperate, you won't have to go to jail now. We just give you a ticket for a court date. Otherwise, we might have to arrest your wife too, and place your kids in foster care." Most of this is bullshit, an attempt to coerce you into confessing and naming other people.

So the answer to the question, "Do you waive your rights?" should be a resounding "No." Tell the police, "I don't want to talk to you. I would like to call my attorney." If you don't have a lawyer, you should say, "I don't want to talk to you. I would like to talk to an attorney." You should try to do this in the presence of other people so that there can be no confusing of the issue when it gets to court. If the police try to coerce a confession, and it is shown that the confession was not willingly given, but was extorted, the case could get thrown out. No matter how abusive, scary, coercive, or bullying the police are, you should never waive your rights.

I. ARRAIGNMENT AND PRELIMINARY HEARING

1. First Arraignment

An arraignment is an appearance before a magistrate (judge) in a superior, municipal, or justice court, where the defendant is told officially of the charges against him/her. Arrestees have a right to be arraigned without unnecessary delay, usually within two court days after being arrested; otherwise, they should be released. A defendant can arrange a self-surrender by sending a letter to the court and the district attorney, offering to show up. This may save you the trouble of arrest and bail.

At the arraignment, an attorney will be appointed if the defendant cannot afford to hire one. The bail can also be raised or lowered. At this time, release on O.R. is considered, even if it was turned down before.

If the defendant is charged with a misdemeanor, s/he can plead guilty or not guilty to the charge at the arraignment. If the court approves, the plea can be "nolo contendere," which means "no contest" to the charges against you. Legally, it's the same as pleading guilty, except that it can't be used in civil litigation.

Before pleading guilty to some first-time misdemeanor offense (such as family violence, alcohol, or drug cases), defendants may want to find out if the state/county has a "diversion" (drug diversion) program. Under these programs, the court may order the defendant to get medical treatment and counseling, or perform community service, instead of being fined or sent to jail.

If misdemeanor charges are not dropped, a trial will be held in municipal court at a later time. If the charge is a felony, the next court appearance will be a preliminary hearing.

2. Preliminary Hearing

A preliminary hearing is usually held within 10 days after the arraignment. At that hearing, the D.A.'s office must present evidence showing "strong suspicion" that a felony was committed and that the defendant committed it. This is done in order to convince the judge that you should be brought to trial.

If the felony charges are not dropped at the preliminary hearing, there will be a second arraignment. This arraignment is held in superior court, where your trial will also be held at a later date and time.

It is at the preliminary hearing that the court decides whether there is enough evidence to hold a person for trial. The term for this is "preponderance of evidence." This means the police just have to prove that it was likely that the suspect committed the offense in order for him/her to be brought to trial. This proceeding is very important. It is here that the defense makes motions (asks the court to consider) to exclude illegal warrants and illegally gathered evidence. In some courts, if these motions are not made at this time, the defendant loses the right to appeal the court's decisions on these bases, even if the reasons are valid.

The preliminary hearing is the best time to beat a case. The whole legal proceeding is nipped in the bud, so long, drawn-out, expensive legal proceedings are eliminated. If there is a good case for motions, the opportunity should not be missed and it should be handled by a high-quality lawyer.

J. FORFEITURE

To seize and forfeit property, the government must present the owner with a notice of the intended forfeiture. Once the government does so, the suspect must file a document with the appropriate court within a very short time, usually 10 days. This is an absolute necessity for anyone who hopes to contest the seizure and avoid the forfeiture. People should be prepared in two ways: First, be prepared to file (or have someone else file) the claim within the brief time the statute allows. Second, be prepared for the bust so you aren't exposed to unwarranted seizures and forfeitures in the first place.

The owner may be faced with the dilemma of whether or not to claim the money or property seized. If you've made your preparations properly, you should be able to decide quickly and correctly whether there is any chance of recovery. This revolves around your ability to answer the questions of where, when, how, and from whom the property came to you without undue embarrassment. Preparedness is vital because when money or property is seized, the paperwork and excuses had better be already in place.

Many pot cultivation cases today are conceived, planned, and executed with forfeitures in the minds of the cops and/or the prosecutor. Most police agencies view forfeitures as a lucrative source of funds in this time of ever-tightening budgets.

Most cop shops have one specially trained person whose job is to take as much stuff as s/he legally can. These people are not fair and are not seeking justice, so things get ugly fast.

Most prosecutors also have an assistant or deputy prosecutor in charge of forfeitures. These people are often unskilled in civil litigation, since they are otherwise engaged in criminal cases. In my county, the job was given to the office geek because nobody wanted it. Fighting over people's money is what civil law is usually about for lawyers. Criminal lawyers, however, usually view the debate over life and liberty as more critical than the money. That's why they're not in an insurance defense firm, or chasing ambulances. A civil lawyer may be required for the civil litigation.

The cops and prosecutors are ready, willing, and able to take toys, cars, and homes if the suspect is not prepared.

GOOD HOUSEKEEPING

Should the cops come to your little corner of the world, the scene they find will be, to some greater or lesser degree, fixed in time. Recorded in photographs, videotapes, evidence lists, diagrams, and police reports, that scene will be referenced by the cops, prosecutor, judge, and jury, as well as your attorney, throughout the case.

That's why it's vitally important that the scene the cops find truly reflect your innocence, lack of sophistication, desire to grow only for personal use, medical necessity for growing or use, or whatever the defense hopes the judge and jury would like to hear and would believe about you.

Large-scale growers and dealers, who have all the nasty stuff around that proves their status, are usually difficult to defend. Platform and triple-beam-balance scales, lots of Baggies, and the like require great explanations. Smart people don't keep a history of their cultivation or dealing. That includes photographs of prior deals and crops, diaries of the deepest, darkest secrets, including the deals, and the Eternal-Hope Seed Bank from 20 years of saving seeds.

One disabled Vietnam vet had calculated his life expectancy (shortened by various war-related factors) and his use patterns and was growing a lifetime supply. The cops found the paperwork and seized it without knowing what it was. When the suspect and his attorney reviewed the evidence, the defense was obvious (and successful), and 240 marijuana plants were found to be for personal use.

On the other side of the scales, so to speak, were the poor growers with historically significant scales (old, old, high-school-chemistry/yard-sale items) and hundreds of very small plastic lock-top Baggies, remnants of a coin-collecting hobby of yesteryear. The court needed to be rather forcefully shown that if one defendant really did have a 200-pound crop, she wouldn't sell it in 1-gram bags. If she had done so in the past, and was intending to do so with this pot, it would create a nonstop flow of customers night and day, deal lists, lots of cash, pre-bagged pot—all the bad stuff. The prosecutor hoped his fishing expedition would bring forth admissions of white-powder dealing (in some former life, I guess), but he was unsuccessful and the case was resolved very favorably.

The Search

A. GENERAL INFORMATION

A law enforcement officer can search you, your clothes, your purse and/or wallet, your car, and your home. The officer can make a search if you consent, with a search warrant, or under exigent (emergency) circumstances. The officer can, under some circumstances, search you without either your consent or a warrant.

If you're arrested, the cops can search you without further warrant or cause. This search is limited to weapons, evidence, or illegal or stolen goods. In general, this search must be of your person, or closely related in time and place to the offense you were arrested for.

If you're arrested and taken to jail, you may be subjected to a full search, including your most intimate body cavities, without any further supervision or paperwork. You have a right to be searched in a manner that is not offensive to common decency, usually meaning that female officers search female arrestees. Ladies, if any men want to search you or to be present when you're being intimately searched, scream like hell and demand to see the highest-ranking official who is available. Sexual molestation is not an appropriate part of an arrest for any crime. Custodial voyeurism is not legal.

You have much less protection from police intrusions into your life if you're driving your car. Any time the police stop your car for any legitimate reason, any contraband they see or smell could lead to a search and to your arrest without a warrant.

B. ILLEGAL SEARCHES

If you, your home, or your car is searched illegally, a judge may say that any evidence found during the search cannot be used against you in court. In order to punish the police for illegal conduct and to protect citizens' rights, the "fruits," or results, of an illegal search are not admitted into evidence in court. This is called suppressing the evidence; it's an increasingly rare occurrence.

If neither you nor your lawyer objects to the evidence before or at the trial, the court will allow that evidence to be used against you. The court will not say on its own that the police violated the law. You must object to the evidence and ask the court to throw it out. If you don't make a pretrial motion to suppress the evidence, you can't say on appeal that the search was illegal. You must pressure your lawyer to carefully consider all possible grounds for suppression of evidence. Don't let the lawyer say, "I don't think you'll win, so I won't try." If there's any reasonable theory, make the motion. You can't win if you don't play.

C. EXPECTATION OF PRIVACY

The courts have decided that the Constitution protects us from police searches only in certain circumstances. The Constitution guarantees the right of the people to be secure in their persons, homes, and effects from searches without a warrant that is sworn by the cops and signed by a magistrate.

The law recognizes your rights to keep the cops out in circumstances where you have a reasonable expectation of privacy. This must be subjectively held, which means you must believe the cops are invading a protected area. In addition, you must objectively manifest this belief of yours. This means you've got to make some effort to keep people (and the cops) from seeing that which you claim is private. If the grower has taken no precautions to conceal the crop, the law will have trouble finding a legitimate expectation of privacy. The last part of the "reasonable" equation is that society must be willing to recognize privacy as a legitimate concern. Many people believe that too many bad crooks get off if we stop the cops from doing something on the order of battering down the doors of crack houses, so we shouldn't stop them, and they need not have any reason to intrude.

Concrete examples of reasonable, protected interests are backyard fences and greenhouses. If the fence is there, it is evidence of your expectation of privacy. If the plants grow up over the fence, steps haven't been taken to objectively manifest the expectation of privacy, and the case is lost. It's a much closer case if the cops look over or through a fence.

Cops suspect all greenhouses of containing pot. It doesn't matter if you are a member of the Indoor Orchid Growers of America, raise and sell tomatoes year-round, or propagate world-class roses. If you have a greenhouse, the cops all think you grow pot somewhere, somehow. Though the law does not make such an assumption, the cops regularly use the "open-fields doctrine" to trespass and inspect greenhouses. The United States Supreme Court has said you must have something covering your crop for you to have a manifest expectation of privacy. We all know about airplanes, so how could you expect it to be private if you don't cover it? Hard choices, no easy answers.

D. CURTILAGE

The law regarding searches is based on the concept of curtilage. The courts have decided that your house is protected from unwarranted searches but that the rest of the world, including your property, is not. The idea that property beyond the curtilage is unprotected by the need for a warrant was initially promulgated in order to stop Prohibition-era bootleggers and moonshiners. Revenue agents roamed the open fields at will and the court ruled against suppression of the evidence. No warrant was needed unless the curtilage was invaded, regardless of the fences or "No Trespassing" signs everywhere.

The judge who wrote that opinion probably didn't foresee how the cops would use it. Squads of goon cops going house-to-house to search the entire property, save and except the curtilage, paints an ugly picture of Nazi Brown Shirts on the rampage. This occurred in Humboldt County, California, 1993. The ever-vigilant attorney, Ron Sinoway, was able to stop this practice when he showed the court that the cops there had violated people's basic rights. The cases were thrown out of court, but the judge, who seemed righteously indignant, did nothing to the cops.

Curtilage is the area that is associated with the everyday activities of the household. It includes the front and back yards (fenced or not) to some greater or lesser extent. The barn is not generally in the curtilage, but a garage may be, depending on whether it's attached or not and how close it is to the house.

In the oldest English cases, the curtilage is described as the area within a bow-shot of the front door (and presumably the back door), the theory being that I could use my bow to protect myself without waiting for you to break down the door. No shooting is allowed these days, but the concept of curtilage is still with us.

Historically, curtilage was defined as the area intimately associated with the common household endeavors and the domestic economy. Your personal-use vegetable garden or henhouse may be part of your curtilage. The way in which the land is fenced and cross-fenced may be significant. Today the definition usually refers to the backyard or a well-fenced front yard.

You can establish that the cops invaded your curtilage by presenting facts to the court that connect the area searched to your private household endeavors. A chair and table in the garden may show that it was a place of calm refuge and contemplation; you spent your leisure time there, resting. The swimming pool is probably in the curtilage, but if it's a fertilizer mixer, then it's probably not.

Cops often draw their own conclusions about whether or not the places they've gone to are within your curtilage. Don't let them win this point without a challenge. What you considered to be and used as your front or back "yard" is as important as the number of feet between the greenhouse and your front door. Cases are won by a field investigation bearing out the relationship of the garden to the curtilage.

E. STANDING

The term "standing" refers, among other things, to a person's right to ask the court to suppress the evidence. Recent incarnations of the Supreme Court have decided that if your own individual rights have been violated by the cops, you may be able to eliminate the evidence from the trial. However, if it was not your place, or not your stuff, then what's it to you? Saying "It ain't mine" doesn't guarantee that the jury will agree. However, it will surely remove your standing—that is, it will keep you from successfully challenging an illegal search.

You must show the court that your relationship to the place searched and/or the things seized was such that your personal toes have been trodden upon. If you say nothing beyond your name and address when questioned, the cop will establish standing for you: It's yours, you had it. That is normally enough. That the stuff was in your bag, car, or house is normally enough if you don't disclaim any interest in the particular box and its contents.

You don't need to admit knowledge of any crime or contraband to order to exercise your right to privacy and exclude others from a place or a package. If you have the right-now right of control, you have enough of a protected privacy interest to tell the cops "No" and make it stick.

It may be necessary to testify that you have standing in order to make a realistic motion to suppress. This testimony is not admissible at your trial unless you testify differently the second time. This is a major tactical decision, to be made with the help of a lawyer.

The most common standing problem occurs when the cops search A's house and find drugs and other stuff that indicates B is involved. Even if the cops had no warrant and have conducted an illegal search with no probable cause, B has no standing unless s/he can establish a personal expectation of privacy.

5

The Arrest

A. WHAT IS AN ARREST?

You are arrested if a law enforcement officer, or sometimes even a private citizen, takes you into custody. This means you're no longer a free person; you can't just walk away from the scene. The officer who arrests you should say that you're under arrest and tell you why. If you're stopped for a short time, you may have only been "detained," or held for questioning, rather than being arrested. Do not respond to questions such as "What do you think you did?" Ask questions if you want, but don't give information beyond what is necessary.

1. What Is an Arrest Warrant?

An arrest warrant is a piece of paper telling law enforcement officers to arrest a certain person. The arrest warrant must be signed by a judge or magistrate. The judge must have good reason to believe that the person named in the warrant committed a crime. If the suspect is unknown, a name like "John Doe" can be used, but the warrant must contain a particular description good enough to allow any cop to (probably) recognize you as the person described. If the cops have a John Doe warrant for the 6-foot-tall, 180-pound, dark-haired guy living at 123 Bust Street, they will look at you and ask your address. If you match the description, you go with them. If it's close, but ultimately not you, you may be released later, but the stash you were caught with probably sticks around. You can be detained while the cops check it out.

Once an arrest warrant has been issued, any law enforcement officer in the state can arrest the suspect. This can happen even if that officer doesn't have a copy of the warrant. The "statute of limitations" applies only to whether or not you are charged with a crime. There is no time limitation on using a warrant to make an arrest.

An arrest warrant must be issued before you can be taken into custody at your home. You can be arrested at home without a warrant only if the police have exigent (emergency) circumstances, such as escape prevention, citizen endangerment, or destruction of property or evidence, or if you are at home and committing a felony in the officers' presence.

A felony arrest warrant can be served at any time of the day or night. A misdemeanor arrest warrant usually cannot be served between 10:00 p.m. and 6:00 a.m., unless otherwise stated.

A traffic warrant can be served on you any time you can be found, usually in your car.

If the law enforcement officers have an arrest warrant, you have a right to see it. If they don't have one, you have a right to see it as soon as they can get it. They won't give a damn about showing it to you, and unless you can show that you were injured (prejudiced) somehow by their refusal, you lose.

SHOULD I RESIST ARREST?

A law enforcement officer can and will use whatever force is necessary to overcome your resistance, to arrest you, and to prevent your escape. A law enforcement officer can pin you to the ground during an arrest. Deadly force, such as shooting, can be used if the officer thinks you'll kill him or seriously hurt someone else. For your own safety, never resist arrest or detention.

Physically resisting arrest or detention is a serious crime. You can be charged with a misdemeanor or even a felony in addition to the crime for which you're being arrested. Even innocent people who are wrongly accused go to jail—contempt of cop. Acquitted on the substantive charge? Too bad about the resisting-arrest charge.

B. ARRESTEES' RIGHTS

Police question you as part of their investigation, often without telling you your rights. If you have actually been arrested and/or taken into custody, you have the right to remain silent. You don't have to answer any questions. You must provide the police with your name and address; you must show identification. Before the cops interrogate you, you should be given your Miranda warnings. You should be told:

1. You have the right to remain silent.
2. Anything you say may be used against you (everything you say will be used against you).
3. You have the right to talk to a lawyer before being questioned, and to have a lawyer present while you are questioned.
4. If you cannot afford to hire a lawyer, one will be appointed for you.

If you are not given these warnings ("Mirandized"), your lawyer can and should ask that any and all statements made to the police not be used against you in a court of law. This does not mean that your case will be dismissed.

C. QUESTIONING

If you're not in custody, the cops don't have to tell you your rights. Don't talk anyway. Don't play a game with the cops and hope your statement will later be suppressed.

Once the Miranda warnings have been given, you will be questioned only if you voluntarily give up your rights. The cops usually have you sign a waiver indicating that you understand what you're giving up.

You can stop the questioning at any time if you change your mind, as soon as you tell the police that you want it to end and/or that you want a lawyer.

D. DETENTIONS

You can be detained and questioned by the police for a brief investigation. The person detaining you must have reason to believe that you're involved in some criminal activity connected with a crime that has occurred, is occurring, or is about to occur. A police officer might be able to detain a person carrying a large box near the site of a recent burglary, or a hiker with a shovel and fertilizer near a garden.

A customs inspector can detain you to search for illegal goods. Shopkeepers can detain you if they suspect you're ripping them off. Librarians can detain you if they suspect you've stolen a book.

Like being arrested, being detained limits your freedom to walk away. However, a detention must be only for a short time. It usually occurs in a public place and does not involve going anywhere.

Once you've been detained, a law enforcement officer can do a pat-down search. This means he can feel for weapons from outside your clothes. He may not go into your pockets without further probable cause. If you're arrested, the officer can search for anything else you have on you.

You have certain rights when you're detained, but the law does not require law enforcement officers to tell you about them. Although you should tell a law enforcement officer who you are and where you live, you can refuse to answer other questions. You can have a lawyer present while you're detained, but you're not entitled to free legal assistance. Make the cops an offer to come see them with your lawyer if they want to talk to you about some crime. Do not agree to go to some "more convenient" place. Ask if you can leave. If not, why not?

E. POST-ARREST

The police can require you to give certain physical evidence without letting you talk to an attorney first. If you're suspected of driving under the influence of alcohol, or of a drug, you may have to take a test to measure the amount of substance in your system. In California, if you refuse, you can lose your driver's license for up to one year. If you refuse a handwriting sample, or hair or fingerprints, the prosecutor will later say you did so because you knew you were guilty.

After you're arrested, you can call a lawyer, a family member, a friend, a bail bondsperson, or any two people. You have the right to make and complete two free phone calls in your local dialing area within three hours of your arrest. This right belongs to everyone, citizen as well as noncitizen, upon arrest. Once they book you, you have a right to make the calls immediately—but ask, don't insist, or they will screw with you. The cops do keep track of who you call, and probably listen to your conversation.

F. TYPES OF CHARGES

You can be arrested if you're suspected of committing a crime—a felony or a misdemeanor—or as an accessory for helping in the planning or commission of a crime or aiding someone to escape an arrest or conviction.

1. Felonies

A felony is usually defined as a crime punishable by imprisonment in state prison or by death. Murder, armed robbery, rape, and so on are felonies. So is cultivation of any number of marijuana plants or sale of any amount in all U.S. states, territories, and so on. Possession may be a misdemeanor or a felony depending on the quantity, the intent, and individual state laws. Both possession and cultivation are also federal crimes.

2. Misdemeanors

Crimes that aren't felonies are misdemeanors, unless they are infractions. Misdemeanors are punishable by a term of incarceration in the county jail or by a fine, or by both. Shoplifting and disturbing the peace are misdemeanors. In states with decriminalized marijuana possession laws, simple possession of small amounts is usually a misdemeanor or an infraction.

3. Infractions

Infractions are "petty offenses." They are minor. Usually a guilty verdict results in a fine instead of incarceration. Many vehicle code violations, such as jaywalking or illegal parking, are infractions. Instead of being arrested and taken into custody for committing infractions or certain misdemeanors, such as possession of less than an ounce of marijuana in California and some other states, suspects are asked to sign a citation or a notice to appear. When you sign a citation, you're not admitting guilt. You're only promising to show up in court at a specified date and time. If you have no ID or refuse to sign the citation, then you probably will end up being taken into custody.

CLEARING THE RECORD

After you're arrested, you'll be questioned. If the police are convinced that you haven't committed a crime before any charges are filed, you'll be given a written release. Your arrest will be considered a detention rather than recorded as an arrest. If the police are not convinced, you may be booked and released on bail, or possibly arraigned and given a hearing or a court date.

Once you're booked, your arrest is written into official police records. You'll be fingerprinted and photographed for the record. Records are checked for outstanding warrants against you, and your fingerprints are compared, by computer matching systems, with those already on file.

Information in your arrest record tells when and why you were arrested, whether the charges against you were dropped or whether you were convicted of the charges in a court of law, and what was the disposition of the case.

Pleading guilty and being found guilty after a trial both count as convictions, as does a "no contest" plea. If you're convicted of committing certain misdemeanors, serve your time, and complete probation and/or stay out of trouble for 1 year, you may be able to have the conviction removed from your record for such purposes as background checks for employment.

Local police departments and the state department of justice keep all arrest records. The law says that they can't show your arrest records to anyone except law enforcement agencies and certain employers that have a legal right to know. A personnel official at a hospital or a similar institution can see your record if you apply for a sensitive job, for instance a hospital job that involves dealing with patients, drugs, and so on.

You have a right to see your arrest record to make sure that all the statements in it are correct.

The only way to remove an illegal or just plain wrong arrest from the record is to have the judge find that you're factually innocent. This involves showing the court that you did not commit the crime, not just proving reasonable doubt or dealing with technicalities. If you can convince a judge to do this, then you have ammunition with which to correct your arrest record and clear your name.

H. WHO MAKES THE ARREST?

Law enforcement officers make arrests. City and town police officers, county sheriffs, marshals, investigators from an attorney general's office or a district attorney's office, or Highway Patrol officers—and any other law enforcement officials—can and will arrest you, whether they are on or off duty, and whether or not they are in their home town or county. Cops from another state may only be acting as private citizens, but they too can arrest you and turn you over to the local cops.

These officers can arrest you even without an arrest warrant. All they need is "probable cause," which means good reason to believe you committed or tried to commit an offense in their presence. These officers don't even have to see you commit the offense.

Private security guards are not law enforcement officers, but they can arrest you as private citizens. A citizen who sees a misdemeanor or felony being attempted or committed can make a legal arrest as long as there is good reason to believe the person being arrested committed the crime. The citizen must take you to a police officer or a judge, who is required by law to take you into custody.

Choosing a Lawyer

A. LAWYERS' LICENSES

A case in a federal court can be defended by anyone admitted to practice law in any state and also in that district. The attorney has to swear that s/he will uphold the rules, follow the law, be respectful, and pay any fees in order to qualify to practice. Usually an out-of-the-area attorney must associate (hire) local counsel to assist to some greater or lesser degree, as needed or required by local court rules.

Cases prosecuted in state courts can be defended by any member of that state's bar or, again, by out-of-town talent associated with a local attorney, and admitted *pro hoc vice* (for that one case). You may not be able to get someone local who can do the job you need, but a local practitioner will save you money and will know his/her way around the court. S/he can be used in conjunction with an "imported" attorney.

B. HOW TO CHOOSE A LAWYER

1. Finding Likely Prospects

For good leads to a good attorney, try the membership rosters of some criminal defense-oriented groups. The National Association of Criminal Defense Lawyers is one such source. Each state has attorneys' associations. In California there are several groups, such as the California Public Defenders Association and the California Attorneys for Criminal Justice. NORML (National Organization for the Repeal of Marijuana Laws) also has a referral service.

An important caveat is that anyone who can afford the dues can join any of these organizations. Some attorneys join everything in sight to network for clients, for status, and for referrals. The vast majority of lawyers in these groups, and in most others, are dedicated, knowledgeable specialists in professional criminal defense—your kind of people, with the access to specialized help and knowledge that you need.

Ask for recommendations from friends, coworkers, relatives, or employers. Business professionals, such as doctors, bankers, and teachers, as well as ministers, may be able to refer you to a lawyer. Look in the Yellow Pages of your telephone directory under "Attorneys" and "Attorney Referral Services." The person who takes your call will be able to refer you to someone who can assist you further or direct you to the proper area. A good reference from a satisfied former client is worth hours of time. However, be careful about hiring an attorney based on a glowing recommendation from someone who had a dissimilar case. Divorce, personal injury, and probate attorneys are probably not qualified to handle marijuana cultivation cases.

Do you belong to a "legal insurance" plan individually, or through your employer, labor union, or credit union? If you have an employer, find out through the personnel department. Perhaps your plan provides for legal services by offering an attorney to represent you.

2. Making Your Choice

Choosing a lawyer is not a matter of diplomas on the wall, a well-appointed office waiting room, designer dresses, $2,000 suits, or a short haircut. Each case is different; each defendant is different; each lawyer is different. Finding a good match is difficult but possible. It's a lot like choosing a life companion from among many possibilities. They may be very much alike, but each will be different and attractive in his/her own way. And, like a spouse, this decision may be one you'll live with for the rest of your life.

Ask the attorney about his/her last jury trial for cultivation. Ask him/her to describe the last five or six marijuana cases s/he has taken to court. You don't need the names, just the cases, the issues, the strategy, the tactics, and the results. You should be able to spot and sift through bull this way. Don't be surprised if s/he is obviously uneasy; keep asking for specifics.

Ask the lawyer about him/herself. "War stories" from prior cases only celebrate victories. Attorneys rarely discuss losing cases with their clients. Every case—including yours—is different. If an attorney concentrates on his/her war stories and you can't get a straight answer about your case, s/he's probably not for you.

Don't pass up a lawyer just because s/he is new and inexperienced. Old and inexperienced may be worse. But do hire someone who regularly defends criminal cases, drug cases, pot cases, pot-growing cases. If the lawyer is inexperienced, s/he may still be a good lawyer, who will work hard, but perhaps you should adjust the fee. You shouldn't pay for the lawyer's education.

You can go to see most lawyers for a brief consultation. This should be free, but "brief" is the key word. Be prepared to talk or listen as required, and take all your paperwork with you.

Don't choose a less-than-enthusiastic lawyer. Personality does count. You must feel comfortable with this person, because you'll come to rely on him/her emotionally as well as legally. Pick someone who has some empathy toward you and your situation. A lawyer must have the spark of life, the "warm zeal" for defense, but must also remain a somewhat detached tactician.

When you're shopping for a lawyer, be aware of your own psychology. You'll want to be reassured by the person you interview, and will crave the slightest indication that you'll win the case and go free. Nevertheless, resist the impulse to hire the most optimistic player.

No one can predict, let alone guarantee, the result of your case. Anyone who seems to do so is stretching the truth, probably to get you to cross the "green line" — the point where you start paying. If the attorney seems too enthusiastic, get his/her claims in writing (an informal opinion letter, perhaps). Later his/her opinion may change and you may get an expensive lesson in misplaced trust. If your attorney decides not to do something that you've discussed and that you believed was going to happen, be sure to get a real explanation—in writing if you suspect a sellout.

You'll probably decide which lawyer to hire before you or s/he has any police reports or court papers. A "realistic" assessment of your case, provided by an attorney without these documents, can only be a cruel fantasy. The most that a competent lawyer should do is suggest the possible strategies or tactical maneuvers that could be useful to your case.

Imagine yourself confiding your deepest, darkest secrets to this man or woman. Like a medical doctor, the lawyer often must know the truth, however bad. No lawyer should be judgmental or belittle you for your acts or omissions. You don't need another mother, or two judges on the case. You need someone who will work hard to learn and master the facts, research the law as necessary, figure out things to do that may get you off, and then do them well and effectively.

Shop around. You're entrusting this person with your life and your freedom. Talk openly about fees, strategies, experience, and anything else you think is relevant to making a good choice. You may be swayed to a choice because one lawyer drives a BMW and another drives a Jeep. The decision will probably be made because you feel comfortable with a particular person.

RENTER BEWARE

Attorneys are a lot like cars. You can get one out on the road for a few hundred dollars, but a reliable one, which also gives you a smooth ride, costs more—and there's no limit to what you can spend on an automobile. Lawyer-shoppers face the further problem that choosing a lawyer may be more like choosing a used car. Even an expensive lawyer can still be a lemon.

Be aware that your choice of an attorney will determine just how the case is pursued. A lawyer who doesn't know the law can do you irreparable damage by waiving rights, not making motions regarding police actions that might cause the case to be dismissed, or not representing you. When you're shopping around for the right attorney, there are some ways to sort through the lists.

It's best to choose an attorney who specializes in marijuana or drug cases, or at least in criminal cases. They can be asked about their record, their general strategies, whether they usually plead clients out or turn them into snitches. This may be the most important decision you'll ever make.

Before you hire a private attorney, you can make inquiries to the state board, the consumer affairs department, and the state bar to see if there are complaints or actions against him/her. The attorney's colleagues can be asked their opinions of him/her. If they have disparaging remarks to make, they'll usually couch them in subtleties, so you'll sometimes have to read between the lines. "Jones has a unique style, but hasn't yet perfected his technique" means he loses cases that could have been won. Former clients can also give you references. The attorney you're considering can also be asked to provide references.

Think of lawyers as if they were surgeons. You want to use one to cut away a disease. Certainly if you were planning on major surgery to fight a serious disease, you'd get the opinions of several doctors regarding the case. Don't be awed just because a person has professional credentials. Lawyers are humans, just like everyone else. They'll have different opinions about the case and will suggest different strategies. The best attorneys are creative, knowledgeable, and enthusiastic. If an attorney lacks any of these qualities, s/he usually should not be considered. No one strategy is necessarily right or wrong; there may be several valid alternatives. It's up to you to decide which strategy suits you and which attorney seems most compatible with you.

I'm always suspicious of attorneys who think they know it all and are not interested in input from the client. In my experience, clients often have interesting and useful insights that help make a case. The best attorneys I've worked with confer closely with their clients while putting the case together.

Local attorneys sometimes discourage clients from hiring out-of-town or well-known attorneys. Their theory is that a high-powered defense will in itself raise suspicions regarding the defendant. My experience watching judges and juries has not borne out that belief. I've found the courts to be impressed with good-quality counsel. They seem to feel that it reflects on the importance of the case, rather than on the defendant's guilt.

During the Vietnam War, the U.S. increased its troop strength incrementally, moving slowly from a few thousand soldiers to fifty thousand. This slow buildup gave the enemy time to adjust to the situation and learn how to deal with it. A marginal attorney might say, "Let me do the preliminary hearing and the motions; then if you don't win, get a trial lawyer." I think this is a bad strategy. Rather than increase force gradually, which gives the prosecutor time to prepare, you want to blast them out of the water as fast as possible. It will cost less in the long run, since less attorney time will be used, the case will end faster, and there will be less pressure on the defendant. A good attorney may be able to quash the government case at the preliminary hearing and thus put an immediate end to the prosecution.

D. QUALITIES OF GOOD DEFENSE LAWYERS

Successful criminal defense requires the stamina of a fighter, the willingness to take on the state, the love of a good intellectual fight, and a passion for winning. Most good defense lawyers consider themselves outlaws; often they hang out with other outlaws.

Much like the knights of old England, your lawyer is a paid champion, sent to do battle with the forces of the government. The other side usually has the big horses, the best armor, and the white hats. If the knight you've personally chosen to champion your cause is too close to the political or social establishment, s/he may not have the requisite fighting spirit. I've never understood how someone who challenges and tries to defeat the prosecutor on an intensely personal basis can then ride home, lunch, or play golf with him/her. It seems to be a sellout to me.

How your lawyer looks may or may not matter. A good-looking lawyer isn't worth anything without all the other qualities we've discussed. Obviously, competence doesn't come with the purchase of clothes, cars, or office furniture. The best lawyers are often unaware of, or don't care about, those petty things. Your life and liberty may be worth the effort to look past appearances to the substance of the person.

Tony Serra, the role model for the movie "True Believer," has long hair, wears nondescript clothing, and drives old cars. Mike Stepanian, noted San Francisco attorney and author of "Pot Shots," has called pot defense lawyers the Samurai of the counterculture, and that captures somewhat the flavor of a good attorney.

E. DO YOU KNOW YOUR LAWYER YET?

It's not illegal, nor is it evidence of guilt, to know the law and its ramifications. Going to a reputable criminal defense attorney and paying for a consultation makes good sense. You must have a couple of dozen questions you'd like to ask someone who knows.

No lawyer can (or should) give you advice on how to break the law successfully, how to evade prosecution, or how to cover your ass if you're busted. Charges of obstructing justice, aiding and abetting, or counseling the commission of various felonies have all been brought against defense lawyers who were not careful as to what they said or to whom they said it.

This is why good criminal defense attorneys are careful. If an attorney has a successful private practice, the chances are good that the cops have tried to bust him/her for some real or imagined indiscretion.

Lawyers must follow the rules of ethics. As a matter of basic self-protection, a lawyer will be very hesitant to advise you if no case is pending and you don't sound right, feel right, and look and smell right. You don't have to confess all your indiscretions to a lawyer. If your brother Joe is breaking the law, you might ask a lawyer about it. If you have a fictional scenario in mind that will help to illustrate your questions and make the answers meaningful, it's okay to talk about that. Often a person who is thinking about growing pot will consult a lawyer and decide that the risks and penalties outweigh the probable benefits and decide not to grow. (Remember the conspiracy laws!)

It's better to get the feel of a lawyer as a person when there's no emergency pending in your life. It's also better to get a realistic assessment of your contemplated actions than an after-the-fact monologue from the lawyer about how you screwed up.

Most attorneys don't charge for a brief consultation about a pending or potential case, because they want to be hired for that actual case. But if you haven't been busted and don't expect to be, you should pay the lawyer's regular hourly rate for a consultation.

Prepare all your questions and then, during the consultation, make notes and get new ideas. The difference between good and bad lawyers will be more evident if you're not stressed out and searching frantically for someone to save you. Ego-trippers, especially, are easier to spot when you're not twisted. The "Trust me, I can help you" aspect is not there, and the true grit becomes visible.

It's possible that you'll find one lawyer who's obviously better than the others you've seen. If you're fairly certain that this is the person you would turn to in case of a bust, then you can think about that great American institution, the lawyer on a retainer. If you give a lawyer money, s/he can treat it either as an opening move on a particular matter, or as a fee to insure his/her later availability.

The best lawyers tend to be the busiest, and may be busy elsewhere. A single lawyer or law firm can defend only a limited number of clients competently. Your retainer fee helps the lawyer pay the bills in lean times or pay for a toy or a trip, or buys you some number of hours of representation later, if you need them. The lawyer earns the money for being available if needed. If you do get busted, you know who to call. Lawyers are happy to hear from someone they know. Most important, they'll feel obligated to begin work immediately.

F. RETAINERS

Attorneys are required to tell the Feds if you pay more than $10,000.00 in cash. The fee for a decent attorney in a serious case will seriously exceed this limit. Simple problem, simple answer: Don't pay in cash. A check from you or from some third party is all the preparation it takes to avoid this potentially embarrassing problem.

G. FEES

Before hiring an attorney, you should discuss price, find out exactly what s/he will do for that price, and get a written statement and a receipt. People who wouldn't think twice about trying to negotiate the price of a stereo in a store often feel too cowed to discuss money with a lawyer. It somehow seems out of place to them. This works to the lawyer's advantage, and makes it easy for him/her to set a price. There is no reason for you not to discuss the price, the terms of payment, and in what form the fees are to be paid. In some cases, attorneys are required to report cash payments of as little as $3,000 to the government, so they should be paid by credit card, check, or money order.

Establish a budget with the lawyer. Revise it regularly; stay informed as to what your money has bought. There is a universal requirement that lawyers keep records of things they do and the time they spend on your case. Even in a flat-rate-fee arrangement, you should be able to see the file grow thicker, and the pleadings and paperwork from both sides should be given to you as a matter of course. You should keep abreast of your case. Even the busiest of lawyers can call you back, if necessary after business hours, or the paralegal assistant/secretary can meaningfully relay your concerns and answer your questions.

H. DO YOU NEED A PUBLIC DEFENDER?

The question of whether or not you can afford to hire a lawyer means simply this: Do you have money? Mom and Dad aren't required to help you. If you don't have a substantial bank account, a partially paid-for home, or a regular job, you probably qualify for the public defender. You don't have to mortgage your property or spend yourself into poverty for a lawyer. The public defender (or a court-appointed counsel from a list on a panel, or a private lawyer or law firm with a contract) will do his/her best for little or no money.

If you can't afford to hire your own lawyer, the court will appoint one for you. You may be required to pay some or all of the fees charged by this lawyer, usually less than $250. This depends on your financial status.

1. P.D. Realities

You do need the assistance of an attorney. The key word is "assistance." All the requirements we've discussed so far apply to a public defender as well.

Usually these lawyers are talented and dedicated. The problem is that they're underfunded and overworked. This means that a marijuana case may not get the attention it requires. This is understandable, especially if the overworked public defender or court-appointed lawyer is also handling murder 1, manslaughter, assault, and robbery cases, which are considered much more serious.

A defendant has several options, even if s/he has no money to spend on attorneys. You could shop around and try to make a deal to get the court to appoint the attorney of your choice. For instance, in one case of a married couple in California, the public defender was appointed to defend the wife. To avoid a conflict of interest, the husband could not use the PD's office, so he shopped around for an attorney (who was paid by the state) until he found one who shared his idea of a defense.

Even if there's no choice but to use a PD, all is not lost. A squeaky wheel gets the most attention. By letting the PD know that you're taking the case very seriously and that a certain level of service is expected, you may get much more attention.

At the very least, you have to tell the attorney the facts. In addition, you can be the "gofer" and research assistant. The only things that limit your participation are your interest and your lawyer's time and patience. Helping the attorney to prepare the case can save him/her enormous amounts of time, and gives you insight into how the battle is fought. Some things you can do are to develop a theory of the case, examine and critique the police and prosecution documents, make a detailed investigation of crime-scene data, find experts, and help locate and identify witnesses (but not serve subpoenas, since you're a party to the action).

All appointed attorneys are hideously overworked and disgustingly underpaid. Many counties prohibit public defenders from working overtime (the budget, you know) on the hundreds of cases they have. Some are great lawyers performing a valuable and noble public service; some are dweebs, punks, creeps, and dump trucks hiding from real work behind the skirts of a government paycheck.

The problems are these: (1) It's not always easy to tell what kind of lawyer has been assigned to you. (2) You'll have very little control over the particular attorney you get from the court. Even the great public defenders and Criminal Justice Act panel attorneys are far too busy to treat you like a private, paying client. Government funds for court-appointed attorneys have always been tight, and the prosecution's budget always outweighs that of the defense. With an appointed attorney, it's not a fair fight.

2. Helping Your P.D.

There are many ways you can help your (appointed or retained) attorney represent you well.

1. Be professional, helpful, and caring. Be on time for appointments with the lawyer. Get the names, addresses, and paperwork you have access to before they're needed. Communicate this information. Write it down so that you and your lawyer won't forget.

2. Be awake, involved, calm, and centered. It won't help to be overly emotional. Tears or yelling may be necessary to reach a real turd, but it's rare that they'll help.

3. Write things down. This may seem stupid, but your word that something was told, promised, planned, and so on will carry much more weight if your notepad shows when, and with whom, you discussed it. Such a trick also helps keep you calm in the crunch. When you get very upset, take a deep breath and make some notes.

3. My Appointed Attorney Won't Call Me Back!

If you've been pleasantly insistent, and have done everything you were supposed to do, you'll most likely be so unusual that your attorney will quit ducking your calls. If you call and are put off, call again. Make an appointment to call and talk. Attorneys have a legal duty to meet and confer with clients. It is partly up to you to make sure that your meeting is not just the one minute before your case is called in court each day. Be nice, but be insistent. Keep notes of when you called and who you spoke to.

If you feel you aren't being represented by your appointed lawyer, and s/he won't talk to you about the case, you may be able to have another one appointed. Here's what to do:

After too many unsuccessful attempts to see or talk to your attorney (or at least to some attorney from the office who is knowledgeable about your case), you can start to complain. How many times are too many? It depends on how complex the case is, and how soon you go to court again. An "interviewer" or an investigator may routinely be used to get your story, but you have a right (and an obligation to yourself) to talk to the lawyer. Only the lawyer can evaluate your case and give you legal advice. If you have diligently tried to see him/her, take notes on your attempts, then try to see a supervisor or even the office chief of staff.

This usually produces an upset attorney who's been ordered to see you. Better for him/her to be upset now than for you to be upset later on. If the lawyer is mad because s/he has to talk to you and explain your case, perhaps you should suggest s/he give the case to someone who will help you and not get mad about it.

4. Changing P.D.s

If all your efforts to communicate fail, and you come to court without having had any contact with the attorney, tell the judge. Have your notepad detailing the many, many attempts you made, and then you can make your attorney tell the court what the problems have been, why s/he hasn't talked to you, and when s/he will do so.

The judge will undoubtedly start by oozing praise for the attorney who's trying to sell you out. I've heard judges lie shamelessly to defendants about their feelings or opinions about a lawyer. The judge probably knows that the so-called attorney has not really represented anyone in years. However, a judge will say, "S/he's an experienced, competent attorney." What this may really mean is that the attorney has not yet been disbarred, but is neither competent nor experienced. The court is trying to protect the record. The judge is only interested in getting you in and out of his/her court A.S.A.P. and making whatever happens stick.

Reversals for incompetent counsel are very rare, even though incompetent attorneys abound. Don't let the judge talk you into withdrawing your objections to the lack of real assistance from your attorney. Be strong, ask for someone else, and make a record of your objections and efforts.

The grounds (the reasons you must allege) for getting a new attorney are that your wishes and desires about the defense of the case differ from those of your attorney and a conflict has arisen, so that you and s/he can't cooperate to prepare and present the defense you want to present. If your lawyer "thinks you'll be convicted," and therefore refuses to prepare a defense, get a new lawyer. You can tell the judge the problems in his/her chambers without the prosecutor present. This maintains confidentiality and protects your case. Please remember that the truth may be that you're screwed. Even so, your attorney should still try to get you off.

The obvious downside of asking for a new attorney is that you may get the very worst attorney, who is assigned to deal with difficult defendants. However, you may wind up with the best and brightest if you demonstrate that you're aware, awake, and interested. A fair amount of knowledge on your part may also persuade the powers that be that you're serious and that you deserve adequate representation.

Let me say without qualification that a bad public defender may be better by far than an expensive, incompetent private attorney. At least PDs practice criminal law exclusively, day after day, and have access to knowledgeable help. An alcoholic divorce lawyer may get a big fee and not only do nothing, but also know nothing.

I. LAWYER-CLIENT RELATIONSHIPS

1. Types of Relationships

There are no set rules that control how much or how little you participate in your defense. It's a matter of agreement and capabilities. Your attorney should be willing to discuss the degree of your participation.

Don't expect the attorney to give you a law school education, but a complete explanation of all the important issues is mandatory. If you have the desire, the next step is to read the relevant case law.

If you find, as many clients have, that your lawyer has changed from a gung-ho fighter to someone who tells you, "You're guilty, take the deal," be very careful. It's a common cheap trick for lawyers to take a case—and all your money—and, after doing little or no real work, to dump you to the Public Defender or try to plead you out. Lack of money is not a controlling factor. You have to be able to afford what you want done, but money is not a good enough reason in and of itself to dump you.

Even a competent, thorough defense attorney can't always win. If the facts are incriminating, there may be no defense against the charges. The true role of the defense attorney is to think up ways to get you off. Be careful that your attorney doesn't lie to you about your chances of winning just to get the case and then tell you later that you have no defense.

If you and the lawyer have talked about a motion to suppress, it should be made, heard, argued, and (if appropriate) denied by a judge. Your attorney should not say, "I thought it had no chance, so I didn't try."

As I've noted, the duty of the defense attorney is to think up ways to get you free. If you want to pursue any of these options, the attorney's job is to do the best preparation and presentation possible. If it turns out to have been an unsuccessful choice, at least it was your informed choice of action. It's often true that your strength and determination will motivate an attorney to do well, and just trying, just fighting hard, may turn up some angles that were not apparent at first blush. It's never too late to fight, according to some experienced, successful defendants.

Most good lawyers I know will take time to explain the justice system to you, to acquaint you with the basic principles, and to get some idea of your particular story. Don't expect to tell all during the first meeting. The relationship will grow and there will be time, soon, to talk some more.

2. What Is Client Control?

Client control occurs when a lawyer uses her/his superior knowledge and skills to steer the client in any particular direction that the lawyer wishes him/her to go. By steering the client's opinion for the sake of the attorney's own wishes, s/he is able to force or allow clients to plead guilty to crimes and sentences they do not deserve.

The problem for the layperson is that it's difficult to spot a lawyer who puts his/her interests before the client's. A second opinion is always acceptable to a real lawyer who's being square with you. Clients rarely hear this question, commonly asked of one lawyer by another: "Do you have client control?" If I hear this question and tell my colleague "No," I'm usually smothered with sympathy. If you ever hear one lawyer ask another, "Do you have client control?" and they're talking about you, run like hell.

A lawyer with client control can negotiate a deal and then to sell it to you as if it were in your best interest. The case is resolved as the lawyer thinks it should be. This might be laudable, but I don't know any lawyers who offer to serve the time for the client because it was such a great deal.

The Courts

A. GENERAL INFORMATION

Some people think that hearings and trials are genteel affairs because there is a certain decorum and many of the players are wearing suits and ties. In reality, trials are verbal street fights. The lawyers try to beat up each other's witnesses, discredit each other's theories, and show who is the toughest by winning the case. The sad part is that people's lives hang in the balance while such pettiness is indulged.

The burden of proof in a trial is greater than in a preliminary hearing. Instead of "the preponderance of the evidence," it is "guilty beyond a reasonable doubt."

Most cases don't actually go to trial, and most attorneys are afraid to fight jury trials. One reason for this is that the court is likely to impose a harsher sentence if the defendant is found guilty at trial than if s/he pleads guilty beforehand. However, sentencing guidelines are mandatory for federal defendants, so that the court has little leeway. The best opportunity may be a trial. I have found that most jurors take their responsibilities seriously and try to render fair verdicts.

There are many strategies for winning at trial. If the facts are on the defendant's side, the object of the defense strategy is to prove those facts to the jury. However, other issues may be important. Trying the police is one good strategy. If the cops messed up their investigation, the defense should let the jurors know about it, so that the jury develops reasonable doubt.

The courts are terribly out of contact with the realities of society and have no idea of the impact of the drug war on people's lives. At one trial a judge asked me, "Do you mind if we go off the record for a moment?" I replied, "No." He continued, "So you earn a living legally from marijuana, writing articles and books and taking photos and testifying?"

I replied, "Yes, your Honor. But all of us here today are earning a living from cannabis. You, the prosecution and defense attorneys, the bailiff, secretary, court reporter, janitor—"

At this point the prosecutor said, "Your Honor, I object to this line of reasoning. I don't—"

The judge interrupted him. "I understand Mr. Rosenthal's line of reasoning. This proceeding wouldn't be taking place if marijuana were legal, and none of us would be here. Let's go back on the record."

B. STAGES OF LITIGATION

Arrest
Bail
Arraignment in lower court
Discovery and investigation
Motions
Preliminary hearing (probable cause hearing)

or

Grand jury indictment
Arrest
Bail

then in either case

Arraignment in superior court (trial court)
Motions
Pretrial conference
Trial
Sentencing
Appeal

Each state has its very own rules of criminal procedure, and each judge has his/her own way of doing things. The listing above is a general outline. Details vary in each jurisdiction. Timing is often critical in criminal cases: You can snooze and lose.

What happens at each stage is largely determined by the case, the lawyers, and the court. Don't take a rigid view of what should be done—that's what a good lawyer is for.

> You should remain acutely conscious of your bail status. If you post bail or are released without bail, you must make all your appearances, and be on time—and properly dressed. If you do all this, then the judge usually can't put you back in jail or raise the bail. If you're convicted, then the judge can put you in jail. Ask for bail pending (awaiting) sentencing. After sentencing, ask for bail pending the resolution of your appeal. You must, of course, file an appeal to stay out on bail, and this costs money, but you can try for release without bail—the worst they can do is say "No."

Sentencing is a stage of the case. If you lose the case, you're going to be sentenced. If you ignore this part of litigation, the consequences of your conviction may be more harsh than necessary. I have employed the services of sentencing consultants to investigate and prepare a report. You or your attorney can do the same. The report that is prepared by the probation officer will be based largely on what the police said you did. If you wish to contest the facts of the case as set forth in the police reports, you must prepare your own presentence investigation and report.

Do not expect the probation officer to be sympathetic when you accuse the police of lying. Although probation officers are required by law to be impartial and unbiased, it is the rare bird who is able to see the truth in a defendant's assertions when the police report says the opposite.

In many ways the probation interview is an attitude test. You must demonstrate remorse—be repentant and contrite—if for nothing more than all the trouble you've caused yourself, your family, and the system. If you're wrongly convicted, you still can be sorry for causing them so much hassle, while still softly proclaiming your innocence.

C. NEATNESS, ATTITUDE, AND VOICE

Your dress and attitude in court may suggest to the prosecutor and the court that you're a good person—or some kind of Charles Manson mass-murderer character. To act in the play, you need the appropriate costume. If you want to keep your identity, beard, hair, jeans, or whatever, be sure to discuss it with your lawyer.

You don't have to become someone different and try to fool the court. Your honesty and your centered awareness of who you are and what you were (and were not) doing may be the greatest forces you can employ to help yourself.

You and your lawyer can present the most favorable image and make the best impression on the court without guile or artifice. If you're neat and clean, you can look like yourself and not be offensive. You can buy good, clean clothes at a thrift store. If you're completely broke, you can usually borrow clothes for court. Most public defenders' offices have a limited stock of dress-up-for-trial clothes. Simple rules: Do not wear a T-shirt. If you're a man, wear a pair of slacks (not jeans), a shirt with a collar, shoes, and socks. Carry your hat. No bandannas. No visible jewelry except wedding rings. Women should wear a modest dress or skirt and blouse appropriate for an office. It's best to wear a suit. This is a very important, very serious moment in your life; by appearing in a suit, you're telling the court that you recognize that.

If you're already an in-custody defendant, you have no right to wear street clothes for court appearances, unless it's for trial by jury. Have your friends bring you street clothes and shoes to wear for your trial. If the sheriff and the judge will let you, dress out for all your appearances. Get up early enough to shave. Pull your socks up. Walk straight, stand tall. Look as if you care and are worthy of respect. I have worked in court with tattooed and hairy bikers who have charmed the judge and jury by being so pure and so honestly themselves that they were respected; the judge believed them when they said they would be good. You'll have very few chances to speak on your own behalf in court, but the judge, prosecutor, and jury look at you, closely, every time your conduct or sentence is mentioned. If you're atten-tive, awake, and polite, and participate meaning-fully in the process, you can show them your most favorable side. The courtroom is, after all, a stage where you're acting. Playing the part of the defen-dant to a tough, tough crowd, you must be con-vincing in look, word, and deed.

CONTRITION

One way to show the court that you're repentant and contrite is to be seeking help for your "drug problem." If you're busted, the legal system will presume that you have a drug problem. Even the most shallow of intellects will acknowledge that if the jail door slams, and it's because of use, possession, or association with drugs or drug users or sellers, then drugs + jail = problem.

Coupled with this elementary logic is the watchword of drug treatment: *denial*. If you don't admit you have a problem, you're "in denial." This is the first, most obvious *symptom* of drug abuse/addiction. The more you say you don't have a problem, the more the system's psychobabblers will insist you do. Worse than a problem is an *unacknowledged* problem, which is by definition untreatable.

If you would rather be treated and rehabilitated instead of jailed, you should consider acknowledging your errors to a counselor or shrink early on in the proceedings. This can be done with a fair certainty that your conversations with the doctor will not be made public or used against you.

Be careful if the Pretrial Services staff representative in federal court recommends that you undergo counseling as a condition of your release. If the wrong papers are signed (you'd better read them, and get a copy to keep), or if you admit to something you shouldn't, you may see this in your pre-sentence report to the judge, and you may regret it. This is one of those moves that require tactical preci-sion, but are strategic plays. If your strategy and the-ory of the case is "personal use," then acknowledg-ing such use is not a bad thing. If you don't know what they're talking about, the moves are different.

The majority of convicted drug offenders say to the judge at sentencing, "I'm better now." The judge would like to believe it's so, but will not unless you show him/her that you are and have been *doing*, not just talking. A religious revelation may be helpful.

Show the court and/or probation officer that you have set your mind straight. It may be helpful to demonstrate this at a very early stage of the case. It may be necessary only after conviction, before sen-tencing. If it's still just a proposal at sentencing, you're probably going to lose. If you have a demon-strated track record of AA (Alcoholics Anonymous) and/or NA (Narcotics Anonymous) meetings, a pri-vate or public mental health meeting you've regularly attended, or some such program, you have a pretty good chance of convincing the judge that you're not a threat to society, that you can control yourself, and that you may not need to go to jail. If not, the judge can and will try to protect us from you, and send you to jail.

Rarely is it a problem to admit you have a drug problem and seek help, and yet at the same time to maintain that you're innocent—or at least not as guilty as they say. Be very careful about statements made under penalty of perjury. (Pretrial release ques-tionnaires frequently list this admonition.) If you mis-state your drug use patterns, or change your tune later, someone will notice and comment to your detriment. Be sure your story fits the "evidence" and is the truth. To convince the judge, you must tell the truth—and you must appear to be telling the truth.

Basic Steps to Defend a Drug Case

Suppose you were arrested and charged. You know you'd have to defend yourself. If you had a knowledgeable, diligent, competent, and caring lawyer, and an iron disposition, nerves of steel, resolve, moves, luck, and good karma, your defense might succeed.

You do have to know what to do. How do you make sure the minimum steps are taken so that your luck and karma have room to operate?

If you follow these steps, both as an analytical framework and as a procedural guide, you'll give yourself the basic blocks upon which to build your successful defense.

A. THE FOUR ELEMENTS OF A DRUG CASE

Any drug case has four basic elements: cops, crooks, drugs, and money. If cops and two of the other three elements have been in the same room at the same time, it's a tough case. If all four have been together, it's a very difficult situation. The success of your case depends on proof in court of the four elements.

B. THE BASIC SIX-POINT PLAN

In order to defend a drug case, a plan has to be followed. Here is the one I use:

1.   Look at the evidence. Both the attorney and the expert should thoroughly examine the evidence. Depending on the issue at trial, this effort may win the case.

2.   Look at the police reports, photos, and/or video and study the evidence list.

3.   Visit the scene of the crime. Important evidence can turn up there.

4.   Talk to witnesses mentioned or suggested by steps 1 through 3.

5.   Identify the prosecution's theory, adverse evidence, and inferences from facts. Develop a defense theory of the case that accounts for the evidence, drawing favorable conclusions from physical evidence.

6.   Decide if the defendant is to testify. This can be very helpful at trial, but it must be weighed against the possibility of letting unfavorable information be admitted into the court proceedings.

1. Look at the Evidence

Though this may seem too elementary to need stating, I have observed that very few attorneys take the time and trouble to look at the physical evidence in the case.

Almost every time I ask the cops and the prosecutor for an evidence view they don't know whether to defecate or go blind. While it may be regarded as "unusual" in your town to show the defense attorney and expert the evidence, your attorney must wade through the bureaucratic BS and firmly but politely insist on seeing what the cops have as evidence. Looking at the evidence list in some police report will not do. This is simply some cop's opinion of what the evidence is. It is rarely a complete, accurate listing of the specific items taken.

Often the report contains characterizations such as "papers, records, and documents," omitting the specifics. It is tremendously important to know whether one of those papers is a pay/owe sheet or contains other damaging information. Do not allow your attorney, or your case, to be blindsided in court later by failing to insist strongly enough that the defense be shown all the items seized from you, your house, and your codefendants. Don't wait to look at the stuff until the cops bring it to court. You need to be prepared.

There are times when the evidence that ends up at the cop shop doesn't match what was found. One case in Humboldt was favorably resolved when the evidence technician showed us a big, empty bag that had contained the buds, saying, "Don't get mad at me, but there is no evidence." The previously supplied photographs had shown 35 glass jars stuffed with beautiful buds, one pound in each jar. The evidence had shrunk to 28 pounds by the time it got to the Laytonville substation (I swear to God that the cops said, "It loses weight when it dries"), and had "dried" to nothing by court time.

Presented with these problems, the prosecutor was more than reasonable in agreeing to a disposition of the case that involved no time and no fine (although he didn't undertake any investigation of this $100,000 "evaporation").

One Redding, California, case resolved favorably when the defense insisted that the pot be brought to court. Someone had taken the buds that were clearly described in the police report. No buds, no case. Because of the evidence view, the attorney knew about this and was able to use it at the right time.

In a federal case in Kansas, personal use or sale was the issue. A close examination of the evidence indicated the presence of male flowers. This proved that the plants had not been sexed and that half the plants would be eliminated from the garden. The police "expert" identified all the flowers as females, proving his ignorance to the jury once they were educated.

2. Look at the Police Reports, Photos, or Video

Once you get to court (usually at the bail hearing or arraignment, whichever comes first), you or your attorney will most likely get access to the police reports. Sometimes they will be given to you outright; sometimes you have to ask, pay, and wait. Eventually you get some or all of the reports the cops made up when they sat around after your arrest and waxed poetic about your real and imagined sins.

"Discovery" is the general name for this sort of stuff. You must get all the discovery you're legally allowed in your particular case and jurisdiction. Push for everything, obnoxiously insist they produce each, every, any, and all papers, records, documents, and names. Make formal motions to the court so that it issues orders that they turn everything over to you. Then if they don't, you may get some relief.

> Many cases have been won by pressing for more complete discovery of police reports. I once heard a cop say to a federal judge, "Oh, you wanted all the reports from that file. I didn't understand." After two months and two hearings, we finally got the name/address of the informant. The Judge understood, and so did the prosecutor when he soon thereafter (after we subpoenaed the informant to come and play and he failed to appear) made a six-month offer to the heavies and I got my poor client a walk-away. The "branch office files" in Louisiana had lots of discoverable stuff in them, once we knew who to ask and how to politely and correctly phrase our inquiry.

The reason you need all the reports is that the prosecutor most likely has (or will be given) all of them. The case against you is based on the information in the official reports. To establish the bureaucratic paper trail, the cops write it all down and send it to the prosecutor, who reads it and asks for more work and/or information if necessary. Supplemental reports are often withheld from the defense. Sometimes the cop doesn't give the report to the prosecutor until very late in the case. Sometimes the prosecutor neglects, forgets, or whatever.

You must insist that the prosecutor ask the cops if s/he has all the reports, or you must give the cops notice of the discovery hearing and order of the court. I like to include the cops as noticed parties or agents of the party; that way, they're more likely to give up the whole set of reports the first time we ask. They'll only be sleazy and sloppy if you let them get away with it.

The reports that are written become the script for the cops' testimony. If you know their reports, you can usually figure out the case against you. Your defense efforts will include finding things and people to contradict the official version of the events. You may be able to show that the cop is stupid or lying through "impeachment" (presenting contradictory evidence) of almost anything s/he has put into the report. If you can make the issue in the case the reliability of the reports, not your guilt or innocence, you may be ahead of the game.

You should also get all the reports of tests or analyses performed in your case. These are regularly done because the cop usually isn't qualified to identify pot (or any drug) for purposes of trial. An expert, usually a forensic criminologist or some such person, will perform a few visual (microscopic) examinations and a chemical test or two, and then deliver the opinion that it is whatever it is.

The visual test for marijuana involves looking for hair structure on the leaf surfaces. The chemical test is usually a Modified Duquenois-Levine. The technician mixes the pot with a reagent (a substance) that produces a light blue or purple color.

S/he adds chloroform and watches the color go into that layer. Other chemical tests that are used in pot cases are thin-layer chromatography and the use of a gas chromatograph/mass spectrometer. These are increasingly sophisticated tests; each of them has its own set of problems. If there are any issues here, get a defense expert to examine the pot and the reports of the prosecution expert. You can pursue more thorough discovery about the reagents and machines used if you think there's an issue there. Even if you don't foresee that this will be an issue, it may be to your advantage to cross-examine the forensic chemist.

In one case, the defendant had tight green buds and the forensic chemist said he examined loose brown ones. This discrepancy in the evidence caused a dismissal. Usually the chemists are honest, so they may provide you with interesting information.

The cops almost always take pictures and/or videos of the crime scene. It's such a basic thing that if they don't have lots of photos, you ought to be very suspicious. You need to see them as soon as possible, and you need to get copies for your own use.

Call to mind any number of television cop/lawyer dramas, and you'll see how careful examination of photos and/or videos may lead to your freedom. The camera records what was there (and also what was not there), creating a frozen moment in time. You must be careful here, because in some cases this frozen instant is not truly indicative of *reality*, which is a changing, continuing, evolving thing, *not* a frozen moment in time.

There is no doubt that photos and videos taken by the cops are vitally important. If you don't get your very own set of those photos, you (or your attorney) must at least look at them. Getting copies is better, because then you and your attorney can sit in the calm quiet times and talk about them under the protection of the attorney-client privilege. If your attorney is knowledgeable about pot growing and use, s/he will need little explanation of the photos; if not, of course, more explanation will be necessary.

Ignorance about the basic processes, procedures, and implements for growing, use, and sales is an indication of lack of personal experience (not at all required for your attorney, but perhaps a plus) and of professional experience (which could be fatal) with these types of cases. Presenting a marijuana case poorly, many times over, may not be a plus for a lawyer. Mere experience is not enough.

In a case in Humboldt County, California, the public defender had the good sense to send an investigator to videotape the scene of the bust. The tape showed that the alleged grower had put out salt blocks to attract deer to his house, and that he had also spread barrels of spoiled apples from a local orchard to attract bears. Mr. Animal Lover was acquitted at trial when it was pointed out that marijuana growers protect their crops from wild animals; they don't befriend them and leave food out for them.

The real growers nearby (who were undoubtedly upset about Mr. Nature's practice) had also made a trail from a public access road to the project. The cops had overlooked this in their investigation, but the defendant's investigator took the right pictures.

3. Visit the Scene

Field investigation: You need a person other than yourself or your lawyer to testify and authenticate (confirm that they're for real) the pictures you've taken and the maps you've prepared. It would be even better for the investigator or expert to take the photos, draw the maps, and so on. The cops may not always be fair or accurate in their investigation, and they won't agree with you and your documents and, ultimately, your theory of the case, just because they're true. Professional investigators familiar with marijuana should be used.

Viewing the scene with an expert or investigator familiar with marijuana is the most often overlooked, ignored, or rationalized-away aspect of cultivation litigation. Most lawyers are usually unwilling and occasionally unable (physically or timewise) to go to the scene of your particular crime. However, this may be the single most important aspect of the case.

The investigation may not turn anything up, but unless the lawyer goes and looks, and assesses the situation with his/her superior intellect and knowledge, s/he can't be sure. This is why you hired him/her, isn't it? The ability to get the information from the scene, and to work with it, is the basis of a successful defense. In your initial interview with your lawyer-to-be, which should include a discussion of what is to be done, this step should be included. The scene may be far away, yes, and it may be that a bit of time has passed, yes, but unless you're willing to give up a point that could be important, the visit should be made. I'd think twice about having a lawyer who couldn't, or wouldn't, go to the scene.

The court, or the jury, must hear the defense's version from a fairly impartial investigator who has been to the scene. It can't be your lawyer, and your own self-serving testimony will not be given as much credence. In addition, the story (the theory) must be coherent and consistent. You may have to face a very difficult cross. Exposure to cross-examination, if you're not prepared, can wreck your case. Also, your motive to lie is strong. If the perjury is detected, your case is blown.

Having an investigator go instead of, rather than with, your lawyer is a far worse alternative. The eyes and mind of another person act as a filter between what was there and what your attorney "knows" about the case. Just as your knowledge is filtered by the necessity of choosing what to tell, and how to tell it, an investigator relating to the attorney his/her version of what was there is better than nothing (especially if accompanied by pictures that can be shown), but is certainly not the best.

To recap an already-told story, the salt-lick defense was solidified only when the defense expert saw the video and the salt cubes. If the lawyer had visited the scene and observed the salt blocks, perhaps his curiosity would have been aroused and he would have asked the accused about it. When it was brought to his attention, he understood its importance. The defendant was not in fact a dope grower, so he didn't understand the importance of this evidence to his case, and he hadn't mentioned it to the lawyer. The investigator had seen them, but had forgotten to notice and report them.

4. Talk to the Witnesses

Never rely on a cop's opinion of what the witnesses said or did. The police are not fair and impartial observers and reporters. They're usually trying to filter things so that their script will match their theory of the case. They know the minimum statutory requirements necessary to charge you with any particular crime.

Soon after they have assessed the situation, they usually decide who is the crook and who are the victims or witnesses. Then they gather facts, and notice and record things, that support their theory. Your case will be won or lost by investigation and preparation apart from, and in addition to, the official reports in the case.

In many cases the police do not put everything said by the witnesses into the reports. You can use this to your advantage strategically and tactically. If a witness says the police report of what he/she said and/or did is not true, complete, and accurate, you can use this fact in court to show that the police script is not the truth, and that perhaps the conclusion the cops had in mind isn't the right one!

In marijuana cultivation cases, this tendency of cops to slant the evidence is often manifested in their ignoring other trails and modes of access to the garden site. If "the" trail from the project to your house or road is not the only trail in the area, which is usually the case, perhaps the frequency of use of this trail—and of alternate trails—should be investigated. It's not illegal for you to walk by someone else's project on your way somewhere else.

Some Northern California residents were happy to tell the cops that Joe Zingo regularly walked on the trail "to" the project. They also said he was en route to his mom's house to tend to her needs, a fact omitted in the police reports. The trail he took was an established hiking trail that went from A to B, coming close to other trails that led to his house, the project, and his mom's place. He was the first poor soul to come along on "the" trail after the cops had set up surveillance near the project. Overeager as always, they busted him before he touched the plants or even entered the garden.

It was a shame that the defense team had to intimate that he was a pirate who might have just been looking for a ripoff to commit, but the cops and the court understood at least that not everyone in the forest was the grower the cops were looking for. The defendant was acquitted. He did not testify on his own behalf, having nothing to add to his not guilty plea.

The worse the case appears from the police reports of the statements of witnesses, the more important it is to go and talk to the people cited. A head-in-the-sand attitude is a sure recipe for failure. If your situation is really that bad, you have to know it; on the other hand, it could be much better than you imagined.

A most important aspect of this need to talk to the witnesses is the need to talk to them *soon*. Investigation and preparation of a defense is like the expanding circles of ripples on a pond. One idea, one thought, one lead, can generate an expanding, at times seemingly endless, pattern of necessary followup. Finding a good lead too late to follow it is the bane of trial lawyers, who are generally one half step short of where they could be—and scrambling.

Don't let your lawyer be, and don't you be, slow about getting around to talking to the witnesses. If they're friendly and cooperative, you can gather them at your house and when the field investigation is in progress, the initial witness interviews can be conducted at the same time. You can gather up everyone and take them to your lawyer's office, to the court, or wherever—whatever it takes. Your lawyer should be an active participant in this process.

An investigator who will serve as a witness is necessary if the police witness is not friendly or cooperative, or if the story s/he tells is critical or might change for some reason. Be like the cops and make notes or tape-record it, but be aware of discovery rules.

According to these rules, you'll probably have to give the witnesses' prior statements to the prosecutor at some time.

Your version of what the prosecution witnesses will say probably is not discoverable, at least prior to trial. Once a witness has testified, you'll probably have to disclose any statements your witnesses have made for so prosecution can use them during cross-examination. Be sure to consider this rule in deciding whether or not to make a "hard" record of the witnesses' statements.

5. Prosecution and Defense Theories of the Case

Once you have the police reports and have seen the evidence, you should be able to identify the prosecution's theory of the case. Just as in the parlor games, the "crime" consists of a person (or persons) who did thus and so, in such a place, with certain tools/implements/weapons.

Usually the prosecution's theory is obvious and is rarely stated as a theory. Most prosecutors try to establish the "facts" without any true analytical framework. This gives you an open field to run on.

The formation, and the importance, of the prosecution and defense theories of the case will be discussed in Chapter 9.

THE TRUTH

There are times when the truth, ugly and unvarnished, will set you free. Any time you try to manipulate the truth, you court disaster by losing the moral high ground. Therefore, you should always tell the truth. However, it is equally important to prepare so that you will *appear* to be telling the truth. Only you and God know what the truth is, and S/he probably won't come to Earth, much less to court, soon enough to affect your case.

---

6. The Defendant's Testimony

"Do I have to testify?" is a question lawyers are often asked. The question comes from the natural fear of being on the spot and of being forced to talk to and in front of people who have power over you. Most defendants are not comfortable with public speaking, especially to authority figures. The very real fear you feel will be confirmed only if you and your lawyer do not adequately prepare for your testimony.

Preparation for your testimony includes, at the very least, going over all the police reports and all of the physical evidence in order to rehearse, refine, shape, and color your words and memories so that they fairly and fully reflect the truth of the points you wish to assert.

Many defendants and lawyers feel that they can't or shouldn't talk to other people about what happened. Though there's a time and a place for everything, it is not suspicious, nor does it in any way imply criminal intent or behavior, for you to prepare your case. If you're asked, "Did you talk to anyone about [your story] before you came to court?" you may be inclined to hear the question as: "Did you and some other fool get together and cook up this bunch of lies?" Before you get to the point of in-court testimony, discuss at length with your attorney what you're going to say. Talk to your lawyer, in private, about all the good and bad things you will be asked and might say.

The lawyer has to follow the rules of ethics and law in preparing your testimony for public airing.

If you decide to take the witness stand and lie about something, and tell your attorney that, s/he is not allowed to put you on the stand to commit perjury. S/he is required to try to talk you out of your foolishness, or to get the judge to do so. Failing that, if you assert your right to testify, but the lawyer thinks you're lying, s/he "should" do some pretty bizarre things, such as refrain from asking you questions, and refrain from arguing to the jury that your testimony is true. If the jury doesn't think something strange is going on, they're sleeping or dead.

Problems arise when you say "ABC" and then later it appears that you might win if it's really XYZ. If you then decide that it was XYZ all the time, your attorney is likely to wonder if you're just lying. Some attorneys are very unwilling to address this issue; they may well decide that you're guilty, and give up on your defense, without ever discussing it with you.

There are a lot of gray areas to be resolved before anybody is suspected of lying, but you must be aware of the rule against lying under oath! Perjury is taken seriously and is severely punished.

You may not remember the details correctly. Your normal, natural intense desire to win your case will influence you as you try to figure out your defense: your recollections may be filtered and colored by this desire. Together with a limited understanding of the law—and of the police version of the facts—this may cause you to be wrong. If you insist on telling your story in detail, early on, you may feel (or your attorney may feel) later that you have a vested interest in sticking with that story, rather than changing it in mid-case.

You may think that the sun rose at midnight on the day of your particular problem, and that you're therefore innocent. Your lawyer will present that testimony to the jury if you insist, but s/he will try to show you that the rest of the world believes a 6:00 a.m. sunrise is more in line with reality. The local newspaper, or your friends, or other sources, may also have some information on that. The kicker is that often your lawyer will conclude that your best shot is to claim that a 6:00 a.m. sunrise is the truth.

The best way to avoid this problem is to be orderly in your approach to the case. You and your attorney should discover and analyze the prosecution's case and theories, and the physical evidence, *before* your story is cast in stone. I don't even ask what my client thinks the facts are until well into the case. It is just his/her opinion, not necessarily the truth, because the client might be right, be wrong, or be lying.

As far as your attorney is concerned, his/her first task is to discover, analyze, and discuss the evidence against you. Though it may be important at the proper time to establish your side of the story, it's rarely productive for you to decide when and how to relate the minute details of the incident—to the cops or to your attorney. It's never helpful to allow the story to become fixed before you know as much as you can about the case against you.

When a suspect talks to the cops at the scene, his/her story is on record. Usually, defendants' selective recollection and their desire to talk themselves out of the problem creates more problems for them. Talking about seemingly innocent things and telling the whole, unvarnished truth will not set you free. The cops at the scene are not required to believe you when you tell them and, worse, they may hear it wrong, they may interpret it badly, or they may lie. They may be more interested in making an arrest than in finding the perpetrator.

In a recent federal case, a national park ranger insisted the defendant had admitted to owning a boat (illegally on a closed lake) and a backpack full of plastic starter pots, and had said he was there to grow marijuana. (The defendant said he'd told Smokey the Bear that he "knew how the game was played" and "wanted a lawyer.") Six hours later, the cops finally read him his official Miranda rights and he officially invoked them.

The lying cop changed his story all three times he told it, and the judge ruled that the defendant's statement had been illegally obtained, but the defendant had to live with those lies at trial. His attitude probably got him that courtesy from the cop. Without those police statements, implausible as they were, the case would have been much easier.

The Fresno, California, jury decided that having seeds and equipment, and going somewhere to see if it's okay for growing, is not an attempt to grow. The defendant successfully testified that he never went from thinking to intent plus action.

The United States Attorney and the prevaricating ranger were extremely upset, since they thought it was a dead-bang case. Help from experts and a good lawyer changed a 10-year mandatory minimum prison term case into a 6-month maximum in a halfway house. A nasty aside from that case was the bold assertion by the Assistant United States Attorney that each and every unsprouted, unplanted seed was the equivalent of a kilogram (2.2 pounds) of dry, manicured bud.

You can prepare for your testimony by reading the law you're accused of violating, then accounting for the physical evidence in a favorable way. If the Feds charge you with attempted growing, for instance, they must prove you went from just *thinking* about doing it to some *substantial* step toward the commission of the crime. If you know that, you're better prepared to analyze your actions and verbalize your intent in the way most likely to set you free.

Approach the case with knowledge of the sentence you face on the charges. If you say things that are better left unsaid to a cop, judge, or jury, you can be sentenced for what you say you did, even if no one ever sees you with any contraband. If a defendant testifies that s/he has been a grower for years, and has sold a bit here and there, s/he may talk him/herself into a huge prison term.

C. PLEA BARGAINING

Plea bargaining may take place during most of the stages of the case, any time your attorney and the prosecutor are together. If you think it is possible and/or advisable to try to cut a deal, use every opportunity to push your position. Even if they don't agree, you can plant seeds in their minds.

The official time to cut the deal is the hearing just before the trial, usually called the pretrial conference, the jury call, or some such. You must be prepared before this hearing if you hope to sell your case to the prosecutor. It usually won't work, and you do not want to reveal anything the opposition can check on and "disprove" at trial later.

At the federal level, the crucial fact of a plea bargain is the "relevant offense conduct": How much product are you going to be connected with? If you can get an agreement that the "conduct" amounts to less than 100, 1,000, or whatever number of kilos, you may be able to have some control over your ultimate sentence.

In one federal case in Oregon, the snitch had set up five projects and put the "growers" in place, with lights, equipment, and plants. When busted, "Toni" had lots to say about my client and the four others. Each got a long prison term for his/her own garden of over 1,000 plants. The snitch had come over and demonstrated cloning, thereby making 8 mother plants into 732 babies, and then told the cops to come on down.

The judge let us put on experts at the sentencing hearing, and decided that over 700 of the "plants" were not plants because they were cuttings with no root hairs on them, so they were not to be considered plants. He knocked 8 years off the recommendation/guideline for our defendant.

When the snitch was sentenced, he didn't get the usual walk-away with thanks. The judge added up the number of plants from the five projects, and since no one contested the plant count, all of them were considered plants. The judge assigned 100 grams of weight to each mature plant (under the 1987 guidelines) and each day-old cutting (a total of 2,500 of those in the five projects) and gave the snitch the required long-term sentence.

The judge thanked the government for recommending a lenient sentence for the snitch, but the court is not required to follow the prosecutor's recommendation. The guidelines called for 21 years, and it was really a 20-to-life crime, so the judge felt that a sentence of "only" 21 years was the right thing to do. I had argued mightily that the federal district court judge was not just a glorified clerk, adding up numbers and going to a scorecard for the sentence, but "Toni," the snitch, didn't argue anything.

During the sentencing hearing, I reminded the judge of the concept of Constitutional democracy. It had been developed to protect citizens from unbridled government power over their lives. I covered the need for an independent judiciary, with discretion and power of its own. The judge replied somberly that it was clear that the law put him in the position I described, and proceeded to add and subtract "points". He expressed no sympathy with my client's situation, but he did follow the law and knock off the cuttings—for my guy only.

You can be sentenced for things you've been found not guilty of doing. As I've mentioned, the standard of proof at a sentencing hearing is "preponderance of the evidence;" at trial, "beyond a reasonable doubt." This means that if you only "probably" did it, the jury may have to acquit you, but at sentencing, the judge can find the act to have been proven.

Another example of wretched excess at sentencing is the case in which you talk to the cop about a much larger deal (buy or sell) than you actually carry out. The issue is whether or not you *could have* done it. If you sell an ounce and talk about a truckload, and have some real or apparent ability to score the big load, you can be charged for it. The truck that was only in your mind may come to the sentencing hearing and run you over.

The Theories of the Case

A. THE PROSECUTION'S THEORY

Every case has at least one theory—the prosecution's. It reads like the board game *Clue*. "He did it in the bedroom with fluorescent lights and sold the stuff in Baggies weighed on the scale." In order to win a case, the defense has to prove either that the prosecution cheated or that their theory is wrong.

The prosecution's theory of the case is detailed in the complaint or indictment. If you look at what the law forbids and what it is alleged that you did, you can see how the theory developed. To make a comprehensible summation argument to the jury, the prosecutor must arrange the facts and the law so that they fit together to show that you're guilty.

A competent, ethical prosecutor will not urge the jury to convict a person because s/he is a long-haired, no-good layabout. S/he may intimate that or tap-dance around it, caress, stroke, and play peek-a-boo with the idea, but ultimately your alleged conduct, not these other things, will be the basis for the prosecution's argument.

Proving the prosecution cheated, for instance with a bad warrant or an illegal search, usually causes the state's case to be severely damaged or dismissed. Proving the state's theory wrong at trial usually results in an acquittal or conviction on lesser charges. To be assured of winning, the defense should have its own theory: "It wasn't his bedroom, there were no sales, and the police destroyed the evidence so there is no way of knowing how much was actually there." If every case has a theory, then the proof or disproof of that theory usually depends on just a few unanswered questions about which the two sides disagree.

In a case in South Dakota, under pre-1988 guidelines, the Feds charged an individual with growing for sale. Their proof was that the grower had 47 female plants. They claimed that each of these plants, which were growing in a total space of 25 square feet, would ultimately produce a pound of bud—47 pounds. The defense disagreed, claiming that based on the small area used for growing, only 1 pound or less was involved, clearly for personal use. He was convicted only of cultivation, not intent to distribute.

* * *

A man was charged with possession for sale based on the theory that he intended to plant all the 10,000+ seeds he possessed and that the result would be too much for personal use. The defense argument was that there was no indication of any intention to use the seeds. The judge agreed with the defense expert.

* * *

A lawyer was growing a few plants on his property. The state contended that the plants were for sale because the police had found a postage scale and some Ziploc bags. The defense's winning strategy was to show that the defendant had a disincentive to sell because he could not have made enough on his few ounces to risk losing his law license.

* * *

In one case, the cops said they'd smelled growing plants from outside. The defense contended the cops couldn't smell them because the only vent was on the top of the house and the hot air would have gone up into the slight breeze, away from the place where the police were standing. The warrant was found to be invalid.

* * *

The 1990 federal sentencing guidelines by statute state that any person growing 100 to 400 plants must be sentenced to a mandatory minimum of 5 years in prison. In one case, the question was whether newly cut clones were considered to be plants. The government claimed that the clones had roots and that even if they did not, they should still be considered plants. The defense claimed that the clones didn't have roots, that court precedent had declared unrooted cuttings should not be considered plants, and that therefore they shouldn't be counted. They weren't.

In each of these cases, the prosecution had a theory and used an expert to expound on it. These experts can opine on intent (personal use, weight, yield, or quality). In other cases, the "witness" to the crime may have the crucial (mis)information. In either type of case, to win, the defense must discredit the testimony of the key prosecution witness, or make the witness's testimony irrelevant. First the defendant and the defense lawyer must set realistic goals. If the defendant was caught in the garden picking plants, s/he cannot deny involvement. The key question could also be: Personal use or sale? Other questions at trial might involve weight or yield.

> Police have a tendency to exaggerate. This is often helpful in eventually discrediting them. A classic example occurred at a trial in Visalia, California. Bill Logan was cross-examining the state's expert witness, Charlie Stowell (then head of the marijuana eradication task force of the Drug Enforcement Administration), regarding yield. At Logan's request, Charlie was holding a single-stemmed 2-foot plant in his hand. Charlie admitted that the plant weighed less than an ounce and that it would ripen in 6 weeks. He then insisted that in that time it would grow large enough to produce a pound of buds. By stubbornly refusing to budge from that position, he discredited himself; although his testimony was admitted, his absurd assertions destroyed his credibility.

Logically, one would need only to discredit the testimony of the prosecution to convince the court of the innocence—or at least a reasonable doubt of the guilt—of a defendant. However, this is not always the case. The court may need to hear the defense theory.

The defense must try to poke holes in the prosecution's theory. It may have to redefine the battleground or present a completely different theory that accounts for the facts in a better, more logical way. The best theories satisfy the judge or jury in factual as well as intuitive and emotional ways. This convergence ultimately leads to the unerring conclusion that you're innocent, or at least not guilty beyond a reasonable doubt.

At times a partial defense is easier than a complete one. Sidestepping the charges is often easier than trying to meet them head-on. This is one of the strategic decisions you and your lawyer must make in the course of defending the case. Framing your case must involve addressing, acknowledging (or, rarely, ignoring), and explaining the elements of the prosecution theory and also by redefining the issues to better suit you.

Sometimes it is not possible to convince a jury you're not involved, but the question could be what your involvement or intentions were or whether you had a legally valid reason to commit the act. For instance, a possession-for-sale charge may turn into a charge of possession or cultivation for personal use and you may get drug diversion classes or some other treatment rather than a jail sentence. Perhaps, for instance, the substance is a medical necessity for you or you have or a religious right to use it as a sacrament.

If you can define the terms of the debate—the issues about which you wish to litigate—you can focus your energy and you have a better chance to resolve the case favorably.

B. THE DEFENSE THEORY

It may seem odd to speak of redefining the terms of the debate in a case. However, it's very difficult to win a debate in the head-on contest in which the prosecution wishes to engage you. Rather than engaging in frontal combat, you may be better off if you can alter the usual scenario.

1. Contesting the Charge

The obvious example is a possession-for-sale charge. The prosecution may charge that your stash is really for sale. Your argument might be that it is yours but that it was solely for personal use. In this case, you'd admit it was yours and tell the jury where you got it, how much you paid, where you got the money to buy it, how much you use, and how long will it last, all to show that it wasn't for sale.

In California, "simple" possession of any amount is a misdemeanor, with a maximum sentence of 6 months and a $500 fine. Possession for sale is a felony and carries a lot more jail time and hassles with it. Juries are more likely to compromise to give you a break than to give you a complete walk-away. It's not uncommon for jurors to feel a defendant is being truthful in admitting what is usually the basis of contest, focusing everyone's attention on the real issues. The misdemeanor conviction often carries a fine and no jail time.

If you can get into a drug diversion program—these are available in California and some other states for defendants accused of possession or cultivation—you may even want to emphasize the possession aspects of the case ("It's mine, but not for sale"). You may need to show that the pound in the freezer is from your plants ("cultivate" is often defined as "plant, harvest, cultivate, dry, or process" or some combination thereof) in order to get a court hearing on the issue of the intended use.

2. The Defense Team

Experts are used to assist your lawyer (and you) in identifying, developing, and presenting your side of the story. The range of experts you can use is limited only by your imagination and your budget. Almost every case can benefit from the use of expert testimony to prove the facts. Even if you're guilty, and admit it, a sentencing specialist may be able to present you to the court in the most favorable light and reduce the amount of time you do in jail, or help you get alternative sentencing.

Your lawyer should be knowledgeable about the experts who can be used and are available. You and s/he will eventually make the tactical and financial decisions that are necessary.

It is not uncommon for a lawyer to get ideas about strategy and tactics from the expert. Someone who specializes in a particular area, and who works on pot cases regularly, might see just the point you need to make.

C. USING AN EXPERT

Every defendant in a marijuana case faces at least one prosecutorial witness who is proclaimed to be an expert (the prosecution expert, or PE) regarding marijuana use, sale, or cultivation. The PE usually makes statements such as these: "This is among the most sophisticated gardens we have seen in this area," or "There is no way that this could be personal use. It would take four years to smoke this much."[1] In the absence of a rebuttal, the court usually has no recourse but to accept the prosecution's theory. The best way to bring some truth to the court is to present a witness of your own.

Defense attorneys use experts for three distinct purposes: to frame the case, to help with the cross-examination of the other side's experts, and for direct testimony.

1. Framing the Case

Framing the case means developing a theory that will be considered reasonable by the court. It can be the most important use of the expert. The prosecution's theory may be based on inadequate information or on a misreading of the evidence; it may even rely on the court's ignorance. The defense requires an understanding of the situation, something the expert can provide. S/he will have the training to provide a realistic assessment of the evidence and other aspects of the case.

The prosecution's case is based on a number of assumptions. Here are a few typical ones:

- Each plant has a predetermined yield.
- All parts of the plant are usable.
- There is a set maximum amount that a person can smoke.
- Almost all users have intent to deliver.

Each of these assumptions results from some mythical averaging; they don't deal with the particulars of the case. The defense expert will have a better understanding of what the defendant was doing; once the court hears it, it is likely to be more sympathetic.

In one case in which I participated,[2] a well-paid attorney was charged with cultivation with intent to sell. He had been growing using a Phototron, which is a small hobbyist's garden chamber, and had about 2 ounces of good bud. However, he was a "pack rat" and had saved everything he had ever grown. The police found 5 pounds of fan leaves, stems, and male plants.

Based on that quantity, the prosecution charged him with intent to sell and the main PE confirmed intent to sell in his testimony. The defendant's own lawyer originally believed the defendant had intent to sell and thought the case was lost based on the weight. We were able to show the court at the hearing that the material had little economic value and that the defendant had no incentive to deliver. He was given drug diversion.

2. Testing the PE

Cross-examination can be a painful process for the prosecution's alleged expert. Usually, s/he faces a cross by an uneducated defense attorney and can appear quite knowledgeable about his/her subject. As soon as s/he is faced with a well-prepared cross, however, his/her lack of information becomes apparent.

Charles Stowell, formerly with the DEA, claimed that each plant would yield at least a pound of bud. He testified[3] that the plants would be ripe in 6 weeks. The defense attorney, Bill Logan, had Stowell hold a plant that weighed less than an ounce. Stowell maintained that the plant would grow a pound of usable material in a month and a half. The court took notice of the situation and had Logan continue the cross on another issue. Stowell was obviously discredited.

"Voire dire" is when the court determines if the expert proposed by the prosecution or defense has enough knowledge to provide information to the court. Most prosecution marijuana experts have never faced a real voir dire and do not fare well when they're tested. Here are some questions that will help bring out the lack of knowledge of an alleged cultivation expert, along with typical answers:

1. What drug classes did you attend?

2. In those classes, how much time was spent specifically on marijuana? (Usually not much.)

3. How much of that time was spent on identifying marijuana? (Usually most of the class time.)

4. How much time was spent on cultivation? (A few hours.)

5. How much time was spent on yields? (Some time. I don't remember exactly how much.)

6. How much time was spent on indoor cultivation? (Very little of the class was specifically about indoor cultivation.)

7. Did it cover the difference in yield between indoor and outdoor plants? (No.)

8. Did you use any texts? (Yes.)

9. Do you remember their names? (No.)

10. Who taught the cultivation class? (I can't remember.)

11. Did the class cover use versus sale? (Very little.)

12. What is the difference between indica and sativa? (I don't know.)

13. Have you ever seen a plant manicured to test its yield? (No.)

14. Have you ever testified that a grow was not for sale? (Yes.)

15. In what case? (I can't remember.)

16. Are there separate male and female plants? (All kinds of answers.)

17. How do you tell the difference? (All kinds of answers.)

18. Do growers treat them differently?

19. Why?

20. How do you cause a plant to sex? (All kinds of answers.)

21. How large does a marijuana plant have to be to flower?

22. What is the significance of spacing regarding plant yield? (I don't know.)

23. How do you figure out how much a plant yields?

24. Would it be of significance to you if there were several varieties of marijuana growing in a garden? (No. Marijuana is marijuana.)

25. Do you know what CO_2 is used for? (To grow the plants?)

26. What significance does it have? (I don't know. Makes them grow faster?)

27. How much marijuana can a person smoke?

28. How do you know that? Who taught it? What documentation did s/he use?

29. If you don't know how much a plant yields or how to figure that out, and you don't know how much people smoke, how can you make a determination of intent?

The voir dire should concentrate on other areas according to the crux of the case. If the cop is to testify regarding intent, use, or yield, the questions can be tailored to bring out the lack of depth of his knowledge. Your expert can help you develop the questions for your probe into the abyss of the prosecution's ignorance. It is uncommon (though not rare) that a PE is found unqualified based on this line of questioning. However, a vigorous voir dire does affect the PE's credibility.

The voir dire can test each aspect of the PE's expertise. S/he may be qualified to identify marijuana. Does that make him/her an expert on price, use, quality, and intent? How did s/he get his/her knowledge in this area—by taking a four-hour class and interviewing a bunch of self-serving arrestees?

3. Expert Testimony

Direct examination is used not only to rebut the testimony of the PE, but also to provide new theories to the court. This is important, because in the absence of another plausible explanation, the court is likely to side with the prosecution even if its theory has been damaged.

For instance, in cultivation cases, given the question of personal use versus intent to distribute, which is an important issue in some states, the prosecution will make a conclusion based on several criteria. These are given below.

a. Prosecution Criteria

1. Quantity of Marijuana. This is one of the main factors the prosecution uses to determine whether the marijuana was for personal or commercial use and to increase the sentencing.

Narcotics officers tend to overestimate the amount of marijuana involved. Frequently it's not weighed and just an eyeball estimate is given. "It was a lot of marijuana. More than one person

could smoke." Then they state, "Each plant is capable of producing one pound (or one kilo) of marijuana."[4] PEs try to avoid talking about the specific plants in question; they prefer to discuss the weight the plant is capable of producing and to refer to mythical averages. In some cases, the prosecution experts have never looked at the evidence, but rely solely on their experience.

Weight is subject to dispute. In one case, the prosecution claimed it was 10 pounds. When we weighed the evidence, it was only 5 pounds. With the court's permission, we manicured the plants in the judge's chambers. It turned out to be only $1\frac{1}{4}$ pounds of leaf and 13 ounces of bud.[5]

Before trial, the defense expert should examine the evidence, weigh it, and look for indications of growth stage, condition, quality, and weight. All of these factors are important. If plants were growing from seed and were unsexed, half of them (the males) would be thrown away at the time when they indicated sex. Plants that were grown in the shade tend to be "leggy," with a ratio of fewer flowers to the length of the stalk. This is very important in some states, where mature stalks are not illegal.

Not all marijuana is equal. Frequently growers throw leaf away; it has little value commercially as compared with bud. A grower who has a lot of leaf is not necessarily commercial. S/he may be planning to use it for purposes other than smoking, or the cops may actually have collected it from the trash, where the grower dumped it.

Even if the physical evidence has been destroyed, the expert can analyze photos, videos, and preserved samples to get an idea of the weight.

2. Number of Plants. This is a very important factor in federal cases, where the number of plants determines sentencing. Prosecution experts sometimes miscount plants or count cuttings that are incapable of self-supporting life as plants.

In federal cases, the defense expert's estimate of actual weight has not been found relevant in sentencing for cultivation charges. However, this testimony may be quite important if the court is considering the grower's intent.

In state cases, the prosecution expert may claim weight based on the number of plants multiplied by 1 pound (or 1 kilo). If the grower has a "sea-of-green" garden, which is a technique of growing small plants very close together, the expert might claim that the number of plants indicates that the grower was growing a big crop. Then the defense expert must bring reality to the situation by discussing the actual weight and potential of the plants in the defendant's garden.

3. Presence of Scales.

The PE would have the world believe that anyone who owns an ounce scale is a dealer. The expert can help put the scales in context. Were they postal scales? If a gram scale was found, did the defendant have a specific use for it?

The idea that anyone with a triple-beam scale is a dealer is absurd. The court has to be educated about their presence in many non-drug users' households. It should be taught that some drug *buyers* use these scales to weigh their purchases, since prices are so high. Scales can be discounted when placed in a different context.

Is the scale broken? Did the scale have residue on it? If not, how can it be associated with marijuana? Where was it? Was it was found under dusty, untouched debris in the garage?

4. Packaging Material.

The state would have the court believe that anyone who has some Ziploc bags is a dealer, especially if the bags are found in proximity to marijuana.

The defense expert can bring some clarity and reality to the court. After all, the judge and jury use such bags. Is this an indication that they're dealers?

> The prosecution contended that five Ziploc bags they found in the trash, with residue inside, were packaging material, indicating intent to sell. The bags contained residue of different grades of marijuana, indicating a user who had bought pot. Without a defense expert, the prosecution's theory would have been accepted by the court.

5. Pay/Owe Slips.

Any scrap of paper with people's names and dollar amounts is immediately labeled a pay/owe slip.

> In one case, a few invoices from the store in which the defendant worked were presented as financial records. Once this error was brought to the court's attention, the prosecution's expert lost quite a bit of credibility.
>
> * * *
>
> In another case, the "pay/owe slip" turned out to be the accounts of the defendant's son's lawn-cutting business.

PEs try to turn everything into pay/owe slips. Telephone/address books become "customer lists." Were relatives listed? The doctor, minister, or grocer? Were they all customers?

6. Presence of Large Amounts of Cash.

The prosecution would have the court believe that any large sum of money found by the police is an indication of illegal activity.

There is often a legitimate reason for a large sum of cash. This should be proven thoroughly to the court.

In one case, the police found over $4,000 when they raided the defendant's home. It was mostly in large bills; the prosecution expert testified that this typically indicated sales. The defendant was able to show that he had just sold his car and had not yet deposited the money in his bank account.

7. Indicia of Use. Rolling papers, pipes, and roaches indicate use, which helps prop up the defendant's contention that s/he is a user. In one case, the police did not collect the indicia, but I photographed them at the scene. The presence of indicia, including books, posters, magazines, and pamphlets about marijuana use, also tends to show that the person was using it and was perhaps very involved in it as a hobby, rather than selling it.

In states where nonprofit transfer is not a serious offense, these indicia may indicate that the defendant was part of a subculture and regularly participated along with friends.

8. Indications of Wealth. The police immediately suspect a person of dealing if they see indications of wealth, such as expensive cars or jewelry. It is usually up to the defendant to prove these items were legitimately acquired.

This proof may require the expertise of an accountant or a tax attorney, but sometimes legitimacy is much easier to establish. An inheritance, a high-paying job, or some other source of wealth is often easily proved.

9. Sophistication of the Garden. Prosecution experts think that a sophisticated garden is an indication of cultivation for sale, and use it to establish intent to sell. They presume that only commercial growers have access to this equipment, which is actually offered in general gardening magazines such as *National Gardening*, and not in *High Times* since January 1990. I have never heard a prosecution expert say that a garden was *not* sophisticated.

Although an unsophisticated garden is usually an indication of personal use, since the grass usually doesn't meet commercial standards, a sophisticated garden is not necessarily an indication of intent to distribute. After all, hobbyists often get very technically involved in their interests. Sophistication should not be substituted for potential or expected yield.

b. Defense Criteria

The defense expert brings other issues to the court's attention:

1. The Size of the Garden. No matter how many plants there are in a garden, it has a maximum potential yield based on its space.

In one case, the prosecution claimed the defendant had 94 plants.[6] Half of them would be male, so half of them—a total of 47—would each yield 1 pound, for a total of 47 pounds. The three garden areas together totaled 25 square feet, the equivalent of 5' x 5'. By reconstructing the garden spaces with pressboard, we demonstrated in the court how absurd that contention was. The jury accepted the defense estimate of under 1 pound, total.

2. *Actual Yield and Expected Yield.* The actual and expected yields of the grower are usually much lower than the police estimates. The police usually stick with 1 pound or 1 kilogram per plant. It is unusual to find a plant with more than 6 ounces of usable material.

In an indoor garden, you can figure that for each square foot of growing space, in the flowering area, the yield will be between ¼ ounce and 1 ounce of bud. The variation in yield results from different growing techniques and varieties.

The garden may have had problems such as insects or other pests, or problems maintaining correct temperature, water, or nutrient levels. This would lower the yield and show incompetence.

The DEA's *Cultivation Yields 1992* (Appendix A) offers the only scientific study of plant size and yields. This is a great document to base yields on. The police are unfamiliar with it. On several occasions, I've been in court defending the DEA's study against officers who contradicted its findings.

3. *Different Varieties of Plants.* There are thousands of varieties of marijuana. The spectrum ranges from indicas to sativas. Commercial growers have an interest in uniformity so that the harvest time is the same and the crop is the same for easy sale. On the other hand, personal gardeners have more of an interest in smoking several varieties. Thus, a garden with mixed varieties often indicates a connoisseur who is growing for his/her own use.

A mixed garden may also indicate a lack of sophistication. The grower may have germinated mixed stash seeds of varying quality.

4. *How Much the Defendant Used.* The government supplies medical marijuana users with ten 0.8-gram cigarettes per day. This comes to about 6 pounds per year. Most PEs claim that users can't smoke more than a couple of pounds per year.

Other studies, such as Vera Rubin's *Ganja in Jamaica*, can be used to show that users can go through a lot of pot.

5. *Different Grades of Marijuana, Their Value and Use.* Leaf, although considered as weight in the prosecutor's case, is not generally used and is not a commercial product. Its presence as part of the estimated gross weight is often taken into consideration by an educated court.

Stems are often included in the prosecution's original estimate unless they're challenged. Male plants are considered a nuisance by growers, not a source of smoking material or of sales.

Although the legal weight may include leaf, it's important to define the leaf for the court so that only the weight of the bud is used by the court in considering intent.

Since the expert can help you formulate a strategy in the case, s/he should be contacted as early as possible in the proceedings. S/he may be able to help with pretrial motions, and it gives him/her more time to do research and to develop demonstrative evidence.

D. SHOULD THE DEFENDANT TESTIFY?

The defendant may be the best person to explain the case. His/her testimony can be helpful, especially if s/he comes across on the witness stand as believable and sincere. However, the defense must consider whether the prosecution might be able to bring out damaging information. The reason for this is that a defendant who takes the stand must answer all the prosecution's questions that the court allows. Even if a defendant has no skeletons in the closet, the court looks upon this testimony as at least self-serving, and possibly of dubious credibility. Common folk theory among lawyers is that for a drug defendant to win, s/he must testify. This is just not true. There are many other good ways to develop a case.

If the defense considers the situation too delicate for the defendant to testify, an expert witness can be used to develop the defense theory and counter the testimony of the police.

Consider this police officer's statement: "This was the most sophisticated garden we have seen in this area and the 101 indoor plants would have yielded, conservatively, 101 pounds of bud, worth (at today's street prices) over a million dollars."

The defense expert will give the court a more accurate assessment: "The 76 plants you see in the photograph, each of which is circled, were all growing in an area 8' × 4', an area of only 32 square feet. No matter how many plants were packed into that space, the most that could be grown in that area was one quarter ounce to one ounce per square foot, a total of no more than two pounds.

However, this garden was not very sophisticated and there are indications that it was being grown for personal use. First of all, there was no CO_2; second, a number of varieties were being grown, which suits home growers. They like to smoke different kinds of pot. Commercial growers usually like to stick with a single variety, since when they do, the harvest is uniform and ripens at the same time. In addition, the smoking paraphernalia all around the house leads me to believe that the defendant is a heavy user of cannabis."

In a case of medical necessity, all of the prosecution witnesses' testimony regarding the cultivation as well as the yield may be irrelevant after the defense educates the court as to the medicinal value of the plant to this particular individual, the defendant. An expert can also help the attorney to develop a theory for the case and to develop a cross for the prosecution expert. A knowledgeable expert may have been involved in more marijuana cases than the trial lawyer.

E. PERSONAL USE

The question of whether a person is a big-time criminal pot grower or just a backyard stash grower is the most important issue in many cases. If s/he is distinguished from a drug dealer, the defendant may be treated as a human being, with some dignity and some rights, and may subsequently be able to significantly lighten the heat.

Most real definitions of "personal use" include passing the pipe to your friends and even the occasional send-home present, as well as the smoke that goes into your own lungs. In California, we have the protection of a specific statute that makes the joint pass (furnishing less than an ounce, gratis) a citable misdemeanor (no arrest, $100 fine maximum penalty, no jail). Even given this seemingly obvious statement of legislative intent, a lot of our judges and probation departments have a less expansive definition of personal use, and the shared joint can lead at times to a charge of furnishing (sale).

F. RANDOM THOUGHTS ON STRATEGY

Attorneys should tell clients everything they need to know about the law, procedures, costs, and anything else of relevance. Any questions about the laws or procedures affecting you and your case should be answered by the lawyer in words and terms you understand.

If you can understand the language the lawyer speaks, and can read and understand this book, you have all the intelligence you need to understand what the police and prosecutor will bring as a case against you.

The law and the facts are the two sides of the coin you toss in court. You must plan and carry out your defense in the light of the law and the facts against you. You know many of the facts; your lawyer knows most of the law. Together, you should be able to arrive at a rational analysis of your situation.

A law-school axiom: "If the law is against you, pound on the facts; If the facts are against you, pound on the law; and if the law and the facts are against you, pound on the table." This means that your medical right to use pot may be more important if you can't say "It wasn't mine" and jail is the only other alternative. Your right to be free from illegal search may be more important if the stuff is in your yard or house.

Another axiom: "If trying the case is a lost cause, try the police." This means that what is on trial is not only your violations, but also, perhaps, the cops' violations of law and procedure, which the court can also evaluate.

Most lawyers don't know much about marijuana growing or use, but that doesn't stop some of these incompetents from taking your money and representing you. To have control over your life, you should be aware of the rules of the game you're playing.

Ask your lawyer if s/he has considered the things discussed in this book and the ways in which they apply (or don't apply) to your case. If you know ways in which you may be able to help yourself, you can make a more informed decision as to what course you wish to take in the case. You can also make sure that your lawyer doesn't miss a trick or mess up your case by being lazy, stupid, or political.

IS IT PERSONAL OR FOR SALE?

Pot growers have to choose a number of plants to grow. This decision is usually made without serious reflection on the penalties involved. A little fore-thought can eliminate possible problems in the future.

Growers often think about how many seeds they have, how much room they have available, how many plants can be tended, and how much pot they want to grow. Rarely do they think of the consequences of a bust.

It's not easy to know how much pot will eventually grow from those seeds. It's not uncommon for people to plant all, or nearly all, the seeds they have. These may be old, not viable, or of a mediocre variety. If they all germinate, thinning is required. If the cops come before thinning is done, the extra numbers are added onto your sentence in a federal case. In state cases, they may be used as an "indicator" of intent.

G. SECOND OPINIONS

Before you have surgery, you might seek a second opinion from another doctor. This is a good thing to do regarding your case, too. Many good attorneys will agree to review the case, talk with your attorney, and give you their independent opinions about what could have been done so far and possible strategies for the future. Your attorney should not resist independent appraisal of his/her work. If the course of action decided upon by you and your attorney will not withstand scrutiny by another experienced practitioner, it won't pass in court, either.

Attorneys who resist second opinions are usually the ones who have shoddy work to hide. Attorneys' opinions may differ, especially in the assessment of the chances of success of any particular course of action. Ideally, your attorney will have explored and discussed with you all of the possibilities so fully that the new attorney has no new information, ideas, or opinions for you. If s/he does, talk about it!

The evidence stands or falls on its own. Don't switch attorneys simply because someone gives you a more optimistic appraisal of your case. Discuss at length with both attorneys—preferably together—what errors have been made, if any, and what course of conduct should be followed at this point. Remember, it's specific ideas about strategy, tactics, and budget that are important. If a new attorney has new ideas and expectations of a better result from them, be sure you have a very clear idea of why you were wrong and where the case goes now.

Remember too that the defense attorney has no real control over the results. S/he can make moves, employ strategic and tactical devices, fight hard, and try his/her best to win. The prosecutor decides who to prosecute and for what, the judge decides what the law is and how it applies to you, and the jury decides what the facts are and whether you're guilty or not.

Beating the Warrant

A. INTRODUCTION

Marijuana gardens have provoked law enforcement to respond aggressively with intrusive investigation techniques. These include space-age technology and bringing the eyes, ears and noses of law enforcement into areas American citizens have long considered to be at the hard core of the right to privacy.

All phases of marijuana enforcement have become an issue of primary importance since the Drug Enforcement Agency and local law enforcement have prioritized the war on domestic marijuana. In the State of Washington, for example, where marijuana is Washington's number one cash crop, a well publicized $5000 reward awaits informants who will turn in marijuana gardens. Remarkably, no advertised reward encourages those who turn in murderers, rapists, robbers, child molesters or criminals who prey on the vulnerable. Even hard drug dealers have no advertised bounty on their heads.

The resulting pressure on the privacy of the home are difficult to reconcile with traditional American values such as tolerance, liberty, or pursuit of happiness. However, privacy is a fragile right. No one ever got elected for defending it. It comes as no surprise that it has retreated in the face of two decades in which both media and agencies of government have indulged the drug warriors. Defending freedom is not for the fainthearted.

Even the usually robust rights of private property are no longer secure. Every defense attorney, or intellectually honest federal agent, knows that for those who depend for protection upon the U.S. Constitution, few places remain that are truly private.

In many state courts however, there is room for creative and aggressive response to the war on privacy. Marijuana gardens are a relatively new phenomenon. Many of the intrusions they provoke have not yet been tested under state constitutional theories. Where there has been a test, states have often found enhanced protection in their own constitutions. No defense attorney practicing in state court can afford to overlook those few remaining opportunities to have someone in a robe say the word "suppressed."[1]

When you make constitutional arguments in a marijuana case, emphasize the fact that the Bill of Rights should not be viewed as an impediment to effective law enforcement. This fundamental democratic principle has received so little support from our leaders and jurists that the American Bar Association recently felt it necessary to conduct a study to reaffirm its continued validity. Their findings are particularly relevant: the constitution, and in particular the exclusionary rule,[2] do not impede effective law enforcement. Rather, the committee of prosecutors, police, lawyers and judges concluded, they protect fundamental rights at a very low cost, while encouraging the professionalism which is essential to good law enforcement in a Democracy.[3]

B. SEARCH WARRANTS

The Fourth Amendment to the United States Constitution, and the constitutions of the states all require, in some form or another, that searches of private places be conducted only where a neutral and detached magistrate or judge has concluded that probable cause exists to search, and has issued a search warrant. Search warrants are issued based upon sworn statements from law enforcement officers. The statement is usually in the form of an affidavit. A search warrant based upon an affidavit which does not establish probable cause is not valid. Challenging a search warrant, which is usually based on the adequacy of the facts contained within the "four corners" of the affidavit, is an effective tool in defending some marijuana grow cases.

Recent developments in Federal constitutional law leave application of the Fourth Amendment to these cases a largely academic endeavor. There is, however, the occasional exception, such as *United States v. Mendonsa, 989 F.2d 366 (9th Cir. 3/30/93)*,[4] holding that mere confirmation of innocent static details is insufficient to support an anonymous tip and, therefore, the search warrant lacked probable cause. Even so, "good faith" saved the warrant. Remarkably, the evidence was suppressed because of a knock/notice violation. The officers only waited 3-5 seconds between knocking on the door and forcing entry. This victory was unusual because the federal courts rarely rule for the defendent on privacy issues.

Things are not quite so bleak in state court, where some jurists still remember the prophetic admonition of Mr. Justice Douglas:

> We are not dealing with formalities. The presence of a search warrant serves a high function. Absent some grave emergency, the Fourth Amendment has interposed a magistrate between the citizen and the police. This was done not to shield criminals, nor to make the home a safe haven for illegal activities. It was done so that an objective mind might weigh the need to invade that privacy in order to enforce the law. The right of privacy was deemed too precious to entrust to the discretion of those whose job is the detection of crime and the arrest of criminals. Power is a heady thing; and history shows that the police acting on their own cannot be trusted.[5]

For the process to work, the magistrate must be something more than a "rubber stamp" for the police who want to conduct a search.

1. Informers

Most indoor marijuana cultivation cases commence with an initial tip from an informant. Under the United States Constitution, the test for whether probable cause exists is an easy one for the police. An informant's tip is evaluated under the "totality of circumstances" test of *Illinois v. Gates, 462 U.S. 213 (1983)*. Under this test, with minimal confirmation of a few innocuous facts in the tip, the police can secure a virtually air-tight search warrant for a private residence based upon little more than the pointing of an anonymous finger.

Many state courts have rejected this rule, instead requiring that an informant's tip must still satisfy the two-prong "Aguilar-Spinelli"[6] test, which requires the affidavit which supports the search warrant to demonstrate both the informant's basis of knowledge, and credibility.[7]

The credibility of informants must be established by facts in the affidavit which would support the magistrate's conclusion that the informant is telling the truth. That the informant is named in the affidavit, disclosed to the judge, or, at least, known (and identified) by the affiant,[8] is significant.[9] Where analysis still has constitutional significance, informants come in several different varieties.

a. The Anonymous Informant

When anonymous informants are employed, a showing of veracity is not sufficient without more[10] "corroboration" to bolster the otherwise inadequate tip.

Don't accept the police's claim of an anonymous informant. One clever defense investigator reviewed all search warrants filed by a particular officer, and established a pattern which proved that the officer's informant was nothing more than an "imaginary friend."

b. The Citizen Informant

Where probable cause relies on the word of a "citizen" informant, the requirements to prove the individual's reliability is somewhat relaxed. Questions can be raised regarding the issue of whether it is a true "citizen" informant who may then be presumed reliable.[11] Police must still interview the informant and ascertain such background facts as would support the inference that he is reliable. The affidavit should reveal the reasons for the citizen informant being present at the scene of the crime, since most persons present where drugs are seen are usually criminals, not innocent citizens.[12] As Professor LaFave observed:

> Courts should be cautious in accepting the assertion that one who apparently was present when narcotics were used or displayed is a presumptively reliable citizen-informer . . . This is because as a general proposition it is an informant from the criminal milieu rather than a law-abiding citizen who is most likely to be present under such circumstances. This is not to suggest that a person giving information about the location of narcotics may never qualify as a citizen-informer, for it is sometimes possible to show with particularity how a law-abiding individual happened to come upon such knowledge.[13]

State v. Ibarra, 61 Wn.App 695 (1991), is a hopeful case. It reiterates the *Northness* categories of informants, observing that "the concern that the informant information may be coming from an anonymous troublemaker remains when the citizen informant is unidentified. Therefore, the State's burden of demonstrating the credibility of a citizen informant is not necessary lightened when the informant remains unidentified to the magistrate."[14] This case holds that the reliability/credibility of the alleged "citizen informant" was not established, particularly because the reason why the informant was at the scene of the crime/location of the crime was not given. The case holds that a generic recitation of the officer's conclusions is not sufficient to raise the requisite inference that the informant had a valid reason for wishing to remain anonymous.

c. The Criminal Milieu Informant

Some courts recognize the reality that informants from the "criminal milieu" are likely to lie and should be presumed unreliable: "It is to be expected that the criminal informer will not infrequently reach for shadowy leads, or even seek to incriminate the innocent."[15]

Law enforcement officials and prosecutors are at least privately aware of the likelihood that criminals will lie to stay out of trouble. For example, the Hon. Stephen Trott, when he was in charge of the criminal division at the United States Department of Justice wrote:

> Criminals are likely to say and do almost anything to get what they want, especially when what they want is to get out of trouble with the law. In my personal first-hand experience of over 18 years as a prosecutor, this willingness to do anything includes not only truthfully spilling the beans on friends and relatives, but also manufacturing evidence, soliciting others to corroborate their lies with more lies, double-crossing anyone with whom they come into contact, including—and especially—the prosecutor. A drug addict can sell out his mother to get a deal; and burglars, robbers, murderers and thieves are not far behind. They are remarkably manipulative and skillfully devious. Many are outright conscienceless sociopaths to whom "truth" is a wholly meaningless concept. To some 'conning' people is a way of life. Others are just basically unstable people.[16]

Mr. Trott is now a judge on the United States Court of Appeals for the Ninth Circuit. Remarkably, he has recently reiterated these same feelings in a written opinion[17] which addresses credibility of informants as trial witnesses:

> Our judicial history is speckled with cases where informants falsely pointed the finger of guilt at suspects and defendants, creating the risk of sending innocent persons to prison.[18]

Bernal-Obeso is the exception. Courts have demonstrated rare ingenuity in developing theories by which to support the veracity of these inherently unreliable sources of information. The police may rely on, among others, the following common methods of showing the veracity of the criminal informant:

1. A "track record" of virtually any prior cooperation with the police. This should not be interpreted to mean that if an informant predicted the sun would rise, and then it did, his word may now be presumed reliable.[19] Note that a "controlled buy" does not establish reliability unless the affidavit alleges the informant claimed he could buy at that location, and then did.[20] [21]

2. This theory should not be applied where it doesn't fit (although it often is). The statement must be genuinely against penal interest. Note here that the naming of the informant in the affidavit is not a passport to reliability; rather, it is a prerequisite to a finding that a statement against penal interest supports an inference of reliability.[22] This exception should not be used to make a person who confesses to some crime a more reliable source of information than an honest citizen.

3. The informant is highly motivated to provide accurate information, and will not lightly lead police down blind alleys.[23] These cases showcase judicial logic at its thinnest. A criminal caught red-handed who then makes a deal is presumed to be reliable? Often "prospecting," law enforcement's own term for leading police down blind alleys in the hope of getting lucky and finding something incriminating, is an informant's only hope.

4. Merely giving the name of the informant does not establish reliability.[24]

Many search warrants rely almost entirely on the word of a criminal milieu informant. When dealing with a criminal milieu informant, the lawyer should check possible suspects for recent arrests or convictions. Where there are no clues, check search warrants[25] in the same jurisdiction for similar warrants or warrants by the same officer. Interview other targets of similar searches to see if one name of a suspected informant comes up twice. Then interview that one. Sometimes the informant has been materially misquoted. Perhaps he first misled the police before deciding to "tell the truth." Of course, never interview informants alone. That way there is corroboration of their statements.

C. INFORMATION GENERATED BY POLICE INVESTIGATION

The weight of police observations contained in search warrant affidavits may be minimized by defense investigation. Check whether all of the details are accurately reported. Sometimes a series of superficially harmless errors in reporting by police affiants forms a pattern suggesting the information was intentionally misleading when viewed in its totality.

Marijuana cultivation investigations have incorporated a variety of new investigative indicators, tools and techniques. A thread which seems to run through all of the information offered by police in support of probable cause to search for gardens is the tendency to equate conduct consistent with criminal activity with conduct actually probative of criminal activity. Heat escaping from a building, higher than average power consumption, covered windows or other attempts to protect privacy, even the presence of gardening equipment such as pots and potting soil, or purchasing something from a gardening store are often pointed to by police as evidence of criminal activity. The Washington Supreme Court's well-reasoned opinion[26] may be useful here:

> The independent police investigation should point to suspicious activity, "'probative indications of criminal activity along the lines suggested by the informant".[27] Merely verifying "innocuous details", commonly known facts or easily predictable events should not suffice to remedy a deficiency in either the basis of knowledge or veracity prong.[28] Corroboration of public or innocuous facts only shows that the informer has some familiarity with the suspect's affairs. Such corroboration only justifies an inference that the informer has some knowledge of the suspect and his activities, not that criminal activity is occurring. Corroboration of the informer's report is significant only to the extent that it tends to give substance and verity to the report that the suspect is engaged in criminal activity.[29]

United States v. Mendonsa, F.2d, No. 91-30413, (9th Cir. 3/30/93), is helpful here in that it requires something more than corroboration of innocent details, even in federal court.

Particularly troublesome here is the police practice of surveilling garden equipment stores, then following customers and attempting to establish probable cause. Gardening has become a common form of recreation in America. Thus, not only does this investigative technique raise an issue of the chilling effect upon protected legitimate conduct, it also casts doubt upon police observations which are as probative of a legal indoor garden as of an illegal one.

Law enforcement invariably attempts to persuade the courts that only marijuana is valuable enough to be grown under lights. This is a clearly and demonstrably false premise. Across the country, modern hi-tech gardens refute this dangerous misrepresentation. If your community has no local experts on legitimate indoor agriculture, the American Orchid Society, the Indoor Light Gardening Society of America, and the July, 1992 Sunset Magazine, and most of the major national/international light bulb companies, are but a few of the many good sources of evidence to refute this dangerous lie.

1. Monitoring increased power usage

Examination of power consumption records has become a common investigative tool since indoor cultivation relies heavily on electricity. Above average or increased power use, it should be argued, has too many legitimate explanations to be considered probable cause[30] (accepting increased power use as having some significance where the odor of marijuana was also present).

An attorney can minimize the probable cause value of power usage information with statistics from the power company showing what is average and what the range of power consumption is, and by employing an expert to advise the court of the many other innocent explanations for the high power consumption.

In addition to questions regarding their probative value, police seizure of power records may raise constitutional and statutory issues. In Washington state, the Privacy Act prohibits seizure without a written statement of "articulable suspicion."[31] There is an argument that such a seizure of power records is unconstitutional because it violates individual privacy rights. In an age where computer technology makes every small bit of recorded information available almost instantaneously, realistic protection of the fragile right of privacy requires that prior judicial approval precede search or seizure of information regarding matters occurring within a citizen's home. The seizure of power records is for the purpose of securing evidence of a crime; the evidence is of a nature which reflects the private activities of a citizen within his or her home, and about which the citizen has a reasonable expectation of privacy.[32] In *Hearst*, the Washington Supreme Court observed, (in a non-criminal context):

> Every individual has some phases of his life and his activities and some facts about himself that he does not expose to the public eye, but keeps entirely to himself or at most reveals only to his family or to close personal friends. Sexual relations, for example are normally entirely private matters, as are family quarrels, many unpleasant or disgraceful or humiliating illnesses, most intimate personal letters, most details of a man's life in his home, and some of his history that he would rather forget."[33]

An interesting side issue here comes from the fact that pot growers often divert steal power to keep high power bills from alerting the authorities. Where a diversion is suspected, power companies install "comparator" meters which indicate whether or not all power being used by a residence is flowing through the meter. Good arguments are that the comparator meter requires a warrant, and that probable cause to search for power theft does not constitute probable cause to search the entire house, since power is stolen outside the house, before the wires reach the meter.

2. Infrared Thermal Imagers

Modern technology allows law enforcement to monitor surface temperatures of residences by flying over in a helicopter, or driving by at a distance. When police observe what they consider to be "excessively high" levels of heat escaping from a residence, they point to that factor as a part of probable cause. Many defenses are possible:

It's a search. It should be argued that the use of this technology represents a warrantless search. In *U.S. v. Penny-Feeny, 773 F.Supp. 220 (D.Hawaii. 1991)*,[34] the court ruled that the use of an infrared detector from helicopter was not a search since escaping heat was knowingly abandoned and exposed to pubic view like garbage. In *State v. Binner, Walker, and Walker, Harney County (Oregon)* Judge Yraguen ruled that the use of a thermal imager was a search under the Oregon Constitution.[35] Other cases decline to reach the issue. In *United States v. Kerr, 876 F.2d 1440 (9th Cir. 1989)*, the court declined to rule on the issue, observing that the information from the thermal imager had been of limited probative value. In *State v. Murray, 757 P.2d 487 (Wash. 1988)*, Washington's Supreme Court deferred resolution of the issue, noting that it had been inadequately briefed, and chastising counsel for a failure to recognize either the absence of any "physical trespass" requirement or the greater protection of "private affairs" afforded by the State Constitution.[36]

The argument that the use of this instrument is a search must be founded on a factual showing of the intrusive capabilities of the technology. Local experts can assist an attorney in this demonstration, which, at a minimum, should demonstrate the ability of the instrument to detect matters coming from the home which are not visible to the naked eye, and the ability of the instrument to look through windows, perhaps even walls, to observe that which the residents expect is taking place in private.

The legal foundation for such an argument could begin with *United States v. Karo, 468 U.S. 705 82 L.Ed. 530, 104 S.Ct. 3296, reh den 468 U.S. 1250, 82 L.Ed.2d 942, 105 S.Ct. 51 (1984),* where agents of the Drug Enforcement Administration obtained a court order authorizing the installation and monitoring of a "beeper" in a can of ether that was delivered to the defendant. The ether was taken to a house, and the agents relied on the presence of the beeper inside the house to obtain a search warrant.

The court began its analysis by discussing *United States v. Knotts, 460 U.S. 276, 75 L.Ed.2d 55, 103 S.Ct. 1081 (1983),* in which the court upheld the use of a beeper to track a vehicle to a cabin in a rural location. The court held that no fourth amendment violation was committed by monitoring the beeper during the trip to the cabin, because:

> The record did not show that the beeper was monitored while the can containing it was inside the cabin, and we therefore had no occasion to consider whether a constitutional violation would have occurred had the fact been otherwise.[37]

Justice White went on to explain that *Karo* must be distinguished from Knotts because in *Karo*, the agents used the beeper to gain information about the interior of a residence, information that could not be obtained through visual surveillance alone:

This case thus presents the question whether the monitoring of a beeper in a private residence, a location not open to visual surveillance, violates the Fourth Amendment rights of those who have a justifiable interest in the privacy of the residence. Contrary to the submission of the United States, we think it does.

> The monitoring of an electronic device such as a beeper is, of course, less intrusive than a full-scale search, but it does reveal a critical fact about the interior of the premises that the Government is extremely interested in knowing and that it could not have otherwise obtained without a warrant. . . . Here, was we have said, the monitoring indicated that the beeper was inside the house, a fact that could not have been visually verified...

> Indiscriminate monitoring of property that has been withdrawn from public view would prevent far too serious a threat to privacy interests in the home to escape entirely some sort of Fourth Amendment oversight...

> In sum, we discern no reason for deviating from the general rule that a search of a house should be conducted pursuant to a warrant.[38]

Karo can thus be said to stand for the proposition that electronic surveillance which reveals activity occurring inside a residence which could not be observed with the naked eye requires prior judicially authority.

California v. Ciraolo, 476 U.S. 207, 90 L.Ed.2d 210, 106 S.Ct. 1809 (1986) is in accord with *Karo*. In *Ciraolo*, the court addressed the constitutionality of aerial observation of private property. The court upheld the practice of warrantless aerial surveillance on the basis that such surveillance merely revealed information that was exposed to public view, and that was visible to the naked eye:

> The observations by Officers Shutz and Rodriguez in this case took place within public navigable airspace in a physically non-intrusive manner; from this point they were able to observe plants readily discernable to the eye as marijuana. . . Any member of the public flying in this airspace who glanced down could have seen everything that these officers observed... Justice Harlan's observations about future electronic developments and the potential for electronic interference with private communications,were plainly not aimed at simple visual surveillance from a public place.[39] [40]

The court upheld warrantless aerial surveillance because an aerial search cannot reveal anything other than what might be visible to the naked eye. The court recognized that the outcome could be different where modern technology was used to reveal facts not otherwise detectable:

> The state acknowledges that "aerial observation of curtilage may become invasive, either due to physical intrusiveness or through modern technology which discloses to the senses those intimate associations, objects, or activities otherwise imperceptible to police or fellow citizens."[41]

In *United States v. Taborda, 635 F.2d 131 (2d Cir. 1980)*, the court allowed unenhanced viewing through an open window, but proscribed telescopic viewing through an open window, citing differing expectations of privacy by the average citizen facing developing technology. In *United States v. Christensen, 524 F.Supp. 344 (N.D. Ill. 1981)*, the court upheld the use of binocular observation into a private home, but suggested that infra-red viewing would be impermissible:

> These binoculars do not rely on laser beams or infra red to detect images not otherwise available. Rather, they merely magnify what would in any event be apparent to the naked eye.

The district court in *Dow Chemical Co. v. United States, 536 F.Supp. 1355 (E.D. Mich. 1982)*, rejected the use of a high precision magnifying aerial camera to photograph emissions from power houses at the chemical plant because "the camera saw a great deal more than the human eye could ever see." *Id. at 1367.* In *United States v. Lace, 669 F.2d 46 (2d Cir. 1982)*, the court, again relying upon the "expectation of privacy" test, allowed high technology observation of the defendants because they were, while under cover of darkness, wandering about in open fields.

The government may argue that the technology is no different than a dog sniff. The analogy does not survive inspection:

> While a trained narcotics dog reacts solely to the odor of drugs, a (thermal imager) device reveals any source of heat. There is no law regulating how much heat a residence may emit and the radiation of an unusual amount of heat cannot lead directly to an inference of illegal activity in the same direct manner as the smell of contraband implies its presence.[42]

If this level of intrusion were permitted with-out a warrant, even the Orwellian precautions suggested by Professor LaFave would not suffice to protect the citizens of Washington: ...this approach raises the question of how tightly the Fourth Amendment permits people to be driven back into the recesses of their lives by the risk of surveillance. Mr. Katz could, of course, have pro-tected himself against surveillance by forbearing to use the phone; and — so far as I am presently advised of the state of the mechanical arts — any-one can protect himself against surveillance by retiring to the cellar, cloaking all the windows with thick caulking, turning off the lights and remaining absolutely quiet. This much withdrawal is not required in order to claim the benefit of the amendment because, if it were, the amendment's benefit would be too stingy to preserve the kind of open society to which we are committed, and in which the amendment is supposed to function. What kind of society is that? Is it one in which a homeowner is put to the choice of shuttering up his windows or of having a policeman look in?[43]

It isn't probative of criminal activity. As with any other information which makes up a part of probable cause, it must be "reliable." An infor-mant, a drug dog, or even an officer, whose infor-mation was suspect, would not be tolerated as a source of probable cause. Neither should this device. The results of this device are inherently unreliable, as well as ambiguous.

Local experts can assist an attorney in demon-strating that heat radiating from buildings, even in "excessive" amounts, whatever that may mean, may reflect a number of things, only one of which is unlawful. Poor insulation, a sauna, a legitimate indoor garden, the color of the exterior wall, the direction of exposure, shelter, openness to wind or sun, or even the material from which the wall is constructed, All these are factors which would affect the external temperature of a building wall.

An engineer who is trained in the use of a ther-mal imager, (if he is not in the employ of law enforcement) can testify that it is not reasonable to draw any inferences regarding criminal conduct based upon amounts of heat radiating from a building.

The device is subject to manipulation and misinterpretation by poorly trained, unethical or suggestible operators. Again, this is a matter of reliability. By using this ambiguous information as probable cause, both the risk and reality of intru-sion into the privacy of innocent persons are increased to an intolerable level.

In a surprising number of cases investigated by this writer no grow room was found where law enforcement had predicted that one should be based upon their use of thermal imager technology.

Poor training, too much enthusiasm, or even outright fabrication are among the explanations for the many failures of this technology. Must American citizens refrain from any kind of indoor gardening in order to protect themselves from warrants based upon rumor and suspicion?

Even when the device is properly operated, and its results accurately reported, these results are inherently equivocal, and therefore lend them-selves to law enforcement officers who seek to undermine the magistrate's function by passing off conclusions as facts, and elevating their suspicions to probable cause. Compare *U.S. v. Penny-Feeny*, where heat radiating from building was "consistent with" marijuana grow, with *U.S. v. Kerr, 876 F.2d 1440 (9th Cir. 1989)* where lack of heat radiating from a building was consistent with marijuana farm because "marijuana growers often insulate their growing areas."

Investigating cases with these devices is a complex subject. Try to get a copy of the tape, if any, made by the device. Ask the court to order that the device be made available to you for inspection and testing. Demonstrate to the court the inherent unreliability of the device. The thermal imager is often used by the military, at the request of local authorities.

Where the military have been involved, another universe of defense is opened up. With very little notice to the public, the military has crept into civilian law-enforcement for the first time in recent history. Courts seem ready to stretch the *"posse comitatus"* act, the law which prohibits use of the military, to permit this exception where marijuana is involved. This, subject is also ripe for litigation, but too complex to address here.

3. Smell of Marijuana

Another common piece of evidence in search warrants is the allegation that someone detected the odor of marijuana. If the smell of a contraband item is distinctive and the person who smells it is qualified to distinguish it, that smell provides probable cause.[44] Even where the officer was wrong, but believed in good faith that he was smelling marijuana, this may yet establish probable cause.[45]

Hopeful here is *United States v. DeLeon, No. 89-20230, (9th Cir, November, 1989)*, where one of the officers who claimed to have smelled marijuana was not shown to be qualified to recognize the odor of growing marijuana which differs from the odor of burning marijuana. The court observed that odors can be the basis of probable cause only if the affiant is qualified to know the odor and the odor is sufficiently distinctive.

Factual issues become more important where the odor of marijuana is relied on. Some judges have become suspicious of smell evidence. For example:

Smell experts can testify that marijuana is difficult to distinguish from other pungent plants, that smell is not directional, and that the officer had inadequate training to identify that which he smelled or locate its source.

Physical evidence can also cast doubt on the officer's observations, These include distance from plants, filters, negative ion generators, wind direction, topography, etc.

The analogy to the Ouija board comes to mind. If the officer claimed his Ouija board had never been wrong, could it provide probable cause?

One frequently encountered situation involves a farm so well protected from the escape of a smell that it is incredible that the officer smelled it, yet the claim is made, and marijuana is found. It may well be that the officer had to trespass into the curtilage before getting the telltale whiff. Neighbors, footprints, and hidden surveillance cameras, are among the all too rare sources of information which might establish this trespass. If a trespass can be established, the following section discusses the applicable law.

D. WARRANTLESS INTRUSIONS

1. Trespass onto private property

Sometimes the police trespass on private property to make an observation on which they base probable cause.

Federal law allows police to do whatever they want until they reach the "curtilage." Police, without a warrant, may ignore fences and even "no trespassing" signs which do not define the curtilage[46] is the starting point for this inquiry. In Oliver, officers of the Kentucky State Police went to a farm to investigate allegations of marijuana cultivation. The officers drove past Oliver's house to a locked gate with a "No Trespassing" sign. The officers walked around the locked gate and along a road and discovered a field of marijuana over one mile from the residence. The Court held that this field was not within the curtilage of the house, and therefore was not entitled to Fourth Amendment protection. The court affirmed, and perhaps expanded, the "open fields" exception to the Fourth Amendment that was first announced in *Hester v. United States, 265 U.S. 57, 68 L.ed. 898, 44 S.Ct. 445 (1924)*. Oliver and its progeny address police searches of open fields, areas which are not part of the curtilage of the residence. As the Oliver court states, citing Hester:

> The special protection accorded by the Fourth Amendment to the people in their 'persons, houses, papers, and effects,' is not extended to the open fields. The distinction between the latter and the house is as old as common law.

> We conclude, as did the court in deciding Hester v. U.S., that the government's intrusion upon open fields is not one of those "unreasonable searches" prescribed by the text of the Fourth Amendment.[47]

The Oliver decision reaffirms that the curtilage of a private residence is protected from warrantless search, and that a citizen may still choose to "demand privacy" within that area. This protection is both implicit and explicit in the Court's holding:

> The rule of Hester v. U.S. that we affirm today may be understood as providing that an individual may not legitimately demand privacy for activities conducted out of doors in fields, except in the area immediately surrounding the home.[48]

In *United States v. Dunn, 480 US 294, 94 L.Ed.2d 326, 107 S.Ct. 1134 (1987)*, the Court elaborated. In *Dunn*, police officers entered the defendant's property and peered into a barn located 60 yards from the home. The *Dunn* court held:

> We believe that the curtilage questions should be resolved with particular reference to four factors: the proximity of the area claimed to be curtilage to the home, whether the area is included within an enclosure surrounding the home, the nature of the uses to which the area is put, and the steps taken by the resident to protect the area from observation by people passing by.[49]

The Court in *Dunn* applied these four factors and concluded that the barn in that case was not within the curtilage of the residence, and was, therefore, not protected from trespassing police.

Oliver and *Dunn* leave the curtilage of a residence protected against warrantless trespass, at least to the extent that the owner has taken steps "to protect the area from observation by people passing by."

Does this protection extend to the entry to the residence? Professor LaFave observes that "a portion of the curtilage, being the normal route of access for anyone visiting the premises, is 'only a semi-private area'."[50]

As elaborated in State v. Corbett, 15 Or. App. 470, 516 P.2d 487 (1973)

> . . . In the course of urban life, we have come to expect various members of the public to enter (our property), e.g. brush salesmen, newspaper boys, postmen, Girl Scout Cookie sellers, distressed motorists, neighbors, friends. Any one of them may be reasonably expected to report observations of criminal activity to the police ... If one has a reasonable expectation that various members of society may enter the property in their personal or business pursuits, he should find it equally likely that the police will do so.

Thus when the police come on to private property to conduct an investigation or for some other legitimate purpose, and restrict their movements to places visitors could be expected to go (e.g. walkways, driveways, porches) observations made from such vantage points are not covered by the Fourth Amendment. But other portions of the lands adjoining the residence are protected, and thus if the police go upon these other portions and make observations there, this amounts to a Fourth Amendment Search.[51]

In *United States v. Hatch, 931 F.2d 1478 (11th Cir. 1991)*, the court ruled that "the curtilage that defines the property in question is enclosed in the fencing around the home and taxidermist building even if the fence may not be complete on the north and perhaps east sides of the property."

Contrary to appellant's contention, the extent of the curtilage, according to Dunn does not turn on whether or not the area surrounding the house is completely fenced. The test for determining curtilage is not a bright line determination; nor does the boundary it defines need to be as 'bright line' as a fence or other obvious barrier.[52]

Note here that the area in question was actually separated from the curtilage by a fence.

In *L.A. v. Police Protective League v. Gates, 907 F.2d 879, 884, (9th Cir. 1990)*, the court observed,

> We start with the salutary principle that the Fourth Amendment to the United States Constitution prohibits unreasonable searches and seizures just as it prohibits the issuance of warrants without probable cause... Nowhere is the protective force of the Fourth Amendment more powerful than it is when the sanctity of the home is involved.[53] (en banc). The sanctity of a person's home, perhaps our last retreat in this technological age, lies at the very core of the rights which animate the amendment. Therefore we have been adamant in our demand that absent exigent circumstances a warrant will be required before a person's home is invaded by the authorities. "... Garages are commonly used for the storage of many household items besides automobiles. They are not like distant open barns or open fields to which the general public is given visual or physical access." (this particular garage was attached to the house).

In *United States v. Boger 755 F.Supp. 338 (E.D. Wa. 1990)*, the court held,

> For most suburban residents, the sanctity of the backyard is as important as that of the house itself. One of the real benefits of owning a residence such as Mr. Boger's is the right of the owner to spend time in his backyard without interruption from traffic or trespassers. Any reasonable property owner in Mr. Boger's area would not expect to find or allow strangers to invade his backyard.

In *Wattenberg vs. U.S. 388 F.2d 853, at 357-58 (9th Cir. 1968)*, police conducted a warrantless search of a pile of trees located approximately 35 feet from the back of the building. The court's analysis is instructive:

> It seems to us a more appropriate test in determining if a search and seizure adjacent to a house is constitutionally forbidden is whether it constitutes an intrusion upon what the resident seeks to preserve as private even in an area which, although adjacent to his home, is accessible to the public. . .

> If the determination of such questions is made to turn upon the degree of privacy a resident is seeking to preserve as shown by the facts of the particular case, rather than upon a resort to the ancient concept of curtilage, attention will be more effectively focused on the basic interest which the Fourth Amendment was designed to protect.

The Wattenberg court found that because the occupant had taken steps to protect his privacy, the police search was unlawful (358).

In litigating this issue, beware of *United States v. Brady, 734 F.Supp. 923 (E.D. Wa. 1990)*, where the court held that

> It is particularly true in a rural setting that society finds it reasonable that, if no answer is received at the home, one will approach the outbuildings to ascertain if the resident is working there.

United States v. Traynor No. 92-30079 (April 13, 1993), reiterates that observations made by officers while they are not within the curtilage are admissible, even though the entry road is posted no trespassing, and the officers trespassed onto the curtilage while on their way to their ultimate vantage point. The most recent 9th Circuit case is *United States v. DePew, (9th Cir. 11/4/93), No. 92-30245*, a remarkable case where the court of appeals actually excluded some evidence based upon a trespass.

The courts of the future may find that these cases have gone too far. "The right to exclude others from private property, is 'universally' held to be a 'fundamental element of the property right.'"[54] Where a citizen does not leave any access route to his home impliedly open to the public, but instead by fences, gates, and signs clearly displays his demand to be left alone by everyone, the police may not approach the house, or at least its curtilage, without a warrant.

This is a fruitful area for state constitutional litigation. An Oregon court has required that, for land outside the curtilage, the owner must "manifest an intention to exclude the public by erecting barriers to entry or by posting signs."[55] In Hawaii, courts have held that the Constitution prohibits trespass on land 400 feet from a residence.[56]

In Washington, the court has not ruled on trespass per se, but has emphatically rejected the open fields rule.[57] In Myrck, the court consolidated a number of Washington decisions holding that article 1,7 of the Washington Constitution provides a greater and different protection for the right to privacy than does the fourth amendment to the United States Constitution. Under Article 1,7 analysis, the focus is not the nature of the property involved, but rather the "protection of the person in his private affairs.

The Myrick court therefore rejected both the "open fields" doctrine and the "reasonable expectation of privacy" test, holding that they are but two among many factors to be considered in resolving the central issue: whether the entry onto private property intrudes upon "those privacy interests which citizens of this state have held, and should be entitled to hold, safe from government trespass without a warrant. The ill-considered dicta in *State v. VonHof, 51 Wn.App. 33, 40 (1988)*, to the effect that a "No Trespassing" sign does not increase in owner's expectation of privacy has no basis in Washington law. *VonHof* is based upon the rejected "open fields" doctrine.

The approach to a posted residence is an unresolved question in Washington. The Washington State Supreme Court has ruled that police are entitled to approach a residence on pathways that are impliedly open to the public.[58] However, where an officer strays even slightly from a pathway that is impliedly open to the public, this conduct passes from permissible investigation to unlawful trespass.

In *State v. Daugherty, 94 Wn.2d 263, 616 P.2d 649 (1980)*, an officer who walked around a parked car to look into defendant's garage was unlawfully trespassing. The *Daugherty* court focused on defendant's expectation of privacy in the trespassed area, and determined that the extent of one's expectation of privacy "is determined in any case under a test of reasonableness in light of such characteristics as the exposure of the driveway to the street and surrounding public areas, the use of the driveway for common access to the house, and the nature of the official incursion complained of." (268).

The court went on to note the general exposure of the driveway to public view and its general nature as an access route to the house. However, in spite of this, the fact that the entire driveway was not a pathway to the house, the fact that two trucks parked in the driveway effectively obscured from public view a portion thereof, and the fact that one need not expect the police to "thread around and among the vehicles," led the court to conclude that the police actions violated constitutional protection (268-69).

Using a similar analytical approach, the court in *State v. Petty, 740 P.2d 879 (Wash.App 1987)*, found a technical trespass to be constitutionally inoffensive when the officer simply walked to the front door of a residence, knocked, and made his observations after the resident opened the door. Crucial to its decision was the court's conclusion that "an officer, like anyone else, may approach a residence from an access route impliedly open to the public."

Washington courts have also been consistent in rejecting the argument that, simply because an area is rural, not a part of the "curtilage" of a residence, and may be an "open field" police may trespass at will. Such trespass has only been allowed in cases where it was shown that there was no reasonable expectation of privacy.[59]

The courts in Washington have made clear that police have merely the same license as a citizen: "An officer is permitted the same license to intrude as a reasonably respectful citizen... However, a substantial and unreasonable departure from such an area, or a particularly intrusive method of viewing will exceed the scope of the implied invitation and intrude upon a constitutionally protected expectation of privacy."[60]

Similarly, a Texas court eloquently observed:

> This is simply not a case of open curtains inviting observations, or of an initial aided or unaided investigatory observation... The protracted focus on delving into the contents of the (property) belies such a claim and is easily distinguishable from mere surveillance... Clearly, what a person knowingly exposes to public view is not protected by the Fourth Amendment... However, the Constitution does not require that one erect a stone bastion, or retreat to the cellar to exhibit a reasonable expectation of privacy.[61]

2. Knock and Talk

Unless you never watch television, and haven't since before "Police Story," you won't be surprised to learn that police have discovered a way to search private residences without a warrant, without probable cause, and without a show of force: the Knock and Talk. The courts have apparently had little difficulty approving warrantless searches of residences on later review. One police officer who wrote a training memorandum on the subject commented:

> we (the police) know that occasionally there is a reluctance on the part of some prosecutors and judges to allow officers to enter and search a person's home and belongings without a search warrant. This negative factor is best dealt with through education. Once the concept and success that others have achieved is properly explained, most judges an prosecutors will accept the idea... To date, over 15,000 'knock and talks' have been conducted. Only one case that we know of has been adversely ruled against the people.[62]

The issue here is consent. In addressing whether the consent was coerced, the usual questions are still relevant. Was there a show of force? A threat to come back with a search warrant and trash the house? A threat to arrest everyone, including visiting friends or girl/boy friends, or take children to foster homes if consent is withheld? A prior trespass? Was there other conduct which implied to the citizen that the officers had the right to do what they did, and to demand what they appeared to demand?

Whether a person voluntarily consents to a search is a question of fact to be determined from the totality of the circumstances.[63] The burden of showing that a person consented to a search is upon the state. Although this burden is often met by showing that neither doors nor bones were broken, several factors are relevant to determining whether consent is voluntary:

a. whether consent was given in circumstances that are inherently coercive;

b. whether the person who consents is aware of his right to withhold consent;

c. whether consent is given as a result of prior illegal conduct by the police;

d. prior refusal to cooperate by the person who consents to the search;

e. whether consent is obtained after invocation of the Sixth Amendment right to counsel.[64] [65]

One example of coercion is the threat to arrest a friend, relative or loved one. In *Ferguson v. Boyd, 566 F.2d (4th Cir. 1977)*, the Fourth Circuit held that if a friend or relative of the defendant was improperly detained or threatened, the defendant's confession would be invalid. In *United States v. Scarpelli, 713 F.Supp. 1144 (N.D.Ill. 1989)*, the United States District Court for the Northern District of Illinois also held that if the defendant believed his girlfriend was threatened with arrest the confession would be invalid.[66]

In *United States v. Bolin, 514 F.2d 554 (7th Cir. 1975)*, the police officers told the defendant that if he signed the search waiver they would not arrest the defendant's girlfriend. In that case, the Seventh Circuit held that even though the officer's statement was phrased as a promise, it was really an implied threat that the girlfriend would be arrested if the defendant did not consent to the search. That threat rendered the defendant's consent involuntary and therefore invalid.[67] In *United States v. Talkington, 843 F.2d 1041, 1049 (7th Cir. 1988)* at 1049 which was remanded to district court to determine if consent to a search was due to the threat to body search of defendant's wife, the court said:

> Threatening the physical privacy of a woman to coerce her or her spouse to acquiesce to the government's will has been a familiar tool of totalitarian regimes. It has no place in the United States.

In *State v. Walmsley, 344 N.W.2d 450, 452-53 (Neb. 1984)*, the Supreme Court of Nebraska held that the defendant's consent to a search was involuntary where the sheriff told the defendant that his wife could be arrested if Mr. Walmsley did not cooperate.

While the threat to seek a warrant, by itself may not vitiate a voluntary consent, "it should at least be addressed as one factor under the totality of all the circumstances test enunciated by the Supreme Court in Schneckloth."[68] Mere submission to authority is insufficient to establish consent to a search.[69] Coupled with the express threat to search in a destructive manner, the threat to get a warrant is coercive by definition.

Where the officers begin their discussion at the door by stating that they are investigating drug activity, *State v. Soto-Garcia, 841 P.2d 1271 (1992)*, may be relevant. There the court of appeals held that the defendant was seized at the moment the police officer asked the defendant if he had cocaine, and if he could search the defendant. If those events are coercive on the street, they are even more coercive when they take place at the front door.

The government's burden is at its heaviest when the consent that would be inferred is a consent to enter and search a private home.[70] This is because the protection of the privacy of the home finds it roots in clear and specific constitutional language:

> "the right of the people to be secure in their ... houses ... shall not be violated." That language unequivocally establishes the proposition that "at the very core of the Fourth Amendment stands the right of a (wo)man to retreat into his own home and there be free from unreasonable governmental intrusion." ... In terms that apply equally to seizures of property and to seizures of persons the Fourth Amendment has drawn a firm line at the entrance to the house. Judicial concern to protect the sanctity of the home is so elevated that free and voluntary consent cannot be found by a showing of mere acquiescence to a claim of authority.[71]

Although courts may from time to time infer consent in various other situations, the Ninth Circuit "has never sanctioned entry to the home based on inferred consent."[72]

When police seek a warrant, there is clear authority for a search and a clear record of the basis for the intrusion. Consent searches, on the other hand, almost always involve a factual dispute between the officer's version of the events and the defendant's. In fact, an individual has very little recourse if a police officer claims that consent was "freely given." For this reason, police claims of consent must be closely scrutinized and not automatically approved. The better course for an investigating officer is to obtain judicial approval prior to an entry into a private residence. Society treads on dangerous ground if warrantless police searches are given wide latitude under a consent theory.

3. Garbage Searches

Searches of garbage have become a favorite way to develop probable cause to search a residence. Federal law permits warrantless searches of garbage.[73] Whether this permission extends to actual chemical analysis of items found in the garbage, such as Kleenex, discarded medicine containers, or other personal matters is still unclear. In another context, it seems to be forbidden.

In *United States v. Jacobsen, 466 U.S. 109, 80 L.Ed.2d 85, 104 S.Ct. 1652 (1984)* at 100-101, federal agents acting without a warrant performed chemical tests on a package which had been previously opened by employees of a private company. The Jacobsen Court held that the search and seizure of the package were reasonable because they were limited in scope to the extent of the private search. The court then addressed the warrantless testing of the substance found within the lawfully seized package:

> The question remains whether the additional intrusion occasioned by the field test, which had not been conducted by the Federal Express employees and therefore exceeded the scope of the private search, was an unlawful "search" or "seizure" within the meaning of the Fourth Amendment. . .

> A chemical test that merely discloses whether or not a particular substance is cocaine does not compromise any legitimate interest in privacy... Thus, governmental conduct that can reveal whether a substance is cocaine, and no other arguably "private" fact, compromises no legitimate privacy interest.

Thus, chemical analysis that could reveal an arguably private fact would constitute a search requiring prior judicial approval.

United States v. Mulder, 808 F.2d 1346 (9th Cir. 1987) is such a case. In Mulder, the court suppressed evidence discovered during sophisticated laboratory testing that might have revealed a "private fact":

> We consider Jacobsen determinative of the instant case. The facts here are sufficiently different from those in Jacobsen that we do not believe its "field test" exception to the warrant requirement can be extended to the case at bar. First of all, this case does not involve a field test, but a series of tests conducted in a toxicology laboratory several days after the tablets were seized. Secondly, the chemical testing in this case was not a field test which could merely disclose whether or not the substance was a particular substance, but was a series of tests designed to reveal the molecular structure of the substance and indicate precisely what it is. Because of the greater sophistication of these tests, they could have revealed an arguably private fact ...

> While the circumstances of the visual search and seizure did not infringe the fourth amendment, and undoubtedly provided probable cause to seek a warrant, these circumstances do not justify a further extension of the Jacobsen field test exception to the warrant requirement. Accordingly, the judgement of the district court is reversed, and the cause is remended for further proceedings.[74]

E. *FRANKS V. DELAWARE:* WHERE THE MAGISTRATE HAS BEEN MISLED

1. Does the Constitution Require that Challenges be Permitted?

The rule that a search warrant must be judged by the information contained within the "four corners" of the face of the affidavit is not absolute. Certain challenges to warrants which appear on their face to be valid are grudgingly permitted.

The most frequent avenue, and the most difficult, involves a challenge based upon misrepresentations in the affidavit which have the result of misleading the magistrate who issues the warrant.

The Washington rule on this subject began with *State v. Goodlow, 11 Wn.App. 533, 535, 523 P.2d 1204 (1974)*:

> A defendant is entitled to a hearing which delves below the surface of a facially sufficient affidavit if he has made an initial showing of either of the following:

> a.) any misrepresentation by the government agent of a material fact.

> b) an intentional misrepresentation by the government agent, whether or not material...

> However, once such a hearing is granted, more must be shown to suppress the evidence. Evidence should not be suppressed unless the trial court finds that the government agent was either recklessly or intentionally untruthful. A completely innocent misrepresentation is not sufficient . . . Evidence should not be suppressed unless the officer was at least reckless in his misrepresentation. Even where the officer is reckless, if the misrepresentation is immaterial, it did not affect the issuance of the warrant and there is

no justification for suppressing the evidence. . . However, we conclude that if deliberate government perjury should ever be shown, the court need not inquire as to the materiality of the perjury.[75]

The rule we announce today is intended only to test the credibility of government agents whose affidavits or testimony are before the magistrate. The two-pronged test of *Aguilar v. Texas, 378 U.S. 108, 114, 84 S.Ct. 1509, 12 L.Ed.2d 723*. . . sufficiently tests the credibility of confidential informers. Consequently, defendant may not challenge the truth of hearsay evidence reported by an affiant. He may, after a proper showing, challenge any statements based on the affiant's personal knowledge, including his representations concerning the informer's reliability, his representation that the hearsay statements were actually made, and his implied representation that he believes the hearsay to be true.

This was a practical rule, encouraging truthfulness and professionalism in the process by which the police gain access to a citizen's castle. Search warrants are an area where truthfulness and professionalism need some encouragement. For example, after a study of police conduct made while he was a prosecuting attorney, one author concluded that the temptation for police to distort facts in search warrant affidavits rather than lose convictions was so strong that rules governing searches "should serve to deter, rather than to encourage submission to the strong urge to commit perjury."[76]

Another commentator observed:

Though commentators are not in agreement as to the extent of police perjury, . . . it does seem fair to say that 'the threat of police perjury is much greater than most courts are willing to acknowledge.'[77]

A recent study by a special committee of the American Bar Association reached conclusions which would also argue for the prophylactic rule of State v. Goodlow. After a study which considered the opinions of law enforcement as well as the defense bar, the Dash Committee concluded that the constitution, and in particular the exclusionary rule, does not impede effective law enforcement, but rather that it protects fundamental rights at a very low cost, while encouraging the professionalism which is essential to good law enforcement in a Democracy.[78]

Nevertheless, the rule we live with is much less prophylactic. The United States Supreme Court rejected the rule of absolute suppression where perjury was demonstrated, and adopted the more forgiving rule we must work with today. In *Franks v. Delaware, 438 U.S. 154, 155-56, (1978)* the Court held:

Where the defendant makes a substantial preliminary showing that a false statement knowingly and intentionally, or with reckless disregard for the truth, was included by the affiant in the warrant affidavit, and if the allegedly false statement is necessary to the finding of probable cause, the Fourth Amendment requires that a hearing be held at the defendant's request. In the event that at that hearing the allegation of perjury or reckless disregard is established by the defendant by a preponderance of the evidence, and, with the affidavit's false material set to one side, the affidavit's remaining content is insufficient to establish probable cause, the search warrant must be voided and the fruits of the search excluded to the same extent as if probable cause was lacking on the face of the affidavit.[79]

2. Inaccuracies Which Jeopardize a Warrant

a. Lies

Franks addresses this question specifically. The defendant must show "that a false statement knowingly and intentionally, or with reckless disregard for the truth was included by the affiant in the warrant affidavit." There is a clear difference between this and the Goodlow rule where suppression could result upon the showing of,

1. any misrepresentation by the government agent of a material fact, or

2. any intentional misrepresentation by the government agent, whether or not material.

Under the current rule, the government is only responsible for inaccuracies where the defendant can show either a specific intent to mislead, or reckless disregard for whether or not the magistrate is misled. Negligent misleading, even if it is clearly material or even critical, does not require suppression.

The difficulty of meeting a burden which requires a showing of the state of mind of an officer who may be a professional liar is obvious.

Without commenting about the difference between the Goodlow test and the Franks test, Washington approved the latter in *State v. Sweet, 23 Wn.App. 97, 596 P.2d 1080 (1979)*.

b. Omissions

Franks did not discuss the question of omissions which may have the same misleading result as affirmative misrepresentations. Nevertheless, most courts have assumed that misleading omissions could also result in suppression.

In *State v. Cord, 103 Wn.2d 361, 693 P.2d 81 (1985)*, the Supreme Court observed that:

> the Franks test for material misrepresentations has also been extended to material omissions of fact.[80]

The court declined to adopt the more demanding test of *People v. Kurlan, 28 Cal.3d 376, 618 P.2d 213, 168 Cal.Rptr. 667 (1980), cert. denied, 451 U.S. 987 (1981). Kurland* held that:

> negligent omission of a material fact requires insertion of the fact omitted into the affidavit. If the affidavit then does not support a finding of probable cause, the warrant is void and the evidence obtained is excluded.[81]

Nevertheless, it appears that where material omissions are found, and it is further found that their omission, and their misleading impact, was intentional or at least reckless, the "add and retest" formula appears to be the law. See, for example, *United States v. DeLeon, 979 F.2d 761, 763 (9th Cir. 1992); State v. Garrison, 118 Wn.2d 870, 873 (1992)*:

> If . . . the false representation or omitted material is relevant to establishment of probable cause, the affidavit must be examined. If relevant false representations are the basis of attack, they are set aside. If it is a matter of deliberate or reckless omission, those omitted matters are considered as part of the affidavit. If the affidavit with the matter deleted or inserted, as appropriate, remains sufficient to support a finding of probable cause, the suppression motion fails and no hearing is required. However, if the altered content is insufficient, defendant is entitled to an evidentiary hearing.

c. Whose lies or omissions?

Franks allows recourse only when the misrepresentation is that of a government agent. Informants are not government agents. In rare cases it may be possible to show that the informant's relationship with the government was so close that the informant may be considered a government agent for fourth amendment purposes.[82] Nor can the police insulate one officer's misstatement merely by relaying it through an officer/affiant personally ignorant of its falsity.[83]

Probable cause may not be enhanced in the process of communication between one officer and another. *Whiteley v. Warden, 401 U.S. 560, 568 L.Ed.2d 306, 91 S.Ct. 1031 (1971)*:

> Certainly police officers called upon to aid other officers in executing arrest warrants are entitled to assume that the officers requesting aid offered the magistrate the information requisite to support an independent judicial assessment of probable cause. Where, however, the contrary turns out to be true, an otherwise illegal arrest cannot be insulated from challenge by the decision of the instigating officer to rely on fellow officers to make the arrest.

3. Consequences of Inaccuracies

If it is shown that an affiant was intentionally or recklessly misleading exclusion of the evidence will result only if the false statements were necessary to the finding of probable cause. Where the offending act is that of omission, the same rule applies, although in this context it is the intent to mislead, rather than the intent to omit which triggers the exclusion.[84]

Worthy of note here is that a misrepresentation adequate to require suppression under Franks cannot be avoided by the "good faith" doctrine of *United States v. Leon, 468 U.S. 897 (1984)*, since *Leon* expressly stated that its holding left *Franks* untouched.

4. Procedures

a. The Initial Burden: Getting a Franks Hearing

The first step here is to get a judge to order a Franks hearing. To accomplish this, the defendant must make a "substantial preliminary showing that a false statement knowingly and intentionally, or with reckless disregard for the truth, was included by the affiant," and that "the allegedly false statement is necessary to the finding of probable cause . . ."[85] The showing is difficult:

> To mandate an evidentiary hearing, the challenger's attack must be more than conclusory and must be supported by more than a mere desire to cross examine. There must be
>
> 1. allegations of deliberate falsehood or of reckless disregard for the truth, and those allegations must be accompanied by
>
> 2. an offer of proof.
>
> 3. They should point out specifically the portions of the warrant affidavit that is claimed to be false; and they should be
>
> 4. accompanied by a statement of supporting reasons.
>
> 5. Affidavits or sworn or otherwise reliable statements of witnesses should be furnished, or their absence satisfactorily explained.
>
> 6. Allegations of negligence or innocent mistake are insufficient.
>
> 7. The deliberate falsity or reckless disregard whose impeachment is permitted today is only that of the affiant, not of any nongovernmental informant.
>
> 8. Finally, if these requirements are met, and if, when material that is the subject of the alleged falsity or reckless disregard is set to one side, there remains sufficient content in the warrant affidavit to support a finding of probable cause, no hearing is required.

State v. Casal, 103 Wn.2d 812, 699 P.2d 1234, 1238 (1985) is important where the court en banc held that fairness requires that the defendant's burden under Franks to make a threshold showing be reduced where "the defendant lacks access to the very information that Franks requires for a threshold showing of falsity." In *State v. Thetford, at 109 Wn.2d 403*:

> Although Franks requires a substantial showing that a false statement knowingly and intentionally, or with reckless disregard for the truth, was included by the affiant in the warrant affidavit before a defendant is entitled to an evidentiary hearing, Franks also holds that the showing need only be preliminary. Thus, defendants are not required to prove their charges by a preponderance of the evidence before being entitled to a Franks hearing. It is only at the hearing itself that defendants, aided by testimony and cross examination, must prove their charges by a preponderance of the evidence[86] . . .

Professor LaFave comments:

One thing is clear: in a case involving an anonymous informant, the defendant should not be deemed to have failed in his "threshold showing" merely because he has no information as to whether the informant lied to the officer-affiant (no Franks violation) or the officer-affiant lied to the magistrate. "A number of . . . courts have acknowledged this dilemma in anonymous-informant cases and have refused to apply Franks so inflexibly as to make hearings unattainable" in such circumstances. Another possible way of dealing with this predicament is to afford the defendant discovery on grounds short of those required under Franks for an evidentiary hearing.[87]

Most courts will not accept live testimony as a part of the proffer. Affidavits are the usual format. ER 104(a) allows the court to dispense with the Rules of Evidence, except for privilege.

Your proffer is a matter of your own ingenuity. The blatant cases are easy. Cases where the misrepresentations are more significant in their totality than individually are more difficult. Here is an example of a presentation form I have used:

THE AFFIDAVIT: "Clark brought up to 'Skeeter' the subject of a grow operation he helped maintain in the Maltby area (marijuana grow)."

THE TRUTH: Clark told Skeeter he wanted to purchase marijuana, and Skeeter said he didn't have any, but maybe could get some later. Asked where he was getting it, "he said that, through the conversation, that he was getting it from the same place that he was getting it from and what not like that." Clark admitted that Skeeter made no mention of any particular location more specific than "the same place."

THE AFFIDAVIT: "Clark knew about this as he had previously helped 'Skeeter' in the maintenance of the marijuana plants and had been to the growing location numerous times."

THE TRUTH: Clark stated that he had only been there once, did not help with maintenance, and had not told Detective Bales that he had been to the grow operation numerous times. He also stated that he had never seen anyone pick up any marijuana at the Defendant's residence.

THE AFFIDAVIT: "These outbuildings were indicated by Clark as being where the plants were normally grown."

THE TRUTH: Clark stated specifically that he had only seen marijuana in one building.

b. The Franks Hearing

Franks provides:

> (At the hearing) the allegation of perjury or reckless disregard (must be) established by the defendant by a preponderance of the evidence.

This means that the defendant's initial burden is to prove not only that the challenged statements were in fact false, but also that their inclusion amounted to perjury or reckless disregard for the truth.[88] Where the challenge is to omitted facts, it must be shown that they were omitted with intent to mislead, or with reckless disregard for whether or not the affidavit was misleading in their absence. For some time, the applicable rule acknowledged the fact that the state of mind of the officer would always be difficult to prove, and that therefore, on some occasions, recklessness may be inferred from the critical nature of the statement or omission. In his dissent in *State v. Cord*, Chief Justice Williams observed:

> The materiality of the omission to the finding of probable cause is the threshold issue. Nonmaterial, peripheral omitted facts have no effect on the determination of probable cause and are not entitled to review. However, once a fact is determined to be material, it is very difficult to justify its absence. If inclusion would affect the probable cause determination, then it should be included.

As noted in *United States v. Martin, 615 F.2d 318, 329 (5th Cir. 1980)*:

> It will often be difficult for an accused to prove that an omission was made intentionally or with reckless disregard rather than negligently unless he has somehow gained independent evidence that the affiant had acted from bad motive or recklessly in conducting his investigation and making the affidavit. Nevertheless, it follows from Franks that the accused bears the burden of showing by a preponderance of the evidence that the omission was more than a negligent act. It is possible that when the facts omitted from the affidavit are clearly critical to a finding of probable cause the fact of recklessness may be inferred from proof of the omission itself.[89]

Materiality and recklessness are closely related. When the misrepresentation is critical to the finding of probable cause, "the fact of recklessness may be inferred from the (misrepresentation) itself."

This rule, which on its face makes good sense, was adopted by the *Court of Appeals State v. Jones 55 Wn.App. 343, 777 P.2d 1053 (1989)*. Unfortunately, the rule was short-lived. In *State v. Garrison, 118 Wn.2d. 870 (1992)*, the Washington Supreme Court, En Banc, with Justices Utter and Anderson not participating, adopted a rule based upon dictum in *United States v. Colkley, 899 F.2d 297, (4th Cir. 1990)*:

> To prove reckless disregard of the truth, as is defendant's burden, defendant relies solely on *State v. Jones, 55 Wn.App. 343, 777 P.2d 1053 (1989)* which seems to hold that an inference of reckless disregard must be made from the omission of

facts "clearly critical to a finding of probable cause." The Court of Appeals relied on *State v. Jones*, supra, and dicta in *United States v. Martin, 615 F.2d 318, 329 (5th Cir. 1980)* . . .

Relying on such an inference to establish reckless disregard is not proper. The court in *United States v. Colkley, 899 F.2d 297, 301 (4th Cir. 1990)* cogently recognized the error in such reliance: "Such an inference collapses into a single inquiry the two elements—'intentionality' and 'materiality', which *Franks* states are independently necessary.

The test, according to Colkely, is whether the affiant had an intention to mislead. Since the facts omitted in Colkley were not material, and therefore not "clearly critical" to the probable cause determination, it didn't matter, and the rejection of the rule which would allow an inference of recklessness in certain circumstances is but dictum. Nevertheless, dictum in Colkley became law in Garrison. The defendant must prove that omissions were either made with the intention to mislead, or made with reckless disregard for the misleading consequences of the omission. Remarkably, suppression will not result, even if the omission was clearly critical to a finding of probable cause, unless something can be shown about the affiant's state of mind. This may be an impossible burden, although it may be approached tangentially by arguing that the affiant had reasons to doubt, or in fact "entertained serious doubts as to the truth of his (allegations)."[90]

Recklessness is shown where the affiant "in fact entertained serious doubts as to the truth" of facts or statements in the affidavit.

Davis,[91] at 694 (quoting St. Amant v. Thompson 390 U.S. 727, 731, 20 L. Ed. 2d 262, 88 S. Ct. 1323 (1968)).

Under Davis, such serious doubts can be shown by:

1.   actual deliberation on the part of the affiant,

2.   the existence of obvious reasons to doubt the veracity of the informant or the accuracy of his reports.[92]

O'Connor and its progeny remain good law, and may still be of value in arguing that the clear materiality of the fact gave the affiant "obvious reasons to doubt . . ."

Having established intentional or reckless manipulation of the truth, you have still not achieved your goal of suppression. Clearly, the affidavit must be reconstructed, with the perjury stricken, and the material omission added. Here is where a secondary burden of proof becomes significant. The initial magistrate's decision to approve a warrant is ordinarily reviewed deferentially at every level. The law favors search warrants and close cases are decided in favor of the warrant.[93]

In other words, search warrants, on their face, are presumed to be valid. But what of an affidavit which is shown to be materially misleading? Does the presumption still favor the warrant? Although the issue was not before the Garrison court, it was nevertheless addressed:

The challenged information must be necessary to the finding of probable cause.[94]

The Court of Appeals' statement confuses materiality or relevance as it relates to establishment of bad motive with the separate inquiry whether the information is necessary to the probable cause determination.[95]

A court finding "materiality" in the sense that an omission may be said to rise to the requisite level of misrepresentation under Franks may think it has made the second Franks finding and may invalidate a warrant after concluding only that the additional information might have affected the probable cause determination and not that the supplemented warrant could not have supported the existence of probable cause.[96]

"...omitted information that is potentially relevant but not dispositive is not enough to warrant a Franks hearing."[97][98]

It is unfortunate that our state supreme court chose to venture into this area without the benefit of adequate briefing. Strong arguments support the position that where intentional or reckless misleading has taken place, the presumption which favors search warrants is vitiated, the matter should be dealt with as though there were no warrant: the presumption should favor suppression so holds.[99] In Buccini, a consent search was followed by a search based upon an affidavit which the trial court found to be materially misleading. The court held:

> Although in most instances a magistrate's finding that sufficient probable cause exists to issue a search warrant will not be overturned unless it is clearly erroneous, this rule does not apply when a trial court reviews an affidavit that was submitted to the magistrate and later found to have been supported by false statements... Under these circumstances, the trial court must undertake an independent review of the effect of the false statements on probable cause because "the question turns on the consequences of a fraud on the issuing magistrate which that magistrate was not in a position to evaluate."[100]

The Buccini court continues:

> The rule in non-Franks cases considers the general presumption of validity of a search warrant and the deference given to a magistrate's determination of probable cause in concluding that in a "doubtful or marginal case a search under a warrant may be sustainable where without one it would fail."[101] The same rule, however, does not apply to a Franks case. To the contrary:

> When it has been established that the earlier finding of probable cause was based upon a broader set of "facts," some of which are now shown to be false, there is no longer any reason to give deference to that earlier finding. Thus, when a court reassesses a search warrant affidavit with the false allegations excised, a "doubtful or marginal case" should be resolved in the defendant's favor. That is, in such circumstances the probable cause determination should be made as it would upon a motion to suppress evidence obtained without a warrant.

> The policy underlying Franks seeks to mitigate the dangers of the ex parte procedure used to obtain a search warrant, and to deter over-zealous officers from supplying false information in their efforts to obtain access to the constitutionally protected privacy of one's home or car,[102] ...We firmly adhere to these policies and believe that where the officer has deliberately or recklessly made material misstatement and omissions in the original affidavit, it is appropriate to resolve marginal probable cause determinations in such a manner as will best uphold the integrity of the fourth amendment.[103]

Two wiretap cases also support this rule, although wiretaps, unlike search warrants, begin with the presumption that they are not constitutional. In *United States v. Carneiro, 861 F.2d 1171, 1176, 1182 (9th Cir. 1988)*, the court held that fruits of a wiretap would be suppressed for material misrepresentations where, if given the true facts, "a reasonable district court judge could (not should) have denied the application . . ." *United States v. Ippolito, 774 F.2d 1482, 1486-87 (9th Cir. 1985)* upon which Carneiro is based, holds the same.

The integrity of the procedures before the judge or magistrate who issues a search warrant requires meticulous scrutiny. Since a search warrant is issued ex parte, "the magistrate's only check on the affiant's veracity is a search for internal consistency . . ."[104] Evidence that the affiant has misled the magistrate, and thus undermined the usual presumption supporting the magistrate's decision, properly will result in exclusion:

> . . . The Fourth Amendment exclusionary rule by its nature bars reliable evidence. As the court has repeatedly emphasized, the primary justification for the exclusion is to serve the deterrence function. When the cause of exclusion is the actions of the officer-affiant misleading the magistrate, certainly that function is being served particularly well."[105]

c. Appellate Review of Franks Issues.

The trial court's factual findings are reviewed for "clear error."[106]

A determination of whether such omissions and misrepresentations were material to a determination of probable cause is a mixed question of law and fact subject to de novo review. State law seems to be parallel. Since constitutional rights are involved, the appellate court may conduct an independent evaluation of the evidence.[107] The application of law to facts is a matter reviewed de novo by the appellate court.[108]

5. Future Development of the Rule

State v. Garrison has taken much of the punch out of Franks. The determined practitioner should remember that the Franks rule has been adopted by the Washington courts with only superficial analysis and with very little thought to its inadequacies. Fortunately, Garrison, a case which seizes upon shallow dictum from the most miserly cases among Franks' progeny, did not consider any independent State Constitutional arguments. Garrison's most offensive language is also dictum. Whether recklessness has some relationship to materiality, and whether the presumption shifts when misrepresentations are shown are two issues on which Garrison may be vulnerable.

Professor LaFave criticizes the Franks rule lavishly. His treatise contains many seed from which good arguments may be sprouted. The early favorable treatment of this subject in this state, as reflected in Jones and Goodlow, and the relatively superficial analysis with which this excellent rules were abandoned should be viewed as a challenge; an invitation to State constitutional litigation.[109]

F. OTHER SUB-FACIAL CHALLENGES TO SEARCH WARRANTS

Information tainted by prior unlawful police conduct. Sometimes other defects appear in search warrant affidavits, either on or beneath the face of the affidavit. Where the fruit of a prior unlawful search is included in a search warrant affidavit, the offending information must be redacted, and the remaining information examined to determine whether it still establishes probable cause.[110] This argument is particularly useful where evidence offered in support of the warrant request is the result of a trespass,[111] or other unlawful conduct.

Although the government sometimes argues that even these defects must be tested by the Franks standard, no authority supports this position. Where unlawful conduct taints the elements of a search warrant, those elements are stricken, and the warrant is retested in its amended form. No case has been found by this counsel which addresses the burden of proof or the presumptions which operate in this situation, but the rule of State v. Buccini, discussed above, arguably has application.

If the government had unfettered power to pick and chose which facts to present to the magistrate regardless of how misleading the presentations were, the magistrate's review of the affidavit would be rendered meaningless. The magistrate would not be provided with a fair opportunity to review the government's evidence in making the probable cause determination. He would perform his crucial role at the whim, caprice or duplicity of the governmental agents involved in the case.[112]

Handling the Government Informant

Over the years, we have seen the decline of professionalism among law enforcement officers, while at the same time, a growing reliance upon their use of informants. This unholy alliance has moved progressively forward from the starting place of "detecting crime" to the end place of "creating crime." More and more Federal prosecutions are based on informant induced or created criminal activity, which means that the defense of these cases will often depend on our ability to effectively put the informant on trial.

When preparing to try the informant, it is important to plan a strategy of attack that begins with pre-trial investigation and continues through opening statement, cross-examination, the defendant's case-in-chief, and the closing statement. While you never have all of the information necessary to impeach, until the informant has testified on direct examination, there is still a lot of information that can be compiled, organized, and incorporated into your trial strategy.

A. BASIC PHILOSOPHY

When dealing with the Government informant, *always* keep in mind certain truisms:

The informant, historically, has been referred to as a rat, and embodies many characteristics of his namesake. One of the telling features is how when caught in a trap, he will gladly give back the cheese in exchange for his freedom.

All informants lie some of the time. Some informants lie all of the time. What you need to do is figure out who is who and what time it is (Borrowed from Michael Kennedy without permission).

Everybody has some dirt in their background.

All animals eventually begin to identify with their keepers.

B. INVESTIGATING THE INFORMANT

Obviously, if the money is available to hire a professional investigator, this would be the preferred method to begin the preparation for the attack. However, because many clients do not have sufficient funds to hire a professional investigator, the lawyer, his clerk or even the client will have to conduct it. There are several sources of information that can be tapped into for this purpose.

Criminal record check. This should include pending cases past cases, violations of prior probations and pre-trial bond information. Bond applications and records will include prior addresses, financial information, character references, prior record information and bond forfeitures.

Divorce Records will show the identity of former spouses, the grounds for divorce, financial information, prior addresses, allegations of abuse, drug use, child abuse, failure to pay child support and the names of attorneys who represented the spouse.

Civil Suits show if the snitch been sued for injuring others or has he sued others for injuring him? Has he been sued for non payment of debts? Look for financial information and prior places of employment. They may show a pattern of possibly fraudulent suits.

Property Records will indicate any homes which were bought or sold, the identity of others that have conducted financial transactions with the snitch, information involving loan applications and the identity of mortgage companies or lawyers involved in the transaction.

Assumed Name Records are records of businesses owned by the snitch and the identity of the snitch's business associates.

Marriage License Records provide information about current and former spouses including addresses.

The Secretary of State Office can provide information about corporate charters and the identity the businesses and associates of the snitch.

Credit Bureaus can provide the credit history of the snitch and his businesses.

Newspapers can provide a chronological history. Check the local newspaper "morgues" to see if the snitch has been mentioned in any articles. Use the Datatimes Computer Data Base Service and access information regarding newspapers or magazines where the snitch's name has appeared

Discovery is a fertile field. You can get payment records from all law enforcement agencies. Always request the actual hard copy of the payment requisition forms, as well as summaries. You can also get contracts between the prosecution and the snitch setting out what his obligations are, plea agreements and letters of immunity, transcripts of prior testimony, a list of cases, cause numbers, and jurisdictions where the snitch has previously testified. Other records include the snitch's criminal history and the application of the snitch to enter the Witness Protection Program, the periodic evaluations from the U.S. Marshal's office for the Witness Protection Program and psychological tests performed prior to admittance into the Witness Protection Program.

C. PURSUING INVESTIGATIVE LEADS

Once all of the raw data regarding the snitch has been obtained, the investigation should center around developing those leads. All people referred to in the biographical materials should be contacted in order to learn more about the snitch. In particular, you want to know about, other criminal activity, incidents of dishonesty, incidents of violence or brutality, statements made regarding your client or your case, statements regarding the snitch's relationship with law enforcement, use of aliases, horror stories from the ex-spouse, and the general reputation of the snitch for honesty, peacefulness, etc. The opinion of others regarding the character of the snitch. Perhaps you can find a photograph of the snitch using drugs or displaying vast sums of wealth, drug paraphernalia or other signs of dealing.

The list of people to be contacted is virtually inexhaustible. They should include, but are not limited to neighbors, co-workers and former co-workers, employers and former employers, ex-wives or ex-husbands, girlfriends and boyfriends, officers who have previously arrested the snitch, estranged children of the snitch, probation and parole officers.

D. STRATEGIES FOR THE ATTACK

1. The drug use of the snitch

If you are able to establish a long term pattern of drug usage by the snitch, you can lay a foundation for expert testimony regarding his inability to accurately observe or recall events.

Before cross-examination, discuss with a psychiatrist or psychologist, who is qualified to testify about cocaine/narcotics psychosis, what facts you need to establish in order for him to give an expert opinion regarding organic brain disfunction. For example, if the informant admits that he has used cocaine for 3 years and developed a pattern of use that began as sporadic use and graduated to regular use, you may be able to show that he fits within the classic parameters of abuse that brings about cocaine psychosis. An expert can then explain to a jury what the effect of this abuse is, in terms of the witness's ability to recall events.

Even if you can not afford to bring in an expert, you can bring out his pattern of abuse and his frequency of drug use. This, in and of itself can be used during final argument to point out the snitch's inability to accurately recall and recollect events, as they actually happened.

2. Character Witnesses

If you dig deep enough into the snitch's prior business and personal relationships, you will be able to find an number of people who can testify as to his bad reputation for truthfulness and for not being a peaceful and law-abiding person.

Even if the character witness is unable to testify as to the general reputation of the snitch in the community, he will be able to give his opinion of those character traits, or lack thereof.

3. Payments to the Snitch

After obtaining the payment records of the snitch, look at whether he gave any written statements on the same day that he actually received payments. This can be used to show the pattern of mutual conditioning, when the snitch and his handlers learn how to give what it takes to get what they want.

When payment records indicate that the snitch received money for "security" or "relocation," check to see if he actually moved to another home after getting the money. Often, agents will disguise large payments as "security" in order to make it appear that the snitch was afraid of the defendant and therefore had to relocate.

Check to see if the snitch generally gets a "reward" payment after his testimony. You can show that, although he has not received a reward as of the time of his testimony, he obviously expects to get one if he testifies successfully.

Check to see if payments to the snitch were made in compliance with the DEA guidelines.

4. DEA Philosophy of Snitches

The DEA Manual sets out the Government's view of its creatures. Use this with the agent to set the stage for his snitch's appearance. The agents are natu.ally suspicious of their own informants and therefore rules and regulations have been promulgated to control the use of these informants. Exploit this distrust as fully as possible. The NALDL has copies of the DEA Manual. You can also get it through a Freedom Of Information Act request.

5. The Media and the Snitch

Often, the local media will be as upset with the antics of and preferential treatment accorded the snitch and will be more than receptive to heralding the unholy alliance between the snitch and the Government.

While the Government will always step forward to defend the bribes and blackmail as being "legal," the public perception will always be that this type of conduct is immoral and wrong. But first they have to know.

Just as the snitch has to be tried in court, he must also be tried by the public whenever possible. The media will often cover the opening statements and this is a perfect opportunity to grab their attention by bringing out the immoral deals cut by the Government.

E. OPENING STATEMENT

Always make an opening statement immediately after the Government's opening.

Since the snitch will often be the focal point of your attack, you must use your first opportunity to talk to the jury to tell them just how bad he really is. This is your chance to form an impression, in the minds of the jurors, of a person that they will soon be meeting. Obviously, if they have decided that he is to be distrusted and despised, he will take the witness stand tainted and suspicious, rather than authoritative and likeable. Convey your contempt for this witness and give the jury enough facts so that they will share your feelings.

Let the jurors know up front that this snitch has been bought and paid for. If the amount of the payments is particularly high, write it on the board and talk about how terribly obscene these payments are. This is also a good opportunity to explain how there really is no difference between "information," "expense" and "reward" payments and how these labels are used to disguise the real nature of these immoral and unconscionable payments. Since you usually have low to middle class jurors, they should learn as early as possible how this witness has made a large sum of money for his testimony. Breed resentment!

This is your first opportunity to show the jury the penalty range that your client is exposed to as well as the fact that the snitch was able to escape countless years in prison by cooperating. Bringing out the snitch's deal will often show the jury his true motivation to lie about your client. Freedom is a stronger motivational factor than money, and the jury will find it to be a more likely reason to fabricate.

Everyone looks upon the convicted or career criminal with disdain and suspicion. The jury should know the number of prior convictions that the snitch has had, or criminal acts for which he has not been convicted, but is using as bargaining chips with the Government. The revelation that the snitch is a convicted criminal will normally be the most devastating factor affecting his credibility and believability. Especially if it is shown that he usually is given lenient treatment, when caught, in exchange for cooperation.

Inconsistencies are important to point out during the opening statement, you can tell the jury about glaring inconsistencies between the snitch's testimony regarding a transaction, and the testimony of another witness regarding the same transaction. This can be done when you have grand jury testimony, prior court testimony, or witness statements available. By highlighting inconsistencies at this time, the jurors receive the information as unestablished or disputed, rather than as established and "subject to" dispute or impeachment. It is much harder to erase a fact once it is established than to keep it from being established in the first place.

It is absolutely imperative to make an opening in a snitch case, just as it is also imperative to begin your attack as early as possible. If you have a number of issues available to use for impeachment of the snitch, save some for cross-examination, but keep in mind that during your opening, you must strike first, strike hot, and keep striking at the informant so that when the Government calls him as a witness, the jurors will want to turn away with disgust as he slithers into the courtroom.

While discrediting the informant and his testimony, you must also develop the "legitimate" relationship between your client and the snitch. In nearly every case, there will be a legitimate connection between the two, or at least an apparent legitimate connection and this must be developed very early in the case so that the jury will understand why your client would even know a person as despicable as the snitch.

If only the negative part of the snitch is emphasized or developed, then you have not incorporated the snitch into the advancement of your theory of the case. At final argument, you will have no way to rebut the prosecutor's argument that it was your client and not the Government that chose the snitch.

F. CROSS EXAMINATION

This is where all of your investigation, preparation, planning, plotting, and scheming has led. The prosecutor has finished his animal act, which you must now follow.

Establish control. Many snitches are successful at what they do because they have huge egos and are determined to get what they want, no matter what they have to do in order to get it. Therefore, if you fail to seize control of him at the very first opportunity, you will be playing in his ball park and he will be able to draw you into a contest of wills, ego, and cunning that will diminish your ability to effectively destroy him. While listening to the direct examination, you should consider the best method of attack. While some snitches can be steamrolled and destroyed directly and quickly, others are so cunning and will rehearsed that you will need to wear him down before methodically forcing him to expose his own dishonesty and disregard for decency. This is especially true when the snitch is a true sociopath and cannot distinguish between right and wrong. With this type of snitch, the longer he is on the witness stand, the more the jury will come to understand the lack of decency and morality that this person embodies. This type of snitch will be more inclined to boast of his exploits and general rottenness rather than act shamed by the revelations of his sleaziness. Whatever the case, you need to combine the results of your pre-trial investigation with your observations during the direct examination, in order to determine the best way to proceed.

There are some general areas that should be addressed on cross-examination, regardless of how you ultimately decide to go after the snitch.

1. Deception

Bring out the aliases that the snitch has used during his life of crime and snitching in order to show how easily he can change his own identity, which is the most basic part of his existence.

Discuss his ability to lie during undercover investigations in order to get the confidence of those that he is dealing with. In particular, discuss times when he has been able to come up with lies at the spur of the moment in order to protect himself, the investigation, etc. This will demonstrate his ability to think fast on his feet and his ability to be convincing, even when he lies.

Look for discrepancies between his story and the stories of the other witnesses, even on seemingly unimportant details.

Bring out any and every lie that he ever told his supervising agents.

2. Preparation

Go over each and every time that the snitch met with agents or prosecutors, after the defendant's arrest, in order to show the amount of time that the snitch put in to rehearsing his testimony. Often, he will even begin to adopt your term of "rehearsing." What develops from this is the revelation that the snitch put in an inordinate amount of time preparing to be cross-examined. Inquire into whether audio or video tapes were made of these sessions and whether he was "cross-examined" by some Government lawyer. The answer will sometimes be "yes."

3. Payments

Show the individual payments made to the snitch since he began his snitching. Go through the payments that apply to your case, one at a time, and discuss what the true nature of the payments were. While doing this, look to see if the snitch was paid on the same days that he met with the prosecutors to rehearse his testimony. If the payments add up to an especially large amount, the jurors can then be confronted with the issue of whether the Government paid too much for what they got.

Inquire into the amount of legitimate income earned by the snitch, as well as the illegitimate income. Often you will find that he gets paid more for his snitching than he does for working legitimately, or by engaging in criminal behavior.

Always compare the payment summaries with the individual payment requisition form to see if they match.

4. Continued Criminality

All snitches are documented by their agencies and given a number that reflects the date that they began their new career. When they are first documented, they must sign an agreement which sets out what they can and cannot do. Although they can normally continue to break the law with impunity, their agreement instructs them to never violate the law.

Show each time since the snitch first signed his agreement that he violated it by committing a new offense. Go into whether the agents knew and condoned his conduct or whether he hid his violation from them. If you cannot catch him on anything else, you can at least show that he paid no taxes on his snitch money, although the agents will say that they told him that he had to.

5. Deals

Show the jury how many years in prison the snitch avoided by working for the Government. This not only establishes his motive for lying, but also lets you show what your client is looking at if convicted. The plea agreement itself should be used to show the full extent of the benefits accorded the snitch, but a transcript of his plea will sometimes reveal even more consideration.

Interestingly, it seems that many times jurors are more suspect or offended if the snitch is receiving a good "deal" than if he received money from the Government. So be sure to deal with his expectations, as well as the official version of the deal.

If the snitch is entering the witness protection program, emphasize how he will be given a new identity and money and placed in a community that will not be warned of his propensity to commit crimes at will. You should also show that he is not really in need of protection since he is worse than the defendant.

6. Dueling Snitches

In multiple snitch cases, you need to remember that each child wants to be the favorite in the eyes of his parent. Every snitch believes that he is better, more productive, and more cunning than the other snitches and will generally make no attempt to hide this. Often, one will testify that the other snitch is dishonest, a drug user, etc.

Additionally, there will often be many discrepancies between the snitches. Each will recall events in the light most favorable to himself and these discrepancies can often be used to impeach the next snitch before he testifies. By writing important details from snitch #1 on a board or poster, his story is preserved and can later be used to impeach the version of events testified to by snitch #2 or #3.

7. Why Does Your Client Know The Snitch?

Through the informant, you need to show why your client would know him. Since you have shown that he is basically a worthless individual, you need to have a legitimate reason for being around him, in order for your client to not look as sleazy as him. Sometimes you questions are much more important than his answers; since he will try to minimize or negate any legitimate relationship with your client.

Obviously, if you offer no explanation, the snitch's version will be the only one before the jury and the prosecutor is free to make the standard argument of "we didn't choose the snitch, the defendant did." You will have no way to rebut this.

Look at what the snitch does for a living, or more importantly, what he told your client or others that he did. See if there is an apparent legitimate connection between your client and the snitch and take the time to develop that connection before the jury.

8. Tape Cases

If the snitch wore a recorder or transmitter, you need to determine whether he had an opportunity to cut off the machine at will, and only record what he wanted to record. This is not uncommon and frequently you will find that earlier conversation between your client and the snitch were not recorded. You can make use of the fact that only the later conversations were taped, when the snitch was ready to move in for the kill.

It is not unusual in tape cases to find a tape wherein the snitch is controlling the conversation and making all of the incriminating statements. Normally when this happens, the snitch is trying to get the defendant to agree with or otherwise ratify these statements. When this happens, the emphasis has to shift away from content and towards the issue of who was the instigator and who was in control.

It is also important, in non-tape cases, to point out the snitch's ability to record the conversations, but his failure to do so. This can often be used to show that what the snitch is telling the agents is not always what the defendant is telling the snitch.

G. THE DEFENDANT'S CASE

When you finally have an opportunity to present your case, you should make a point of doing the following, whenever possible:

Dispute every possible statement of the snitch. Even seemingly unimportant details should be rebutted when possible, in order to show that if the snitch will lie about some things, he will lie about all.

Character and reputation of the snitch: If your investigation turned up people that hold the snitch in low regard, bring them to court. Bring as many as you possibly can.

People who know the snitch best are in the best position to tell the jury that he is so dishonest and immoral that he should never be believed by anyone.

Character witnesses may testify as to the snitch's general reputation in the community, his law abidingness (or lack thereof), or other character traits that are in issue. Additionally, they may offer their opinion as to those traits that are in issue. While they may not testify as to their basis for that opinion, if the Government opens the door, they should be prepared to give the reasons for that belief.

H. THE COURT'S CHARGE

In a snitch case, you are always entitled to a charge on the credibility of informant type witnesses, co-conspirators, accomplices, drug users, perjurers, etc. Be sure to request the specific charge that you want and include in your request the specific traits that were raised by the evidence.

I. FINAL ARGUMENT

Rather than reviewing the damaging part of the snitch's testimony, review all of the damaging points that you brought out about the snitch. Do not overlook any of them.

Usually a metaphor or story about the snitch will drive home the point a little clearer than merely giving a factual recitation of what they already heard. A simple analogy can sometime make jurors apply more common sense to their analysis, but always weave it in to your argument gracefully so that it blends in naturally to emphasize the point you are trying to make.

Some examples:

"Imagine that you heard on the news reports that children all over town are dying from eating poisoned mushrooms. As you sit down to eat dinner, Joe Snitch arrives at your door trying to sell you mushrooms. Knowing what you know about him now, would you buy them? Would you eat them? Would you let your kids eat them? Would you trust your life to this man, knowing all that you do? If not, don't trust my client's life to him now."

For years the Government pursued Joe Snitch with a vengeance. The followed him, stalked him, cursed him, hated him, and ultimately caught him. After being such a despised and hated creature, he miraculously underwent a moral rejuvenation that made the Government want to love him, embrace him, identify with him, and join him. The day he plead guilty, he was transformed into a paragon of virtue and honor and went from becoming an enemy of the Government to actually becoming a representative of the Government.

If you are in the type of case where the agents and prosecutor appear to be so clean and innocent that they could never knowingly embrace such a worthless piece of slime, you may need to approach the snitch from the standpoint that he used and manipulated the Government into believing that they really needed him. The approach has to center more around the way that the snitch convinced the Government that he could deliver a lot more than he was actually capable of delivering;

"I want to tell you a story about the fox, the chicken, and the weasel. You see, the weasel looked across the river and saw the chicken and decided that he wanted to eat him. The only problem is he didn't want to get wet crossing the river. So, the fox, who was standing with the weasel said, 'that's okay brother weasel, just hop up here on my head and I will carry you across the river.' So the weasel jumped up on the fox's head and they started across the river. After a while, the weasel started to get wet and said, 'excuse me Mr. Fox, but I'm starting to get a little wet.' The fox said, 'that's okay, just climb a little higher up on my head.' The weasel did and a few minutes later he again complained that he was getting wet. The fox replied, lifting his head straight up in the air, 'that's okay Mr. Weasel, just climb up a little higher on my head.' The weasel did. He fell into the fox's mouth and the fox ate the weasel.

Just like in this case, Joe Snitch saw the Government coming. He offered to carry them across the river and when they agreed, he swallowed them." (Borrowed from Craig Washington).

At this point, the jurors should be reminded that this trial involves significant moral issues, that transcend the charge itself. Remind them of the impropriety of buying testimony, of the general dislike and distrust that we have always had for informants, and of the bad public policy of relying on a snitch's testimony to convict another human being.

You should anticipate the Government's standard argument that the defense is trying to shift the focus away from the defendant by putting the informant on trial. Always point out how you are not trying they informant, but instead you are fulfilling your obligation to the defendant, the court, and the jury by pointing out the lack of credibility that this witness possesses. Once you have established this with the jury, proceed to try the hell out of the snitch.

Guerrilla Trial Tactics

If you have something of importance to say,
for God's sake start at the end.

—Sarah Jeannette Duncan

The purpose of Guerrilla Trial Tactics is to break through preconceived limits on how we try criminal cases. We must re-examine our routine. Which breeds complacency. The criminal defense lawyer must communicate his/her purpose clearly, consistently, and passionately. S/he is all that stands between the client's freedom and the jury's bias. If our determination lapses, we have missed an opportunity and lowered our credibility. A jury should never see the attorney relax or be complacent in the defense of the accused.

A. THERE ARE THREE GENERAL PRINCIPALS OF GUERRILLA TRIAL TACTICS

1. Trying a case should begin as soon as we accept it. Trial tactics extend beyond mapping our opening and plotting our cross-examinations.

2. Contrast the prosecution. With passion, you are in direct contrast with the prosecution.

3. Rattle the prosecutor's cage. Prosecutors are generally not creative and they are quite comfortable locked in a cage of routine. Rattle it!

B. INVESTIGATION

I have never seen a situation so dismal that a
policeman couldn't make it worse.

—Brendan Behan (1923-1964)

Early investigation can make or break the case. It is essential to get to witnesses before the prosecution. After the prosecutor talks to witnesses, they generally acquire or solidify a pro-prosecution bias. They rarely want to talk to you, or your investigator, with candor or spontaneity. Get to them fast.

It is important to do what you can to alleviate a witness' suspicion that whatever s/he says is somehow going to be twisted. Consider offering a witness his/her own copy of the tape of the interview. The other obvious advantage to providing the witness with a copy of what he has said, is that prior to the witness being called upon to testify, the s/he can refresh his/her memory. Also, by providing the witness with a copy of what s/he has said, you have further contrasted yourself with law enforcement. Have the witness acknowledge, in writing, the accuracy of any statement, taped or written, or even the investigator's notes.

Consider the advantages of using a female investigator. First, for whatever nonsensical, stereotypical reasons, sometimes witnesses are more willing to let a female in the door. Secondly, consider the benefits of a female investigator testifying for you, and/or being an advisory witness. The reality is that the complexion of a case will be moderated by a woman testifying for the defense or serving as an advisory witness.

One of the elementary rules of defense is to go to the scene. Do it early. No matter how many photos you examine or how many witnesses you talk to, there is no replacement for the real thing. Going to the scene helps you to recreate the case in your opening. There may be details about the color of things, the layout, or any variety of matters that may be the subject of testimony that you could never know without being there. You need to find every single opportunity to attack the credibility of witnesses, especially when you are trying a loser case or, as we affectionately call it, walking the dog.

It also will help you to demonstrate to the jury that you care enough about this case that you went there and you looked at it for yourself. The prosecutor probably didn't do that, which is another way that you can contrast the prosecution. For every ten times you go to a scene, it may only really pay off once or twice, but the payoff is generally well worth all the effort.

A primary rule of defense is to look at all the evidence. This is such a simple thing, but our routine seems to leave little room for this. We generally get photocopies of the evidence, or we send somebody else to look at it, because it is more convenient. Don't slide into that trap of routine.

C. JURY SELECTION (A.K.A. VOIR DIRE)

The hottest places in Hell are reserved for those who in time of great moral crises maintain their neutrality.

—Dante Alighieri (1265-1321)

When selecting a jury the most fundamental thing is to be true to yourself. Perhaps nowhere in the trial process is that more important.

In serious cases, consider opening your jury selection by saying something about you being afraid or uncomfortable, as long as you can mean it when you say it. In general, you're not going to draw an objection if that is one of the first things out of your mouth. If you do, who cares? Let the prosecutor look like the unfeeling dolt that s/he is.

Assure the jury that everyone has his/her own life experience, and no one's life experience is better than anyone else's. In fact, if the judge were trying this case, the judge would be using his/her life experience as well. No one's is better, and no one's is more right. We need twelve life experiences here. This kind of approach helps set up the more favorable jury, and that is a jury of twelve independent people.

Use the judge's mistakes. If a judge makes an error, you can respectfully refer to that in your jury selection. Say something like, "You saw the judge made a mistake. We're all human here."

If a juror doesn't respond when you are asking a question, you might say something like, "Maybe I asked a peculiar question. I don't even know how I would answer that. Can anyone here help us out?" If somebody does jump in and respond, you know that person is with you.

Consider asking the jury to get up and stretch, especially after a long prosecutor jury selection. Consider asking the court for permission to take a break. The jurors have been drinking lots of coffee to stay awake through this thing, and they always appreciate a potty break. Have your client's children sit out in the hallway with him/her, so that during these breaks s/he can join them. Juries see this and pay particular attention to it.

Assuming you have a case with a family that is respectable and presentable, have them seated right behind you in the courtroom. Introduce them. This is important to do because they are going to be there throughout the trial. Clearly, if someone on the jury panel works or went to school with a family member, we all need to know that because we want to be fair.

Nuts and bolts: Use little yellow memo stickies on your jury chart. As new jurors are called up to the jury box, you can just slap on another sticky to have a clean writing space. Don't take a pen with you to the podium. It is too tempting to start writing, and you need to contrast the prosecutor. Prosecutors ask a question, write it down, ask a question, write it down, and the jury looks at the top of the prosecutor's head more than anything else. If a juror says something that is really important, write it down as soon as you get back to your counsel table, and use it in your closing. It shows the jury that you really listened to them.

Consider, at the last practical moment, asking for a jury of six rather than a jury of twelve. Prosecutors are generally not ready to do their opening before lunch. Their witnesses aren't there and they aren't ready. You may have a judge who asks the prosecutor, in front of the jury, "Are you ready to proceed?" The prosecutor has to say, "No, we aren't ready" in front of the jury.

In addition to rattling the prosecution, you gain the fundamental advantage of talking with fewer jurors. You'll find that it is much easier to develop some rapport with each individual juror. Consider also the number of peremptory challenges. For instance, in Colorado you'll have five peremptory challenges to seat a jury of six.

D. RATTLE THE PROSECUTORS' CAGE

The impossible is often the untried.

—Jim Goodwin

Identify and study the prosecutors' routine and then disrupt it. Cause them to lose their balance in the courtroom. They are way too comfortable there. Rattle their cage. Make them think and work hard. Shake them up.

Read the local rules of procedure. I learned that the prosecutor in a particular case, in a particular courtroom, was by habit sitting at the wrong table. We invoked the rule and made him move. He was obviously disoriented. The added benefit was that the judge, who had routinely relied on the prosecution for procedural guidance, was now looking to us.

Consider making the prosecution explain just why they need to have the cop sit there at counsel table as an advisory witness. Invoke Rule 16 of the Federal Rules of Evidence. The rule says, "At the request of a party, the court shall order witnesses excluded so they can not hear the testimony of other witnesses . . . (unless) a person whose presence is shown by a party to be essential to the presentation of the party's cause."

Consider moving counsel tables before the trial. The prosecution is accustomed to feeling in control of the courtroom. It is so familiar to him/her. Move him/her physically, and s/he is thrown off balance. Moreover, it is important that you are positioned to reduce the prosecutor's ability to block the jury's view of you and your client. Sometimes, we wouldn't mind keeping our client out of view, but the reality is that we need to humanize the defendant to make the guilty vote less comfortable.

Don't let the prosecutor push the podium around, or block your view of the jury or a witness. Interrupt the prosecutor's flow. You've got to be in a consistent posture of advocacy, and you want the jury to see you. Use the word "fairness" in your objection and in your request to have the prosecutor get out of the way. Make it clear why you object.

Another good cage rattler is an unexpected motion *in limine*, a written motion for a protective order against prejudicial questions and statements. Some judges mean it when they prohibit it. Know your judge. The substance shouldn't be frivolous, of course, but it doesn't have to be monumental, either. The point here is to force the prosecutor into a position of responding to it unexpectedly. Object to the admissibility of some particular piece of evidence. Judges like to decide that *in limine*. We want a clean, smooth trial, judge. Object to the advisory witness of the prosecution. The point is, it doesn't much matter. You want to catch the prosecutor off guard.

The bonus points come in when you make the prosecutor angry, and then watch him/her try to turn on the charm to the jury while s/he is also trying to cool off from your unexpected motions. Rattle away.

A series of cage rattling techniques does have accumulative impact. Prosecutors are generally not creative people. They are more than likely comfortably locked in a cage of routine. You've got to rattle it.

E. THE INVISIBLE PROSECUTOR

Silence gives consent, or a horrible feeling that nobody's listening.

—Franklin P. Jones

Talk to the jury, talk to the judge, but don't even look at the prosecutor. The prosecutor should be invisible. Don't watch him/her during arguments or examinations. Don't lend any credibility to him/her. When the prosecutor loses his/her balance because you've got the old cage rattled, s/he'll look at you. It's human nature. Don't even glance back. You have much more important things on your mind. The prosecutor doesn't have innate power and, certainly, don't give him/her power by looking at him/her.

Call the prosecutor for what they are; prosecutors. Don't ever call them the "District Attorney" or the "D.A." or the "State" or the "U.S. Attorney" or the "Government." Names like that give them too much power. Besides, they don't even actually represent the state in most cases. For instance, in Colorado, the Public Defenders are state employees, and the District Attorneys are employees of a Judicial District within the state. Consider bringing that out in your jury selection when the prosecutor claims to represent the state. Call them on it.

F. VALUABLE COURT PERSONNEL

Democracy is the name we give to other people when we need them.

—Robert Pellevue, Marquis de Flers
(1872-1927)

If you aren't friendly with the court personnel now, you should start now. Above all, be genuine. Court employees are valuable in too many ways to list. The advantages result from a long term, sincere relationship. Actually, it is not a guerilla tactic on my part at all, but court personnel know a few guerilla tactics of their own.

> I had a case where the jury panel had been seated, and the judge had not yet come into the courtroom. His clerk came up to my counsel table and, very deliberately, asked me, and looked at my client, if there was anything that we needed, if we had enough water, and that sort of thing. She had concern written across her face plain enough for the whole jury panel to see.
>
> * * *
>
> In another case, a bailiff announced in front of the jury that the prosecutor's witness "didn't even show up" when the prosecutor stood and called him to testify next. The bailiff's tone and expression communicated his lack of surprise.

G. YOUR CLIENT

Curiosity killed the cat, but for a while I was a suspect.

—Steven Wright

If you can't learn to love your client, learn to view him/her as the embodiment of the principles you love. The jury is curious and will watch you interact with your client. The absence of interaction is fatal. You must consult him/her during voir dire, pour him/her water, and teach him/her to pour water for you. Teach him/her court etiquette such as rising when the judge enters the courtroom and to say "excuse me" after sneezing. Give the client a pad and pen to keep him occupied and to make notes rather than tugging at your sleeve, enraged by "those liars."

Preparing your client to testify can be a tedious process. There are two primary dangers. One, it is very likely that you have become too involved to see the weaknesses in your client's testimony. Two, you've got to stop before your client crosses the line of being overly prepared. Perhaps one of the best ways to avoid these two pitfalls is to have lawyers and staff members of your office participate in and observe a mock direct and cross-examination of your client. Have another attorney in your office conduct cross-examination. Permit staff members to ask questions. People who don't know much about the case will point things out to you that you can no longer see.

Have your client sit in the witness box when the courtroom is empty. Your client and you should try every seat in the courtroom. Try the witness box, prosecutor's table and jury box. It is important for both you your client to see the jury's perspective.

H. OPENING AND CLOSING

When you have no basis for an argument,
abuse the plaintiff.

—Marcus Tullius Cicero (106-43 B.C.)

Don't hold back your big guns because you think the impact will be better at some point later in the trial. Think about that first prosecution witness, who gives a very long direct. This is the first testimony the jury hears. The jury has been waiting a long time to finally hear testimony, and is paying very close attention.

Capitalize on the opportunity of the opening's timing. It immediately precedes that first witness. Tell the jury what you know you can show them later. This is the best time to color that first witness as so unbelievable that s/he and prosecutor will face an uphill battle from the beginning. The damage is invaluable to you. Don't hold back when you know you can nail them. Nail the witness as soon as you can: in the opening.

We've all heard the "this case is about . . ." opening. Thinking in those terms is helpful because it helps you and the jury to focus on important issues. Nevertheless, eliminate the phrase "this case is about," and jump right into it. A corollary to this is: don't ever say "the evidence will show" or "we submit."

There are two problems with these phrases. First, they mimic prosecutor language, and you sure don't want to sound like him/her. Secondly, it unnecessarily demeans the importance of what you are saying. Why couch it and condition it? Lay it out as if it is absolutely beyond dispute.

In a first-degree murder case with self-defense, my very first line in my opening was, "There is a victim in the courtroom." This was the whole focus of the case, and it really got the jury's attention because they all thought the victim was the dead guy.

* * *

Another example is a mail fraud case in which I knew I could hammer two snitches. My opening immediately focused on the fact that they were liars, why they lied, and how my client was a "target" of their lies. I later used the word "target" in cross-examination and closing. The grand jury transcripts contained a description of the scheme wherein the word "target" was used. I knew I could get a snitch to use the word "target" for me, so I used it right away in the opening, it came through loud and clear in the cross-examination, and I used the word again in the closing. My "target" client was found not guilty.

Another important thing to remember in both your opening and closing, is to contrast your style with the prosecutor's. That takes some flexibility to do without changing the substance of what you are saying. Change the way you deliver it. If the prosecutor is blasting away, full volume, get up there and speak deliberately and softly, for more impact. If the prosecutor is monotone and boring, as they often are, your delivery should be passionate and alive. Remember that the style with which you deliver your opening and your closing is flexible. Your passion can be expressed in bold terms and volume, or can be delivered in a quiet and intense manner.

You aren't finished after closing. Stay on top of that rebuttal, but don't lend support by watching the prosecutor. Look at almost anything else. Listen carefully. This is when they get sloppy, and it usually deserves an interruption. Make an objection. They almost always shift the burden of proof. Break their tempo. Show the jury you are chomping at the bit, and that it drives you nuts that you can't get in the last word because you're right.

I. EVIDENCE

There ain't no rules around here! We're trying to accomplish something!

—Thomas Edison

For a good defense lawyer, the *Rules of Evidence* almost demand a double standard: the prosecution can't get in any evidence without justifying it pursuant to the rules. They have to get permission. On the other hand, we can get everything admitted. All my relevant evidence is admissible, and there may even be a certain rule that identifies a more particularized reason why it is admissible. This is not to suggest that you actually object to every syllable uttered by the prosecution witnesses. Rather, this should be your mindset.

Read the *Rules of Federal Evidence* regularly. It is amazing what is and is not in there. For instance, Rule 806 says "when a hearsay statement, or a statement defined in Rule 801(d)(2), (C), (D) or (E), has been admitted in evidence, the *credibility of the declarant may be attacked*, and if attacked, may be *supported by any evidence which would be admissible for those purposes if the declarant had testified as a witness.*" Use this rule, and then watch out for prosecutors waking up and using it on us. You can use this rule to get in, for example, even a dead victim's prior felony convictions, *even if your client had no knowledge of the victim's reputation for lawlessness.*

The prosecutor's typical response to your hearsay objection is, "But we're not offering it to prove the truth of the matter." Then it's irrelevant. Use the language in the rule's definition of relevancy. If it is not offered to prove the truth of the matter, then it probably isn't going to make a fact of consequence more or less probable.

Keep the *Rules of Evidence* visible to you and to the jury, on an uncluttered defense table. When you do object, consider actually opening up the *Rules of Evidence*, and citing the rule. You look authoritative when you refer to a specific Rule. The natural inclination of the prosecution is to grab their rules. You've got the prosecution scrambling to keep up with you.

Obviously, if they don't have a copy of the *Rules of Evidence* in front of them, they really have their cage rattled.

It is helpful to maintain a chart for your objections which track the nature of the objections, the rulings, the instructions, etc. This is particularly beneficial if you have to argue the cumulative impact of errors because you can list the errors with specificity. It also reminds you to request instructions. Further, it is one more way to show the jury that you are keeping track of this because the fight is not over.

Visuals have a heavy impact. If you are cross-examining a witness with many prior statements, a big board with the inconsistencies in black and white is very effective. If a witness has a long record, get the computer print-outs taped end-to-end, let it unfold and hit the floor as you impeach on his prior record. Consider calling the prosecutor who prosecuted the witness.

> In a murder case where our client knew the victim was violent, and further knew the victim had been charged with rape, we called the prosecutor in the rape case as our witness in the murder trial. What a cage rattler to see a prosecutor try to cross-examine a prosecutor.

Cops always look at the jury when they answer questions, especially when you are cross-examining them. Don't let them get away with it. Ask them if the prosecution talked to them about looking to the jury to answer questions. Were they taught to do that? Were they taught to do it because it hurts the defendant? Ask them if they can look at you when they answer questions.

Don't let the cops talk about the "offense." Object to it. The cop didn't see it. His source of information is often from other people. He assumes an offense occurred, but that's up to the jury to decide. That's why we're here in trial. The cop was taught that in school, and he's trying to influence the jury. That is not fair. Use the phrase "it isn't fair" in your objections.

Call an expert to testify as to benefits of a snitch's plea bargain, especially when the Federal Sentencing Guidelines are involved. Get the certified documents on the snitch's criminal history and plea agreements. When a snitch is called to testify, consider suggesting that this snitch needs to consult with a lawyer, and be advised of his right to remain silent and not to incriminate himself.

When you know that you are going to be impeaching a witness with a transcript, at some point during the trial, it is helpful to ask a reporter to read back a question. It's a good way to demonstrate to the jury that what the reporters take down is what is said in the courtroom verbatim.

Filing A Civil Rights Action
As Part of an Aggressive Criminal Defense

When an individual acting under color of state law[1] violates the constitutional rights of another individual or entity, 42 U.S.C. 1983 (1982) authorizes the filing of a civil action for monetary damages or injunctive relief. *Bivens v. Six Unknown Agents*[2] creates a similar cause of action against federal actors. Although 1983/*Bivens*[3] actions are frequently employed in settings unrelated to criminal prosecutions, they can be used with particular effectiveness when filed during a related criminal prosecution.

The potential effectiveness of a 1983/*Bivens* action does not depend upon the complexity of the related criminal case. The 1983/*Bivens* action can be effectively used during a simple possession of marijuana case or a continuing criminal enterprise case. Moreover, the effectiveness of the 1983/*Bivens* action should be measured not only in terms of the potential civil verdict, but also in terms of the tactical advantages or disadvantages that it may create in the related criminal prosecution. The ultimate effectiveness of filing a 1983/*Bivens* action during a related criminal prosecution depends upon its *judicious* use.

1983/*Bivens* actions, have both tactical advantages and disadvantages that can result when such actions are related to criminal prosecution.

A. EFFECT OF *STATE V. KELLEHER*

In the foregoing cases, the filing of the Section 1983 actions actually created an issue that effected the outcome of the related criminal case. Moreover, no discovery occurred in the Section 1983 actions that adversely effected the defendant's posture in his criminal cases due to the stay of discovery. Finally, the criminal defendant and his carpenter were able to recover substantial civil judgements which pleased them to no end.

B. COGNIZABLE CLAIMS UNDER SECTION 1983 AND BIVENS

42 U.S.C. Section 1983 (1982) provides in relevant part: Every person who, under color of any statute, ordinance, regulation, custom, or usage, of any State or Territory or the District of Columbia, subjects or causes to be subjected, any citizen of the United States or other person within the jurisdiction thereof to the deprivation of any rights, privileges, or immunities, secured by the Constitution and laws shall be liable to the party injured in an action at law, suit in equity, or other proper proceeding for redress.

Section 1983 authorizes the filing of a civil action for monetary damages or injunctive relief by an individual whose constitutional rights have been violated by one acting under color of state law.[9] An "individual" is defined under Section 1983 to include citizens, aliens and corporations.[10] Although no statute authorizes the filing of a civil action against a federal actor, the case of *Bivens v. Six Unknown Agents*[11] creates such a common law cause of action. Under both Section 1983 and Bivens, then, a cause of action is created when a state[12] or federal actor violates an individual's constitutional rights.

A case study will give you an idea of the contours of these actions.

STATE V. KELLEHER

State v. Kelleher[i] is an example of how the filing of a 1983/*Bivens* action can impact a related criminal prosecution. In *Kelleher*, the defendant lived in Gainesville, Georgia, and was suspected of transporting narcotics from Florida to Georgia by way of boats that he bought and sold. On March 16, 1985 a search warrant was secured for the defendant's residence. This warrant authorized only the seizure of marijuana and cocaine. Numerous state law enforcement officers executed the warrant. The district attorney in charge of the *Kelleher* prosecution accompanied these officers during the search.

As a result of the search, the officers found relatively small amounts of marijuana and cocaine. Along with these narcotics, however, the officers sized over 3,000 documents and items from the residence, including, for example, the defendant's last will and testament, tax records and bank statements. Thereafter, the defendant was arrested on charges of possessing marijuana and cocaine.

After the defendant's arrest, a carpenter who worked on the defendant's house was arrested because a shotgun found at the residence belonged to the carpenter, and it was suspected to be stolen. The carpenter was taken to the local jail, and quickly providing the district attorney with documents showing that the shotgun was lawfully purchased. Nevertheless, the carpenter was held in jail for three days while the district attorney interrogated him concerning the activities of the defendant. Although the charge brought against the carpenter was groundless, the district attorney was able to keep his bail at $150,000 during the three-day period by obviating a bond hearing before a magistrate. When the carpenter was finally allowed to contact an attorney, his bond was immediately reduced to a $1,000, and he was released.

Shortly after the carpenter's arrest, law enforcement officers seized nearly every asset owned by the defendant, including numerous boats, cars and even his lawn mower. This seizure was made pursuant to the forfeiture provisions of Georgia's Racketeering Act. A civil forfeiture action was then instituted, but was dismissed after an evidentiary hearing due to the state's failure to prove that the sized items were acquired, maintained or derived through a pattern of racketeering activity.

Before his indictment, the defendant filed a Section 1983 action against the district attorney and the law enforcement officers who searched his residence. The defendant alleged that these individuals participated in a general search of the residence, in violation of his Fourth Amendment rights.

Approximately two months later, the district attorney presented criminal charges involving the defendant to a grand jury, and obtained indictments for various narcotic offenses. Shortly after the return of these indictments, the defendant's carpenter filed a Section 1983 action against the district attorney seeking damages resulting from his unlawful incarceration and interrogation. This action was predicated upon the denial of his Eighth Amendment right to reasonable bail, and his Fourth Amendment right against unreasonable searches and seizures.

The district attorney next entered into plea negotiations with the defendant. The district attorney made a written plea offer of 15 years. The offer was, however, conditioned upon the dismissal of "all lawsuits against all parties, judges, attorneys, agents for the state and political subdivisions of the state involving any acts associated with the facts of this case, and that the defendant issue a claims release against any and all such parties." This type of plea offer was obviously caused by the pendency of the Section 1983 actions.

The defendant immediately filed a plea in abatement, seeking the dismissal of his indictments on the ground that the district attorney was disqualified from presenting these indictments to the grand jury because he had a personal financial interest in this presentation. After extensive evidentiary hearings, the trial court denied the motion. The trial court subsequently denied various motions to suppress concerning the validity of the search of the defendant's home and certain electronic surveillance issues. The defendant proceeded with a non-jury trial, was found guilty, and appealed.

Discovery in the Section 1983 actions was stayed pending the disposition in the trial court of the criminal action, and was then reopened. The first civil case tried was the carpenter's Section 1983 action against the district attorney. After the three-day trial, the carpenter, though he had only $400 in special damages, was awarded $2,500 in compensatory damages, $47,500 in punitive damages, and $29,462.79 in attorney's fees.[5] This verdict was upheld on appeal.[6] Thereafter, the Section 1983 action based upon the unlawful search of the defendant's residence was settled favorably to the defendant.[7]

On appeal in the criminal case, the defendant contended that the district attorney's conduct in attempting to plea bargain away his personal civil liability necessitated the dismissal of the indictments. The defendant also contended that certain violations of Georgia's electronic surveillance statute mandated a reversal of his convictions, as well as the lack of sufficient evidence to support the probable cause finding for the issuance of the initial search warrant. The court of appeals reversed the defendant's conviction upon the probable cause issue, and did not reach the other issues.[8]

An extremely broad range of actions can be brought under Section 1983 or *Bivens*. For example, actions may seek to enjoin school prayer; improve prison conditions; challenge the discharge of a governmental employee because of a violation of his or her due process rights; or challenge the taking of property pursuant to an eminent domain proceeding. Section 1983/*Bivens* actions related to criminal prosecutions most frequently include challenges to the legality of a search or seizure;[13] the use of excessive force by an arresting officer;[14] false arrest or malicious prosecution;[15] defamation;[16] the unconstitutional seizure of assets pursuant to a forfeiture proceeding;[17] and unwarranted incarceration because of the denial of the right to reasonable bail.[18]

Under both Section 1983 and *Bivens*, no action lies for a random seizure of property if an adequate remedy under state law exists.[19] Thus, if an action is brought solely to redress property damage suffered during an unlawful search, the claim is not actionable.[20] Also, an action will not lie solely for the negligent deprivation of liberty or property rights.[21] Furthermore, an action generally will not lie for *de minimis* constitutional infringements, such as the failure of a law enforcement officer to read *Miranda* rights to a defendant.[22] Additionally, actions will not lie if they challenge the alleged perjury of a state or federal actor who testifies during criminal proceedings.[23]

Unlike *Bivens*, actions under Section 1983 may be brought in state court. Related pendent state claims can accompany a Section 1983 claim.[24]

A plaintiff may receive both compensatory and punitive damages in 1983/*Bivens* actions.[25] Injunctive or declaratory relief is also available. A plaintiff who prevails in a Section 1983 action is entitled to recover attorney's fees.[26]

The prospects of the recovery of attorney's fees and punitive damages make cases that are strong from a liability standpoint, but involve relatively minor special damages, economically viable. In determining whether to file a 1983/*Bivens* action during a related criminal case, however, the potential monetary recovery should not be the single most influential factor in determining whether to file suit. Rather, the potential monetary recovery should be considered in light of tactical advantages or disadvantages that can result in the related criminal proceeding. Moreover, the potential deterrent effect, or inflammatory effect, that a 1983/*Bivens* action can have on the law enforcement officers or prosecutors who are involved in the criminal action must be considered.

The statute of limitations for 1983/*Bivens* actions is the same as the statute of limitations that applies to personal injury actions in the state where the cause of action arises.[27] Under Section 1983, no requirement exists for the exhaustion of alternative state remedies.[28] *Bivens* also does not contain an exhaustion requirement, although a *Bivens* action will be barred when "special factors counselling hesitation. . ." in creating a remedy exist.[29] The entry of a plea of guilty in the related criminal action, or the entry of a verdict in the criminal action, generally has no res judicata or collateral estoppel implications in the related 1983/*Bivens* action.[30]

As with any civil action, counsel should carefully evaluate a 1983/*Bivens* claim before filing such an action, especially in light of the sanctions that can be imposed upon counsel for frivolous actions.[31]

In Robeson Defense Committee v. Britt,[32] counsel filed a Section 1983 action that related to the criminal cases involving Eddie Hatcher and Timothy Jacobs (who staged an armed takeover of a newspaper office to protest corruption and police misconduct). Counsel, because this action was held to be groundless, were sanctioned in the amount of $122,834.28 by the trial court, although the amount of the sanctions was reversed on appeal.

C. IMMUNITY

The doctrine of absolute and qualified immunity bar actions against certain individuals in 1983/*Bivens* actions. Judges are absolutely immune from liability as long as they were acting within the scope of their judicial function.[33] Similarly, prosecutors are absolutely immune from liability so long as they are performing tasks that are "intimately associated with the judicial phase of the criminal process."[34] If a prosecutor acts outside of the scope of his or her traditional judicial role, however, the prosecutor is shrouded only with qualified immunity. Under the doctrine of qualified immunity, an individual is not immune from suit if he or she violates "clearly established statutory or constitutional rights of which a reasonable person would have known."[35] Thus, if a prosecutor acts in an investigative capacity, such as by accompanying law enforcement officers during the search of a residence or by interrogating a potential witness, the prosecutor can be sued if he or she violates clearly established constitutional or statutory rights. Law enforcement officers and other governmental employees engaging in discretionary functions enjoy only qualified immunity.

State or federal actors who are supervisory official can be held liable in a 1983/*Bivens* action only if they are personally involved in the wrongful actions, or if they have either established, or allowed to prosper, policies, customs or usages that caused the wrongful actions.[36] Vicarious liability, in and of itself, is inoperative in 1983/*Bivens* actions. Pendent state claims may, however, involve laws that allow for such liability.[37]

D. TACTICAL ADVANTAGES AND DISADVANTAGES OF FILING

When determining whether to file a 1983/*Bivens* action during a related criminal prosecution, counsel should not only determine whether he or she has a legally viable action, but also whether the discovery consequences militate in favor of the filing of such an action. Once a 1983/*Bivens* action is filed, parties to the action are afforded the broad discovery authorized in civil actions by Fed. R. Civ. P. 26 or a similar statute in state court.[38] The civil plaintiff, who may also be a criminal defendant in the related criminal prosecution, should not expect to discover information prior to the trial of the criminal case that is otherwise not discoverable in that case. If the civil plaintiff seeks to discover such material, the civil defendant can move to stay all discovery in the action pending the disposition of the criminal action, or to limit discovery in the civil action only to matters that would be discoverable in the criminal action. Generally, such motions are granted upon the theory that a criminal defendant should not be able to use a 1983/*Bivens* action to circumvent the discovery restrictions inherent in criminal proceedings.[39]

The civil defendant in the 1983/*Bivens* action may inundate the civil plaintiff with discovery requests relating to the criminal prosecution. Discovery relating to the offense(s) involved in the criminal prosecution, as well as discovery relating to the prior criminal history and drug use of the civil plaintiff (who may be the criminal defendant), should be expected. If the civil plaintiff is the criminal defendant in a related criminal prosecution, or has an otherwise valid basis for doing so, the civil plaintiff can assert a Fifth Amendment privilege against self-incrimination in response to these discovery requests. So long as the assertion of the privilege complies with the usual restrictions, the privilege should be honored in the civil proceeding. The assertion of the privilege, however, may result in the dismissal of the 1983/*Bivens* action due to the plaintiff's non-compliance with discovery requests.[40]

If the civil plaintiff is a corporation, no Fifth Amendment privilege can be asserted, and this consequence must be considered carefully prior to the filing of the civil action. Moreover, although the civil plaintiff is allowed to assert a Fifth Amendment privilege, it may be appropriate for the jury in the 1983/*Bivens* action to be instructed that a negative inference may be drawn from the assertion of this privilege, whereas such an instruction would create reversible error if given in the related criminal prosecution.[41]

Another discovery consequence arises when the civil defendant attempts to depose a civil plaintiff who may also be the criminal defendant for the purpose of orchestrating a perjury prosecution. The civil defendant may, for example, possess statements made by the civil plaintiff when the civil plaintiff was being electronically monitored in connection with the criminal case, and may attempt to cajole the civil plaintiff to testify in a contradictory manner to the statements during the deposition. Additionally, the civil defendant may have access to an informant or cooperating witness who will be willing to contradict almost any statement made under oath by the civil plaintiff.

The civil plaintiff has several options available to attempt to defend against this tactic. First, the civil plaintiff can refuse to be deposed until all pertinent electronic surveillance is disclosed. Second, if appropriate, the civil plaintiff can assert a Fifth Amendment privilege in response to such questions. Third, the civil plaintiff can refuse to answer questions that fall outside the ambit "relevant" evidence as that term is defined in Fed. R. Civ. P. 26. Finally, the civil plaintiff can simply refuse to answer questions, although no privilege justifies this refusal, thereby risking sanctions, including possible dismissal of the civil action.

A further discovery consequence is the possibility that privileges that protect the criminal defendant from the disclosure of information in a related state criminal prosecution may be overridden by federal common law.

In *Walker v. Lewis*,[42] the defendant in a Title VII action sought to depose the plaintiff and her estranged husband concerning allegations of misconduct made by the husband. The information underlying these allegations came from confidential husband-wife communications. The plaintiff objected to the taking of the deposition of her husband upon the ground that F.R.E. 501 directs a court to apply the forum state's rules regarding privileges, and the forum state (North Carolina) allows a non-witness spouse to assert the husband-wife privilege to bar the testimony of a witness spouse.[43] The defendant contended that, because the case was pending in federal court and raised federal claims, federal common law governed the privilege determination.[44] The assertion of the privilege by the plaintiff for her husband was therefore ineffectual because federal common law allowed only the spouse from whom the testimony is sought to assert the privilege.[45] The court agreed with the defendant, finding that the predominance of federal claims necessitated the application of federal common law.[46]

A final discovery consequence occurs in 1983/*Bivens* actions involving the excessive use of force by a law enforcement officer. Discovery relating to the officer may include information pertaining to the officer's arrest record, use of excessive force on prior occasions, acts of dishonesty in the performance of duties, and incidents in which the officer has violated office policy.[47] This information can be introduced by the civil plaintiff pursuant to F.R.E. 404(b), 608(b) and 609 (or similar state rules) during the civil trial. Counsel in a criminal action who is used to being bludgeoned by 404(b) evidence may discover the advantages of this rule when he or she uses it offensively in the civil proceeding.

In addition to the discovery consequences of filing a 1983/*Bivens* action during a related criminal prosecution, counsel must consider the possible tactical advantages created in the related criminal prosecution. If the prosecutor who is handling the criminal prosecution is a named defendant in the 1983/*Bivens* action, s/he will violate the due process clause of the Fifth and Fourteenth Amendments if a plea bargain requires the dismissal of a civil action pending against him/her.[48] In all likelihood, the prosecutor will be disqualified from continuing to represent the state in the criminal action if he or she takes such an action.[49]

Moreover, the indictments that the prosecutor procured against the criminal defendant may be subject to dismissal, if the 1983/*Bivens* action was filed before the indictments were returned, on the ground that the prosecutor had an improper personal motivation when presenting evidence to the relevant grand jury (i.e., obtaining an indictment against the criminal defendant/civil plaintiff in order to plea bargain away the civil suit).[50]

The filing of a 1983/*Bivens* suit may equalize the balance of power in the criminal proceeding. The civil defendant(s) (*e.g.*, a law enforcement officer or prosecutor) may become more concerned with their personal liability than with any aspect of the criminal case. The filing of the action may embitter the civil defendant(s), and thereby ensure that plea negotiations in the related criminal case will be futile. The defense team should evaluate the potential effect the filing of the action will have on the prosecutor and law enforcement agents in the related criminal case.

One way to deal with upsetting counsel is to have out-of-town counsel file the civil action in order to minimize this effect, or in order to instigate a particular negotiating posture. Counsel in the criminal action may also be a witness in the civil action, thus presenting a conflict in handling the civil action, and requiring independent counsel to handle this action.

E. *KELLEHER* REVISITED

The tactical considerations discussed above played a prominent role in the *Kelleher* and *Reeves* cases.[51] When Kelleher was deposed, Fifth Amendment and relevancy objections were asserted to a majority of the questions asked by opposing counsel. These objections were asserted to limited Kelleher's potential criminal liability. Further, little discovery was obtained from the civil defendants in *Kelleher* that was not revealed during the related criminal cases. By comparison, Reeves was allowed by counsel to answer every question asked of him by opposing counsel during his deposition. Virtually no limitations were placed on discovery in the *Reeves* case due to the related criminal case. In both *Kelleher* and *Reeves* there was little hope of settlement prior to trial, as the filing of these civil actions galvanized the polar positions of the parties in both the criminal and civil actions.

Counsel must carefully evaluate the potential consequences of the filing of a 1983/Bivens action during a related criminal prosecution. Judiciously used, however, such an action can crate substantial tactical and substantive advantages in the criminal case, as well as result in civil judgment for monetary damages or injunctive relief.

Demonstrative Evidence

A. INTRODUCTION

A jury trial, twelve local citizens making a judgement, often provide the accused with a better chance of a fair decision than any other option. With a jury you have the chance of an acquittal, a hung jury or the lesser included offense. Trials often whittle down the prosecution's case and expose the weakness of their evidence. Exposure to the light of a trial can make the prosecution's evidence look less severe than it might when heaped into the record through a presentence report. This article is intended to help you present a more effective case to the jury.

B. DEMONSTRATE/SHOW WHEN YOU TELL

The use of demonstrative evidence, or, as I like to call it, show and tell, is an important tool which many criminal defense lawyers under utilize. Jurors today are part of the TV generation. It is hard to find a jury member who does not have one, two, or more televisions. They are accustomed to watching it several hours each week at a minimum and over an hour a day on the average. The TV viewer is comfortable with the visual image and the short bite of information. S/he is not accustomed to reading, listening and absorbing information over a long period of time. They are more passive than critical and are influenced by images and impressions more than by dry facts. This proposition is readily evident from even a cursory examination of modern advertising and political campaigning.

Many jurors get lost in the lengthy, verbal nature of a trial. Use of show and tell techniques can help the defense communicate better with the jury. You need not use something that is introduced into evidence. It can be no more than a prop that demonstrates your point. Charts, diagrams, lists, photographs, videotapes, and audiotapes work well and are available at reasonable cost and effort.

You can use show and tell beginning in the opening statement. Usually one cannot put exhibits in front of the jury in the opening statement; however, you can use a chart, key word list, or diagram to illustrate your opening and emphasize the facts you intend to present.

There are many ways in which demonstrative evidence can be used to illustrate your case. When impeaching the narc with documents, project them to the jury via an overhead projector. Let the jury see, not just hear, the narc's life of lies and crime. The years in prison s/he is saving him/herself by telling tales against your client can be depicted visually by a graph. Financial charts can show how much "expense" or "reward" money the narc is paid by the police for testimony as well as the amount the prosecution is protecting from forfeiture or tax penalty in exchange for the narc's story about your client. This kind of graphic brings home to the jury the fact that the prosecution's witness is bought and paid for.

You can use show and tell to help the jury see why police testimony is not credible. Police frequently testify that they saw into, over, around and through things which mere mortals would find impossible. Employing a police officer's prior testimony at a preliminary or a bail hearing as a guide, one can re-enact the events on film or videotape to demonstrate their impossibility.

> In one jump out case, photographs demonstrated that the police observer could not possibly have seen the drug transaction. An obstacle was directly in his line of sight. Using a wide angle lens, photographs were taken of the officer's location at the time of observation in comparison to the alleged position of the accused. The preliminary hearing testimony was used as a script. After taking that shot, the photographer assumed the position claimed by the officer and took photographs looking at the location where he claimed to have seen the sale. The pictures made it quite clear that one could not see what the officer claimed from his vantage point.

Still cameras are very useful for this purpose but video cameras work equally well. Polaroid's are okay but 35mm single lens reflex cameras produce a much better, enlargeable image. Video has the advantage of creating the TV image to which the juror is most accustomed.

Audio tapes can demonstrate that the officer could not hear what he claimed from his location. Since most video cameras now have decent condenser microphones, one can also use a video camera to provide the jury with an audio-visual show and tell that brings your message home clearly. An example of this is the video taken inside the dwelling where the individuals are arguing, the music is loud or the voices are raised. In one fluid shot, the video camera backs out with the door being closed. The reduction in capacity to hear from outside is seen and heard on TV. This is much more effective than someone merely testifying that it is not possible to hear from outside as the officer claims. Jurors often believe in the TV screen before they believe the officer. Judges are also susceptible to the TV image.

Given the predisposition of many jurors to believe the prosecution, show and tell can strengthen even the alibi defense. A blowup of the defendant's timecard showing the jury s/he was working at the time of the offense helps enhance its significance. Some good things bear repeating and the facts contained on the card can be repeated more than once to the jury as you go through it with a pointer explaining what the various indications represent. Projectors can also be used to present other kinds of evidence corroborating an alibi such as time tables, shift schedules and the like.

In some cases, the most we can hope for is conviction for a lesser included offense. Show and tell helps there as well. In an effort to enlarge small drug cases, the prosecution always wants to claim how many dosage units can be manufactured, produced or sold from whatever it is your client might have. When your expert testifies that the amount involved is consistent with personal use, this testimony can be illustrated with a bar graph or other chart showing, with cocaine for example, that dosage and use increase over time. The charted rise in use over time can show that a person with a bad affliction can easily use what your client had in no time at all. The chart visually explains your expert's testimony that the amount is consistent with personal use, not distribution.

Use of a chart showing weights and measures of packaging versus content can assist in reducing the amount when seeking to get below a mandatory minimum sentence based on weight.

> In one case, a courtroom weighing exercise demonstrated that once the packaging had been removed the actual weight of the substance was sufficiently less than the prosecution claimed. The time saved for the client was significant.

C. TECHNICAL APPLICATION

When preparing demonstrative exhibits and show and tell props, keep in mind the great variety of new age marvels which facilitate presentation of this sort of evidence. Photo enlargement, computer graphics, Polaroid cameras, idiot proof 35mm and video cameras, sophisticated video and photographic equipment, and the like are readily available. You can buy, borrow or rent these items.

Copiers can enlarge, reduce and make full color copies as well as transparencies for overhead projectors. Transparency paper, available from most stationers goes through the copy machine. Use it for charts, diagrams, book illustrations, or transcripts.

> In Nancy and Pete's case, the officers testified that the plants were all sensimilla females based on their observation of "female" flowers which they described as having little balls hanging down. They also made outrageous yield statements. Overnight, we put together a 12 page bound booklet using computer and copiers. It included color photos copied from a marijuana grow book, showing charts based on the 1992 DEA Yield study (see appendix) and other pertinent material. During recesses and other waiting times, the jurors had nothing else to read or look at.

Your office computer is another source of modern graphics. Using your office computer and a readily available program, you, or more likely your elementary or junior high school child, can make bar graphs, pie charts and other diagrams. These graphics can then be photocopied onto overhead projection transparency sheets. You can create a projection of the alibi's time sheet or the narc's false credit application where s/he lied for money, or the chart of how much prison time the narc is avoiding by selling his/her tale about your client.

> We used a computer to make large charts for Nancy and Pete's case, printed on several sheets of paper. We pasted them onto a foam core.
>
> The charts were based on "The DEA Yield Report" and contrasted research findings of the yield with the prosecution "Expert's" opinion.

A 35mm camera with a zoom lens can record the crime scene and show the relationship of distance, space and obstacles. Inexpensive Polaroid cameras have the advantage that you can shoot again and again until you get the picture correct. Then shoot the scene with the 35mm camera. With video cameras you can shoot, play back. If it is not an accurate depiction, go out and do it again.

More sophisticated equipment is also available. I use a skilled forensic photographer who is also a good looking, very presentable witness. He can vary the film type and speed to produce grainier or clearer photographs which enhances the depiction of the object or event I wish portrayed.

Jurors are accustomed to the visual depiction of reality so they can see it as well as listen to someone describe it. Using photographs, video tapes and the like makes your case appear more organized, more efficient, more effective and more familiar.

> Audio should not be overlooked. In one case, audio enhancement was used to let the jury hear the police lusting after the client's B.M.W. as they waited for him to enter the room for the taped sting. Hearing the police in an honest, unguarded moment helped in excluding some evidence and casting the agents for what they really were. It also helped the client keep his car in a later forfeiture effort.

Experts can help you understand the nature and method of government orchestrated tapings. They may be able to take some of the sting out of the government's case.

Set up the equipment in the courtroom and make sure you know how to use it before trial Position it so the jury has the best view. Work with it before use so that your courtroom presentation is smooth and effective.

D. SHOW AND TELL AND THE RULES

The use of demonstrative evidence is usually guided by the admissibility versus unfair prejudice tests of Rules 401 and 403 of the Federal Rules of Evidence.[1] Beyond the fundamental balancing test of Rules 401 and 403, the admission of demonstrative evidence generally falls within three categories, each has its own level of scrutiny.

The first category of demonstrative evidence is that used to show physical properties and/or dimensions. This category often includes, films, diagrams, maps and charts to scale. Courts are usually receptive to admitting demonstrative evidence for this purpose.[2]

Maps and diagrams are the most common forms of demonstrative evidence used to demonstrate a physical property such as distance, height, etc. One example is the diagram showing that the police observation point does not provide a clear field of vision of the location at which the alleged drug transaction occurred.

When using diagrams, unless an engineer, architect, or surveyor prepared the diagram to scale, you should be prepared for a limiting instruction from the court to the effect that the jury should not view the evidence as accurate to site and should consider it only as illustrative.[3] If you wish to introduce a chart or graph into evidence, then Federal Rule of Evidence 1006 does not necessarily require that all of the evidence supporting the chart or graph also be introduced before the chart is admissible.[4]

When preparing a reenactment or representation, it is imperative that the conditions in the demonstrative exhibit substantially comport with the conditions in existence at the time.[5] Differences between the depiction and the events at the time should be clearly and carefully explained. When using a video, you can explain by a voice over on the audio portion of the tape as the video is being shot. You may, for example, read the transcript you are using as your script while the video is taken.[6] Whenever there is a difference between the depiction and the scene at the time, be careful to lay it out for the jury. Bear in mind that this goes to weight, not admissibility.

In order to authenticate a photograph or video tape, the following elements must be established:

1. The photograph must be relevant in accordance with Federal Rule of Evidences 401 and 402.

2. The presenting witness must be familiar with the scene portrayed in the photograph.

3. The presenting witness must be familiar with the scene at the relevant date and time.

4. The witness must testify that the photograph or video tape fairly and accurately depicts the scene as it appeared at the relevant time.

5. The probative value must exceed any prejudicial effect.

The identification of the persons, objects, or places pictured in a film requires proof that the film is a true and accurate representation as they existed at the relevant time. This includes evidence as to the actual taking of the photograph or film, its developing or processing, and projection. The photographer or other person having knowledge can satisfy this criteria without much difficulty.[7]

Photographs and video tapes may also be authenticated pursuant to Federal Rule of Evidence 901(a).[8] A video is, after all, nothing more than a motion picture synchronized with a sound recording. A complete video tape may be received into evidence if the offering party lays a foundation like that required for a motion picture and a sound recording.[9]

What about business records and the alibi or other defenses? The Rules require a witness who is familiar with the record keeping system to testify that the records were made in the routine course of business at or near the time described.[10] Be mindful of Federal Rules of Evidence 901 and 902 which address the criteria essential to authenticate the records so that they fit the 803 hearsay exception.

When using a records custodian, it is usually best to also use him/her as the witness even though some courts allow someone familiar with the system to testify.[11] Bring the original records from which the projections were made. You can always ask for leave to substitute copies for the originals for purposes of the business's convenience.

A witness in a state case with a business record that is not within your state can be subpoenaed *duces tecum* in accordance with the Witness From Foreign Jurisdictions Act. That Act has been adopted by most states. In order to get the witness from a foreign jurisdiction, your state court has to certify that there is a cause and controversy in which the witness is needed. That certification is transmitted to the trial level court in the jurisdiction in which the witness resides or has the business. The witness is then subpoenaed to their own court at which their identity, the case, etc., is verified. Then they are ordered to appear (with documents) in the requesting state. The requesting party has to tender the witness fee and a check for mileage at the time of the foreign court proceeding.

In federal court, witnesses can be served with subpoenas anywhere in the United States in accordance with Rule 17 of the Federal Rules of Criminal Procedure. Documents may be subpoenaed in accordance with Rule 17(c). One can subpoena documents to the federal court so that they arrive before the actual commencement of trial. This provides an opportunity to become familiar with them, photocopy them and get them ready for the overhead projector or the like.

In trying to put a transcript of a prior proceeding into evidence, you should have a copy certified by the transcribing court reporter. A certified copy of the transcript is a self authenticating document according to Federal Rule of Evidence 801(d)(1).[12] You may not only use prior court testimony but may also use prior depositions if the declarant was subject to the penalties of perjury for false statements.[13]

The transcript pages showing prior lies by the narc can be blown up, photocopied and mounted on 3' × 4' boards to show the jury how the narc lied for money, lied for favor, lied for benefit or lied just because that is what narcs know how to do best.

Enlarged testimony in a perjury trial compared one testimony against the other in parallel columns on a 2' × 4' board. Each transcript was admitted and authenticated as indicated above. The boards were then used to focus the jury on the actual consistency of the two statements. An office computer produced the parallel columns from the two transcripts.

Public records, other than transcripts, such as weather reports from the National Weather Service, are admissible under Rule 802(a) of the Federal Rule of Evidence. These records may require a seal in accordance with Federal Rule of Evidence 901(1) but some records do not require it.[14]

> We hired a local meteorologist to testify regarding wind direction in a case. Then we directed a student artist to draw a depiction of the scene based on the photograph and the meterologist's information. The officers' locations as they testified were also depicted.

Records which are not public records under seal may be admitted under Federal Rule of Evidence 803(6) if they are "data compilations in any form." These data compilations are admissible if made by someone with knowledge at or contemporaneous with or near to the time in which the events occurred, etc. Under that rule, you can often admit computerized records since many agencies and businesses maintain their records on computers.

In United States v. Hutson, 821 F.2d 1015 (5th Cir. 1987), the records custodian did not have any personal knowledge about the records, had not made the entries, and had not compiled the data; however, the data was normally kept within the computer records of the entity and was admissible. This might help you introduce into evidence the narc's lies on his credit or loan report in which he lied for money in an inquiry under Federal Rule of Evidence 608(b) concerning the narc's lack of truthfulness. Under Federal Rule of Evidence 613(b), if the narc is given an opportunity to explain or deny his prior false statement, then, in the interest of justice, extrinsic evidence of a prior inconsistent statement by the narc or other might be admissible.

Offering evidence to establish that a government witness is lying in front of a jury with sufficient indicia of reliability always makes it more difficult for the prosecutor to object and for the judge to say no, the jury should not find out about the lying narc. Ultimately, the judge is the arbiter of admissibility. If the evidence appears truthful, honest and related to an issue that the jury, in their common sense, would think important, then more often than not you can get it admitted.

Forfeiture

A. INTRODUCTION

Beginning in the mid 1980's the government re-discovered a technique that was a major cause of the American Revolution: forfeiture to the government of property based upon an alleged connection between that property and some prohibited activity. Beginning with the drug laws and expanding to currency laws, driving regulations, and now, in Washington State, to any instrumentality of any felony. This practice has perverted the goals of law enforcement. Many police, particularly narcotics officers, are more interested in making arrests that produce forfeitable goods than they are in arresting dangerous offenders. Why chase the dogs that bite when you can loot from the defenseless?

B. TYPES OF FORFEITURE

Forfeitures come in two varieties: "civil" and "criminal."

1. Criminal

Criminal forfeitures are just like criminal prosecutions. The property is indicted in the same document and proceeding in which the owner is charged with the underlying crime. Given the fact that this procedure allows the owner as many rights as a criminal defendant, including the right to proof beyond a reasonable doubt, these have been, until recently, very rare.

In California Donald Scott, a wealthy citizen, was shot dead (assassinated) by police raiding his rural residence ostensibly in search of drugs. The Ventura County District Attorney's Report on the death of Donald Scott showed that Charles Stowell, the officer who "identified" vegetation as cannabis, lied. Investigation showed that the original "tip" was phony, that no drugs were found, and that the deceased was, in fact, a law-abiding citizen.

Mistakes can happen. But in this case the raiding officers, though they had taken little trouble to confirm the tip upon which their raid was based, had secured the assessor's report indicating the value of the multi-million dollar property. Later research revealed that the government had been trying unsuccessfully for years to acquire the park-like land. Rest in peace, Mr. Scott.

* * *

In Seattle, Washington, a woman who had agreed to set up a man by selling him a substantial quantity of cocaine discovered that merely luring the desperate victim into buying cocaine (by offering it for sale at an extremely low price) was not enough; she was also required to involve both the target's corvette and his residence in the deal, so that they could be seized. Apparently one of the officers liked the car. Small wonder that in Washington, as in many places in the United States, non-violent offenders began to outnumber the violent ones in the late 1980s. A remarkable statistic in the face of the public's growing fear of violent crime.

2. Civil

Most forfeitures are based upon "civil" forfeiture laws which require only that the government establish probable cause to seize the property, and then shift the burden of proof to the property's owner. For prosecutors, this is a dream come true; for citizens a nightmare. Property can be seized summarily. Court intervention comes only later, and it is often meaningless. Citizens facing forfeitures will be shocked to learn that their property can be seized based on hearsay, that they have no right to proof beyond a reasonable doubt, to confront the witnesses against them, to remain silent, or even to appointed counsel.

C. WHAT CAN BE FORFEITED

Federal, state, and local laws now allow forfeiture of virtually any personal or real property that has any connection with a crime. Most commonly encountered are forfeitures of real estate, vehicles and cash which are alleged to have "facilitated" a crime, are the "proceeds" of a crime, or are allegedly intended to be used in some crime in the future. Thus homes in which marijuana is grown, or drug deals are consummated, vehicles which are used to transport participants to a drug deal or to haul potting soil to the grow room, and any cash found on a person suspected of most crimes are routinely seized at the time when a defendant is arrested. Neither arrest nor prosecution is an essential precursor to a forfeiture. A citizen can be permanently deprived of property without ever being convicted, or even charged for a crime.

One commentator, also a victim of forfeiture observed:

> Many scholars believe the fairy tale presentation in Alice in Wonderland was an allegorical dodge used by Lewis Carroll to address the real menace of oppression. The most effective way to oppress the People is to take their property — wipe them out of the public dialogue and sweep them into the street transformed into beggars and paupers — a dire lesson to any others that may wish to object to government policy.
>
> One can hardly pick up a newspaper today without reading of forfeitures served upon an ever increasing cast of bewildered unfortunates, who suddenly find their own government has attacked them with "Jabberwocky" — nonsense spewing forth unfamiliar sounding words from "jaws that bite" stupefying the wretched souls while the "claws that catch" seize possessions — forfeited to the government "Bandersnatch."
>
> —from THE SPECTRE OF FORFEITURE, by "Ben There" (Access Unlimited, 1990).

To date the Federal government has seized over $3 billion worth of assets; the local governments boast equally prodigious sums.

Victims whose property is seized are well advised to hire knowledgeable and experienced counsel. This is a highly technical, rapidly changing area, a minefield of opportunities for tragic mistakes. Below is a summary of the area. This article is meant as an introduction, not a roadmap. Please do not rely on it if you find yourself a victim of forfeiture.

D. THE APPLICABLE LAWS

The most frequently encountered Federal forfeiture law is a part of the drug law, 21 U.S.C. sec.881. There are many others. Money laundering, driving while intoxicated, and failing to place the proper sized letters on the proper sized labels for food supplements are but as few of the offenses which will support a forfeiture. A complete discussion of this and many other complexities of the forfeiture industry can be found in David Smith's comprehensive volumes entitled *Prosecution and Defense of Forfeitures*.

Other forfeiture laws generally follow the contours of the Federal law, although recent reforms in some states' laws make the government's burden heavier, and provide for a few more rights for the victims of forfeiture.

E. WHAT TO DO IF YOU ARE FACING SEIZURE AND FORFEITURE

Not all property seized by the government is seized for purposes of forfeiture. Some is merely held for evidence and will eventually be returned. Some just disappears into the pockets of corrupt law-enforcement who don't list it on the required inventory of seized property left behind when search warrants are executed.

When the government intends to keep property, they must give notice. But that notice may come only in the form of a small advertisement published in *U.S.A. Today*. It is wise to contact counsel immediately after property is taken to determine if the government intends to forfeit it.

If there has not been adequate notice, the forfeiture may be challenged.

After receiving notice, the citizen has very little time to respond. Most "notice" documents give instructions. It is unwise for the property owner to try to do it him/her/self. Instead s/he should hire experienced counsel immediately.[1] In most cases failure to respond by putting in a claim within the stated time period, the property is forfeited automatically. Once it is gone, gone, it can't be recovered.

A property owner may fear that s/he may be charged with a crime based upon the same conduct for which the property is seized. That is an additional reason to consult a lawyer before filing a claim. The filing of a claim may constitute an admission of some fact critical to the government's case. Catch-22. Lose property or lose freedom. The Government likes this.

F. DOUBLE JEOPARDY

A victim of forfeiture may want to let the government take property as soon as possible, since that taking may be considered a "punishment" for double jeopardy purposes which might preclude any further prosecution. Few areas of the law are more complex or are changing more rapidly than this. Get a lawyer[2], or risk making some mistakes with extremely serious consequences.

G. DEFENSES

In this rapidly growing area, there are a number of defenses that may be raised. Creativity should be encouraged. Defenses that were once prohibited by the rule against making "frivolous" arguments may soon be the law of the land. Here are but a few:

1. The crime upon which the forfeiture is allegedly based never happened.

This works well if you are represented by Perry Mason. (When Perry Mason tries a case, the person who did it is always sitting in the back of the courtroom. For the rest of us, the culprit is usually sitting a bit closer.)

2. The forfeiture is based upon evidence which is seized unlawfully.

This will not prevent a forfeiture entirely. The rule is that if there is sufficient evidence which is untainted by the unlawful search, the forfeiture may be based on that. This is a difficult burden for the government to meet since it is difficult to establish the ownership of the property if you can't talk about the search and seizure that produced it. Whose is it? Where did it come from? There is seldom any "untainted" evidence to answer those questions.

3. The crime was committed without the knowledge or consent of the owner.

The owner has the burden of establishing his or her innocence.

4. The owner of the seized property has already been prosecuted for and either convicted or acquitted for the same conduct.

This is the classic double jeopardy defense. Until recently, it was not available, since forfeitures labeled "civil" by the legislative body which passed them were not considered to impose "punishment" and were, therefore, not addressed by the prohibition against double jeopardy. In what may be the most significant change in the law in this decade, or even the last three decades, the United States Supreme Court, and the Supreme Court of the State of Washington have ruled that what the legislature said about a law when it was passed is no longer relevant. If a forfeiture is not "solely remedial" then it is at least in part punishment, and double jeopardy law applies. What is meant by "solely remedial" and when this new principle applies, is the subject of a book published by this author, and Brenda Grantland, national president of F.E.A.R. (Forfeiture Endangers American Rights). Those who wish a more in-depth discussion of the subject should contact F.E.A.R.

Now civil forfeitures may be considered punishment for double jeopardy purposes where the penalty grossly exceeds the actual loss, or where the forfeiture, like drug law forfeitures, is one which has traditionally been considered punishment. Most "civil" forfeitures now fall into this category. Given recent changes in the law, this defense to a criminal case is often the biggest club in the defendant's arsenal. Its application to criminal cases, will be discussed later.

5. The forfeiture is disproportional to the crime upon which it is based.

This is a new one, available only since the Supreme Court acknowledged that some civil forfeitures impose punishment. It is no longer appropriate, for example, to seize an entire piece of real estate based upon a relatively small crime committed on it.

6. The forfeiture takes away a defendent's ability to defend him/herself.

The government takes all of the defendent's assets just when they are needed to retain counsel. This defense isn't doing too well, but it is not yet dead.

7. The forfeiture is based upon evidence acquired after the seizure of the property.

This won't work. The government's evidence is essentially frozen at the time of the seizure, and nothing may be added to it.

8. The government failed to give the owner a full adversarial hearing within a time period required.

The government violated its own statutes or by developing principles of due process/speedy trial law.

This list is by no means complete. Creative lawyering here is often rewarded.

H. APPOINTED COUNSEL

The owner may wish to ask that the court appoint counsel to represent him/her in the property forfeiture proceeding. If it were a criminal case, this would be routine. Case law so far does not favor this, but now that the courts have acknowledge that forfeiture imposes punishment, this area of the law will have to be revisited.

I. PITFALLS

The forfeiture laws invite proceedural errors which can be fatal to the case. Not many attorneys specialize in this area so the client must keep a close watch on the case and to make sure the attorney is handling the case according to the rules. Sometimes the client becomes an expert in this area of the law. Here are four of the most common problems that occur in these cases.

1. Self-incrimination:

Few areas of the law offer so many opportunities for the litigant to make a serious mistake. Since the government is entitled to "discovery", i.e., mandatory pretrial examination of all evidence and witnesses, including the owner of the property, it is easy for the owner to make mistakes which may later come back to haunt him/her during the criminal phase of the trial.

2. Blown deadlines:

It is easy to miss a deadline if the attorney does not respond immediately after the property is seized. Often the owner will not realize that a forfeiture is intended. The noticed may be nothing more than a blurb in *U.S.A. Today*.

3. Hiring an attorney that doesn't have a clue.

It may be more of a danger in civil cases than in the criminal law area. Not many attorneys understand this law, and, unlike the criminal law, the Constitution here doesn't give the property owner many breaks. There is the potential of money to be made here, and that makes some attorneys forget their own limitations. Others, who have never done one of these cases, do not realize what a minefield this area of the law is before they leap into it. It is a specialized area, and only a a specialist should be hired.

4. The idiosyncracies of the civil rules and the admiralty rules.

These procedural rules apply in federal forfeitures, yet they are seldom consulted by the criminal defense bar and most attorneys are not familiar with them. Nevertheless, most forfeiture work is done by "criminal" defense attorneys.

J. FORFEITURE AS DOUBLE JEOPARDY

This is the most radically changing area of forfeiture law. Until recently if the legislature called it "civil," it was, and the owner got no rights. Now it is clear that many forfeitures seek to impose punishment, and some of the rights accorded the accused in our society apply. Most important here is double jeopardy. A person may not be tried or punished twice for the same crime in separate proceedings. This law has only developed since 1989, when the United States Supreme Court decided U.S. v. Halper, (490 US 435) which held that a sanction which is not "solely remedial" is punishment for purposes of double jeopardy.

The government has steadfastly refused to acknowledge this change in the law, with the result that there are hundreds of thousands of citizens out there who may be able to get their convictions vacated, or their property returned. If you have had your property seized and forfeited, and been prosecuted for the same crime, whichever punishment came second may well be void. As to future cases, the government now has to either choose between a civil forfeiture and a criminal prosecution where there is only one crime, or else combine a criminal forfeiture and the prosecution in the same proceeding. For most local jurisdictions, this is impossible without new legislation.

For the Federal Government, it just means they will have to work a little harder.

K. THE PIG THEORY OF FORFEITURE

"If you make a hog of yourself, the courts will make a sausage of you." That's how the L.E.D. (Law Enforcement Digest) opened its article forfeiture. I couldn't believe I was reading it, I wished I had said it and they may be right. For the first time since the Fourth Amendment made its cameo appearance in the '60's, the government has to work to have its way in the courtroom when forfeitures are the issue.

1. The New Line of Cases

In a line of cases beginning in 1989, the U.S. Supreme Court has capsized the law of forfeiture. United States v. Halper (490 US 435) held that A "civil" forfeiture which is not "solely remedial" is punishment for purposes of double jeopardy. United States v. Austin (125 Lawyers Ed. 2nd 488, 1993) held that drug related forfeitures are punishment, at least for purposes of the excessive fines clause. Montana Department of Revenue v. Kurth Ranch (114 Supreme Ct. 1937, 1994) applied these prior rulings to double jeopardy protections.

Finally, the Ninth Circuit, without even the assistance of a brief written by a lawyer, put it all together in a case called United States v. $405,098.23. (33 Fed 3rd 1210, 1994) This case holds that drug forfeitures, even of proceeds, are punishment for purposes of double jeopardy. That means that forfeitures which are not solely remedial must be brought in the same proceeding as the criminal case based upon the same conduct. If not, the government must choose between the forfeiture and the prosecution. Opinions vary as to the continued viability of $405K. The issue of whether forfeiture of property based upon its use to facilitate a crime is punishment, seems to be settled (it is) absent a reversal by the Supreme Court.

As to proceeds, while the logic of the 9th circuit is flawless, the practical impact of this rule is potentially so devastating to the government that most prognosticators are guessing that the courts will figure out a way to duck the issue. However, the conclusions drawn by the court in $405k seem to be the inescapable result of the line of cases coming from the Supreme Court.

2. Government Response

The Government response to these court decisions has been to combine criminal forfeiture with the prosecution. The limits, if any, on forfeitures brought in the same proceeding, have yet to be established. But these prosecutions and forfeitures have left a legacy of victims who may be able to claim relief. All courts which have considered this question have concluded that the relief may be retroactive.

3. State Arguments

States which do not have a criminal forfeiture statute, have less recourse since they cannot attach a criminal forfeiture to the case against the indivcidual. If they seek either criminal or civil punishment, they cannot seek the other. State attorneys have mades a number of arguments. The most popular among the prosecutorial set include "it's not the same crime", "the defendant waived double jeopardy", and "those courts really didn't know what they were talking about and you should ignore them".

4. Defense Response

The defense has the more powerful and logical arguments on its side. Once the courts are educated as to the implications of the recent federal decisions, major policy changes will result.

a. Are the two punishments based on the identical offense?

This is a complex highly "academic" issue. This issue has generated an incredible amount of debate. No one can predict where the dust will settle. For now it is safe to assume that the "same elements" test applies: If each crime (the one on which the forfeiture is based, and the one on which the criminal prosecution is based) contains an element not contained in the other, then each proceeding may be prosecuted without offending double jeopardy protections.

b. Did the defendant waive the double jeopardy argument by a guilty plea?

This argument, routinely advanced by the government where post-conviction relief is sought, has been uniformly rejected. It appears that a guilty plea does not waive a double jeopardy argument if the violation is clear on the face of the record without reference to new facts. In most cases the charging document, the presentence report, the judgment and sentence, and the documents supporting the forfeiture will establish the violation without the need to supplement the record. The DEA papers its internal trail well. These internal documents should be sought in discovery where there is debate on this issue.

One case held that a plea bargain which included the forfeiture didn't waive the issue.[3]

c. Can the defendant object where s/he failed to file a claim for the property?

Where there has been a guilty plea, the problem here may be that the "record" is nowhere to be found, since the original notice of forfeiture usually speaks in broad terms, citing only the statute, and seldom even the section. There is, however, some hope in that situation. Federal seizing agents are required to generate certain documents justifying a seizure, even if it is not contested. A habeas corpus petitioner has discovery rights. This is a good place to use them.

An aggrieved owner should argue that s/he has been punished despite the failure to file a claim. If the ownership of the property is obvious, or can be established, that meets the owner's burden of proof. Otherwise, where there is no real defense to the forfeiture, the rule the government asks for here would require owners to file essentially frivolous claims in order to preserve their rights in an unrelated criminal proceeding. The law does not require this.

d. Is the claim defeated where the forfeiture and the punishment were sought by separate sovereigns?

This theory has not been used successfully yet. There is, some room for maneuvering within this argument. If the state puts a person in prison, while the feds take his/her property, the government will argue that the individual has been prosecuted by "separate sovereigns" and that there is, therefore, no double jeopardy violation. Thus the police accused of beating Rodney King were tried again in Federal Court after being acquitted in State Court for essentially the same crime. The courts held that there was no double jeopardy violation since there was no "collusion" between the state and the federal government. (Don't look for even-handed interpretations here. You and I could be convicted of conspiracy on much less evidence of "collusion.")

However, when the feds take property in cases where local law-enforcement has had a role, they are required by law to share the loot with the local agency in proportion to the amount of participation by the local agency. It is a fertile area for inquiry. For example: "How much was the local agency paid? What did they say in support of their request for such a large percentage of the loot?"

e. When does the punishment become final?

It does not matter which comes first, the forfeiture or the criminal prosecution. However, the timing is critical, since it is only the second punishment that can be vacated. Answers vary on this question, and it's too soon to make a prediction about how the courts will work with the various combinations. I have argued that punishment attaches in the criminal case when the jail/prison sentence begins. In the civil context most courts hold that punishment attaches when the order of forfeiture becomes final. It may be fruitful to argue that punishment is final when the owner gives up any claim to the property, either by failing to file a claim, or by signing an agreement to forfeit.

Even more interesting is the argument that, based upon the "relation-back" doctrine — title to the property passes to the government at the time the underlying crime is committed, but only when an actual order is entered by a court at some later date. By this theory, the forfeiture would always come before the criminal punishment.

Since the prohibition is against both double punishments and double attempts at conviction, even a prior acquittal will act as a bar. What about a prior criminal profiteering? Where it is dismissed? This case is pending.

f. What remedies are available?

Many jurisdictions are just giving property back. Getting out of jail is much tougher. Nevertheless, that, too is happening. Cases are mounting, especially in the Western United States. Both return of property and vacation of convictions are appropriate remedies, and that the next few years will see a landslide of just such relief.

Appendix A

Cannabis Yields

June 1992 Drug Enforcement Agency

"Cannabis Yields" is the report of a research project conducted at the University of Mississippi by Dr. Mahmoud ElSohly in 1992 and 1993. The study was funded by the DEA. He conducted a controlled experiment in which he measured the yields of a particular strain planted at different distances.

This is the first actual study of marijuana yields. Prosecution "experts" often claim ridiculously high yields which contradict the findings of this report. Most of them are unfamiliar with it. Unfortunately, he has done no study on indoor cultivation or on "sea of green" yields. His smallest plant grew in nine square feet. Indoors a plant might grow in only one square foot. It would yield only one ninth of the larger plant.

Results from this paper should be extrapolated to circumstance. Planting date, variety, predators, shading, climate and harvest date all affect yield. These factors may lower yield considerably. In Mississippi they had warm, sunny weather, plenty of water and rich fertile conditions. Few guerilla gardens provide these conditions, and the yields reflect that.

SUMMARY

Outdoor *Cannabis sativa L.* (cannabis) yield studies conducted during the summers of 1990 and 1991 have determined that the usable dry weight yield (leaf and bud) for female cannabis plants can be up to 2.3 kilograms (5.1 pounds). Based upon a survey of 15 leading producer states, the average plant yield for mature, domestically grown female cannabis plants in 1991 was 448 grams (1 pound). An accurate yield estimate can be made by weighing the fresh weight of a plant or measuring the plant's diameter at the broadest point in the canopy. A very significant factor affecting yield was planting density.

BACKGROUND

The Drug Enforcement Administration (DEA) during the summers of 1990 and 1991, conducted a detailed cannabis yield measurement program at the university of Mississippi in Oxford. The purpose of the project was to determine the average yield of outdoor cultivated cannabis plants and identify factors to predict usable yield. Prior to the project's initiation, the only quantitative studies undertaken were two studies self-initiated by the University of Mississippi in 1985 and 1986. These two studies made a limited number of observations and did not identify factors influencing plant yield.

METHODOLOGY

The overall intent of the studies was to introduce variation into the research design in order to gain a basic understanding of some of the factors influencing plant yield. The DEA sponsored research used different seed stocks from Mexico, Colombia, Jamaica, and a hybrid of South Africa-Afghanistan origin.

The 1990 effort consisted of a progressive planting of 3 separate areas at 2 week intervals. Each area was planted with the same seed stock at an identical planting density. The varying of the planting date permitted analysis of the sensitivity of cannabis yield and plant development to planting date. The 1991 effort focused on the relationship between planting density and yield. Three different planting densities of Mexican seed stock were studies. Tables 1 and 2 describe the average plant yields which are associated with specific densities.

Yield measurements were made on 90 days or older female plants which duplicated the preference of a majority of domestic growers to cultivate the larger yielding females. However, no attempt was made to cultivate unfertilized female plants, commonly known as "sinsemilla". The vast majority of observations were made on the very common, tall, narrow leaflet cannabis variety known as "sativa". A very limited number of observations were made on the other major variety, "indica". The indica variety is a shorter, more compact, faster maturing plant with larger leaves.

Yield measurements were made on 102 plants during the course of the two year study. Physical measurements were made of the plant's height from ground level and the diameter at the broadest point in the plant's canopy. Upon completion of the physical measurements, the plant was cut at ground level and separated into four component parts - stem/branches, leaves, female flowering tops, commonly known as buds or colas, and seed. The individual components were each weighed to determine a "wet" or "fresh" weight. The material was dried in a convection oven at 70 degrees Celsius. The dried material was reweighed when it had reached a constant weight, typically after 24 to 48 hours. This second measurement is termed the "dry" weight. During both yield surveys, cannabis plants were harvested and measured on a monthly basis to quantify yield throughout the growth cycle. The selection of plants was based upon a determination of their representative physical size, shape, and overall vigor characteristics. The selection process captured the diversity of plant size by including cannabis plants ranging from the larger to the smaller plant specimens. The planting of approximately 100 plants per cultivation area insured that there was a large and representative population from which plants were sampled. If a particular plant was harvested for the measurement program, the neighboring plants were ineligible for future selection which avoided changing the planting density during the study. Similarly, no plants on the outer rows were selected to avoid edge affects which could skew results because of an asymmetrical planting density.

YIELD RESULTS

All measurements recorded in 1990 and 1991 are contained in Attachment 1. Table 1 depicts the average yield for all mature (120 days or older) cannabis plants grown using a dense planting pattern of either 9 square feet per plant or 18 square feet per plant. At this relatively high planting density, the lateral branches of adjacent cannabis plants were touching by the middle of July. Thereafter, the horizontal growth rate decreased in relation to the vertical rate of growth. The results were tall, narrow plant canopies.

TABLE 1

AVERAGE CANNABIS YIELDS AT MATURITY FOR HIGH PLANTING DENSITIES

Sponsor	Year	Density	Yield*	Seed Stock
Univ. of MS	1985	9 ft. sq.	222 grams	Mexico
Univ. of MS	1986	9 ft. sq.	274 grams	Mexico
DEA	1990	18 ft. sq.	233 grams	Colombia
DEA	1991	9 ft. sq.	215 grams	Mexico

* Yield = Oven dry weight of usable leaf and bud from mature 120 day or older plants.

The similarity of plant yields contained in Table 1 is remarkable considering the variation in seed stock, year of cultivation, and other factors. However, if the planting density is decreased, the plants have more room to laterally branch out. The additional space allows the plant to assume a natural canopy shape, somewhat similar to a Christmas tree. The larger branching structure coupled with increased available sunlight, soil nutrients, and water resulted in significantly greater plant yields. Table 2 displays the yields for cannabis at maturity for identical seed stocks at three low planting densities and for different planting dates and years.

TABLE 2

AVERAGE CANNABIS YIELDS AT MATURITY FOR LOW PLANTING DENSITIES

Sponsor	Year	Density	Yield*	Seed Stock
DEA-A	1990	81 ft. sq.	777 grams	Mexico
DEA-B	1990	81 ft. sq.	936 grams	Mexico
DEA-C	1990	81 ft. sq.	640 grams	Mexico
DEA	1991	72 ft. sq.	1,015 grams	Mexico
DEA	1991	36 ft. sq.	860 grams	Mexico

* Seedlings for the 1990 measurement program were planted at two week intervals: DEA-A was planted on 4/17, DEA-B was planted on 5/8, and DEA-C was planted on 5/17. The 1991 plantings were made during the first week of June.

Figure 1 reports select plant height-diameter ratios for the planting densities used in 1990 and 1991. The noticeably high ratio for the 9 foot square planting density confirms that this plant canopy shape is different than all of the other observations which had relatively large amounts of space in which to grow. The height-diameter graph of Figure 1 shows that planting density is a significant factor affecting plant canopy shape, which in turn affects plant yield. The significance of the relationship between planting density and plant yield will be discussed later in this paper.

During both growing seasons, only standard irrigation, fertilization, and weeding activity were rendered as required. However, two plants, identification numbers 107.01 and 103.01 in the 1991 low planting density plots, had extremely high yields in comparison to neighboring plants. The dry weight yield for plant 107.01 was 2,086.9 grams (4.6 pounds) and plant 103.01 yielded 2,308.4 grams (5.1 pounds). These two plants were located in a low area. It is believed that the natural slope of the land caused these plants to receive additional water and possibly additional fertilizers through run on water. The significance of these yields is that they demonstrate that certain agronomic practices can produce higher average yields than those reported in Table 2.

Analysis of the combined 1990 and 1991 DEA yield data shows that usable oven dry weight material (leaf and bud) in a mature cannabis plant is 14.4% of the plant's total (roots excluded) fresh weight. A breakdown of the four types of material found in a mature female cannabis plant is presented in Figure 2.

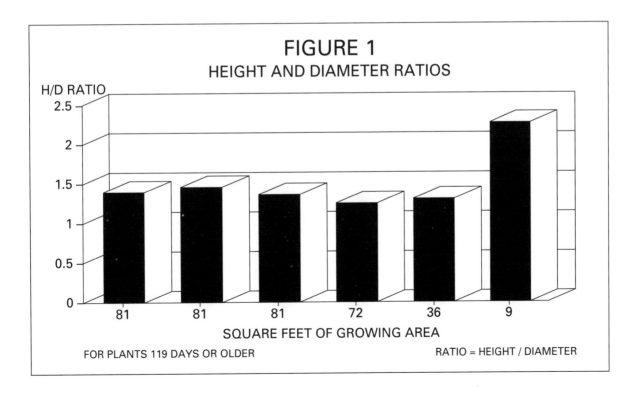

FIGURE 1
HEIGHT AND DIAMETER RATIOS

H/D RATIO

SQUARE FEET OF GROWING AREA

FOR PLANTS 119 DAYS OR OLDER   RATIO = HEIGHT / DIAMETER

FIGURE 2

NON-SINSEMILLA CANNABIS COMPONENTS

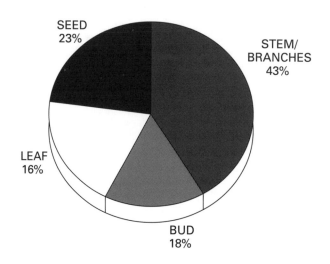

PERCENT OVEN DRY WEIGHT FOR 120 DAY OR OLDER PLANTS

SINSEMILLA CANNABIS COMPONENTS

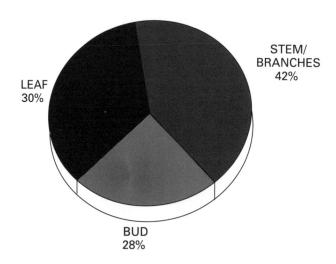

PERCENT OVEN DRY WEIGHT FOR 90 DAY OR OLDER PLANTS
WHICH DID NOT HAVE ANY SEED DEVELOPMENT

YIELD PREDICTION

The plant growth and yield data collected throughout the 1990 and 1991 growing seasons shows that plant yield can be accurately predicted from simple field measurements. Several field measurement techniques were assessed including plant height, diameter, fresh weight, and the number of grow days. The predictive models developed are valid for any sativa variety plants regardless of plant age or planting density.

The best predictor of plant yield was measurement of the plant's fresh weight. Figure 3 depicts the linear relationship between plant fresh weight and yield dry weight. The only required measurement is the weighing of the plant at the time of seizure in a timely fashion to avoid excessive loss of plant water. The fresh weight would not include the plant roots or any soil adhering to the plant. The fresh weight multiplied by the number 0.1437 would result in an estimate of usable dry weight material. This estimating technique is extremely accurate.

Another accurate method for predicting plant yield is based upon measurement of the diameter of the plant at the broadest point in the canopy. Figure 4 depicts the curvilinear relationship between plant canopy diameter and the plant dry weight. The measurement of a plant canopy diameter is simpler than the measurement of the plant's fresh weight. However, the calculation of a yield estimate requires a two step process. First, the measured diameter is entered into the equation: Dry Weight = -3.76786 + (0.06666 * (Diameter ^2)). This first equation estimates the plant's total dry weight. Usable yield is then calculated using the percentages of bud and leaf described in Figure 2.

Neither plant height data or the number of grow days were as accurate a predictor of plant yield as were fresh weight or diameter measurements. However, height was a good indicator of plant age and this relationship may be useful in estimating planting date. The correlation matrix included in Attachment 1 reports on the degree of association among 13 different plant measurements.

MISCELLANEOUS DATA ANALYSIS
Air Dry Weight

The use of oven dry weights, although scientifically acceptable because it can be reproduced, under-represents the amount of usable material in the illicit market. Most illegal material is air dried or at the time of sale, is in equilibrium with surrounding atmosphere which contains a certain amount of moisture. It is estimated based upon the DEA studies that the leaf and bud material of cannabis would weigh an additional 10% to 20% if allowed to air dry naturally and equalize with the surrounding atmosphere.

Water Content

In addition to the yield measurements, the amount of water contained in each plant was measured. A mature cannabis plant has, on a fresh weight basis, 66% water and 34% dry plant matter (leaves, buds, seeds, stems/branches). Plant water content can vary with plant age. Young plants less than 55 days old have a water content ranging from 75% to 82%. Older plants have water content ranging from 60% to 70%.

Plant Height

The average height of a mature cannabis plant was between 270 cm and 350 cm (8.6 - 11.5 feet). A few cannabis plants were measured in excess of 400 cm (13.1 feet). The tallest plant recorded was 430 cm (14.1 feet). Height was determined not to be very sensitive to planting density factors.

Crop Cycle

The crop cycle for the cannabis plants grown at the University of Mississippi was typical of cannabis grown in the contiguous states. The crop cycle consists of two stages. The first stage is the vegetative state which is characterized by a 30 to 90 day period of vigorous growth of sexually undifferentiated plants. Typical plantings occur in April or May and the vegetative stage extends until late July or early August. The transition from the vegetative stage to the second stage, known as the flowering or fruiting period, results from the reduction in day length associated with the photoperiod peaking on the summer solstice of June 21.

The flowering or fruiting stage lasts for the remainder of the plant's life cycle. Beginning in August, male plants form the stamens from which huge amounts of pollen are released. The male plants usually die by the middle of September or soon after they release their pollen. Female plants live a longer time in order to produce seed for the next generation. This reproductive stage is essential for naturally growing cannabis because it is an annual plant and can not survive the winter months. Female plants will produce a protective leafy bud to surround the pistulate reproductive organs and develop seed, if fertilized. The bud structure is highly desired by illicit growers because it contains the highest number of THC producing glans.

Yield Adjustment Factors

There is no need to adjust yield estimations of outdoor mature cannabis crops if at the time of seizure there are no male plants. If male plants are present, then evidence of this fact should be apparent by early August. The estimated yield of a male plant in early August, the point at which it begins to senesce and loose leaf cover, will be approximately 50% of the weight of a female plant of similar age and growth stage. By late September or October, the only harvestable cannabis plants remaining will be female plants.

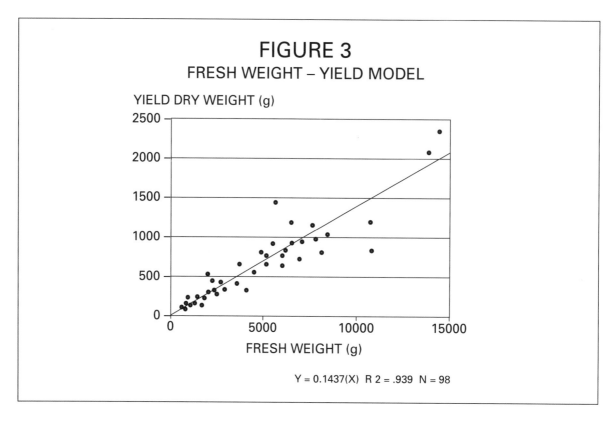

FIGURE 3
FRESH WEIGHT – YIELD MODEL

YIELD DRY WEIGHT (g)

FRESH WEIGHT (g)

$Y = 0.1437(X)$ $R\,2 = .939$ $N = 98$

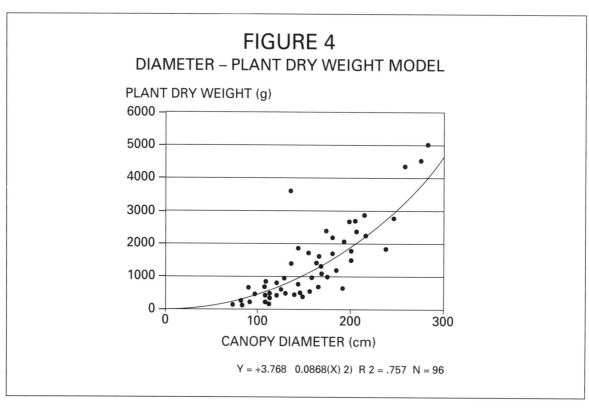

FIGURE 4
DIAMETER – PLANT DRY WEIGHT MODEL

PLANT DRY WEIGHT (g)

CANOPY DIAMETER (cm)

$Y = +3.768$ $0.0868(X)\,2)$ $R\,2 = .757$ $N = 96$

TABLE 4

ESTIMATED CANNABIS PLANT YIELDS

State	1991 Eradicated Plant Total	Avearge Diameter*	Estimated Non-Sinsemilla Yield(g)	Estimated Sinsemilla Yield (g)
Alabama	163,294	4 ft.	369	630
Arkansas	106,405	4 ft.	369	630
California	151,529	3.5 ft.	284	484
Florida	92,190	4.25 ft.	420	716
Georgia	300,583	4 ft.	369	630
Illinois	337,730	3.25 ft.	243	414
Indiana	206,494	4 ft.	369	630
Kansas	21,751	4 ft.	369	630
Kentucky	809,366	3.25 ft.	243	414
Louisiana	79,009	3.5 ft.	284	484
Minnesota	191,790	4 ft.	369	630
Missouri	104,493	3.5 ft.	284	484
N. Carolina	198,470	4 ft.	369	630
Tennessee	508,816	4 ft.	369	630
Texas	22,997	4.5 ft.	466	795
Average:		**3.85 ft.**	**345 grams**	**589 grams**

*Source: DEA Cannabis Investigations Section Survey May, 1992.

If the female cannabis plants are unfertilized, then no seed will be produced. The average usable yield (leaf and bud) of a mature female plant will be 57% of the plant's dry weight whereas the yield for a typical fertilized, seed bearing cannabis plant will be 34% of the plant dry weight (Figure 2).

DOMESTIC ESTIMATE

The identification of accurate plant yield estimation methodologies makes possible the opportunity to estimate the average domestic yield using eradication statistics and plant canopy diameter information. A survey of 15 leading producer states was conducted by DEA to determine the average diameter of mature plants eradicated in September 1991. Table 4 lists the average diameter or mature plants observed in that state as reported by the DEA state eradication coordinator. The estimated usable yield for each state's eradicated plant total was calculated using the predictive methodology described in Figure 4. This methodology uses average plant canopy diameter information as the predictor variable to estimate plant dry weight. The plant dry weight is adjusted to estimate usable air dry weight yield by first taking 34% of the dry weight to calculate usable yield, and adding 10% to the oven dry weight to obtain the air dry yield. This estimate is valid for female cannabis plants at maturity which contain seeds. An estimate for seedless cannabis (sinsemilla) is derived by first taking 58% of the plant dry weight, and then adjusting upward by 10% to convert from oven dry weight to an air dry yield.

The average yield for the entire outdoor domestic cultivated cannabis crop can be calculated by averaging the non-sinsemilla and sinsemilla yields in the same proportion as reported in the 1991 end of year eradication program results. The total number of cultivated outdoor cannabis plants eradicated in 1991 was 5,257,486. The number of sinsemilla plants was 2,251,735 or 42.8% of the total, and the number of non-sinsemilla plants was 3,005,751 or 57.2% of the total. A weighted average using the yields reported in Table 4 results in an average domestic plant yield of 448 grams or approximately 1 pound per plant.

CONCLUSIONS

The application of detailed field measurements and mathematical analysis techniques has shown that cannabis plant yields can be accurately estimated. Continued field observations at illicit cultivation locations, both domestically and overseas, will provide the opportunity to further validate the relationships reported. Development of cannabis yield methodologies is essential for understanding of the size of illicit cultivation problem and the drug abuse threat.

1990-91 DEA YIELD DATA

Productivity Data for Mississippi Field Plots, 1990-1991

Index Number	Grow Days	Density #/m2	Plant Ht. cm	Plant Diam. cm	Plant Fresh cm	Plant Dry cm	Plant Water %	Stem Fresh g	Stem Dry g	Yield Fresh g	Yield Dry g	Seed Fresh g	Seed Dry g
Mexican Variety - Plot A, 1.8x2.7 m Planting, 1990													
1.00	55	0.20	25	20	11.0	2.1	82	4.7	0.7	7.2	1.4	0.0	0.0
2.00	55	0.20	47	36	57.4	17.3	70	24.0	5.2	33.4	12.1	0.0	0.0
3.00	55	0.20	45	42	72.9	19.8	73	31.7	6.3	41.2	13.5	0.0	0.0
4.00	55	0.20	27	24	12.3	2.7	78	4.7	0.6	7.6	2.1	0.0	0.0
5.00	93	0.20	145	110	590.2	166.2	72	311.3	79.0	278.9	86.5	0.0	0.0
6.00	93	0.20	156	107	967.6	251.4	74	511.9	112.9	455.7	138.5	0.0	0.0
7.00	93	0.20	228	147	1793.0	500.2	72	1004.3	266.0	788.7	234.5	0.0	0.0
8.00	94	0.20	142	111	660.2	177.7	73	307.2	70.7	353.0	107.0	0.0	0.0
9.00	111	0.20	172	124	1110.9	369.6	67	582.8	190.2	528.1	179.4	0.0	0.0
10.00	112	0.20	238	202	5906.0	1699.3	71	3280.7	951.6	2625.3	747.7	0.0	0.0
11.00	111	0.20	341	265	7581.4	2523.0	67	4362.4	1532.5	3219.0	990.5	0.0	0.0
12.00	152	0.20	245	203	3586.8	1384.6	61	2428.4	957.6	1158.4	427.0	0.0	0.0
13.00	153	0.20	303	245	8010.0	2737.9	66	4545.7	1639.7	3464.3	1098.2	0.0	0.0
14.00	146	0.20	324	170	7781.2	2287.0	71	4798.9	1481.6	2982.3	805.4	0.0	0.0
Mexican Variety - Plot B, 1.8x2.7 m Planting, 1990													
15.00	36	0.20	16	16	4.1	1.1	73	1.3	0.2	2.8	0.9	0.0	0.0
16.00	36	0.20	25	25	14.5	4.2	71	5.2	1.0	9.3	3.2	0.0	0.0
17.00	36	0.20	20	20	13.0	3.9	70	4.0	0.8	9.0	3.1	0.0	0.0
18.00	36	0.20	34	34	27.9	7.6	73	11.1	1.9	16.8	5.7	0.0	0.0
19.00	64	0.20	117	112	689.0	199.8	71	323.6	83.4	365.4	116.4	0.0	0.0
20.00	65	0.20	137	121	923.1	237.5	74	484.7	111.3	438.4	126.2	0.0	0.0
21.00	65	0.20	137	132	1040.7	273.3	74	513.7	116.8	527.0	156.5	0.0	0.0
22.00	91	0.20	255	190	4196.6	1199.9	71	2270.7	597.2	1925.9	602.7	0.0	0.0
23.00	93	0.20	205	160	3243.2	940.6	71	1684.6	438.7	1558.6	501.9	0.0	0.0
24.00	127	0.20	255	215	9856.9	2985.6	70	5771.6	1844.3	4085.3	1141.3	0.0	0.0
25.00	134	0.20	328	180	6770.1	2177.7	68	4339.0	1448.1	2431.1	729.6	0.0	0.0
Mexican Variety - Plot C, 1.8x2.7 m Planting, 1990													
26.00	56	0.20	63	56	103.4	23.5	77	45.8	8.2	57.6	15.3	0.0	0.0
27.00	56	0.20	68	65	153.7	32.4	79	75.3	11.3	78.4	21.1	0.0	0.0
28.00	56	0.20	90	85	239.9	49.5	79	132.4	19.9	107.5	29.6	0.0	0.0
29.00	83	0.20	175	145	1802.9	523.9	71	939.1	260.4	863.8	263.5	0.0	0.0
30.00	82	0.20	140	110	1186.9	308.8	74	565.0	127.5	621.9	181.3	0.0	0.0
31.00	124	0.20	301	185	4942.9	1652.0	67	2624.9	906.6	2318.0	745.4	0.0	0.0
32.00	124	0.20	230	150	4293.2	1340.4	69	2489.8	791.8	1803.4	548.6	0.0	0.0
33.00	124	0.20	220	180	3304.8	1086.1	67	1797.3	621.4	1507.5	464.7	0.0	0.0
34.00	124	0.20	210	190	5944.6	2008.3	66	3557.4	1205.7	2387.2	802.6	0.0	0.0

1990-91 DEA YIELD DATA (continued)

Productivity Data for Mississippi Field Plots, 1990-1991

Index Number	Grow Days	Density #/m2	Plant Ht. cm	Plant Diam. cm	Plant Fresh cm	Plant Dry cm	Plant Water %	Stem Fresh g	Stem Dry g	Yield Fresh g	Yield Dry g	Seed Fresh g	Seed Dry g
Mexican Variety - 2.4x2.7 m Planting, 1991													
107.02	30	0.15	30	16	6.6	2.2	67	2.0	0.6	4.6	1.6	0.0	0.0
108.02	30	0.15	40	25	22.2	6.7	70	7.1	1.6	15.1	5.1	0.0	0.0
109.02	30	0.15	100	64	166.9	44.9	73	70.4	16.6	96.5	28.3	0.0	0.0
108.04	64	0.15	150	167	2691.8	706.0	74	1163.2	276.0	1528.6	430.0	0.0	0.0
107.04	64	0.15	170	100	459.5	128.9	72	184.6	41.1	274.9	87.8	0.0	0.0
106.04	64	0.15	170	143	1608.6	440.8	73	816.4	201.2	792.2	239.6	0.0	0.0
106.06	91	0.15	200	229	6829.0	2026.6	70	2517.8	816.2	4311.2	1210.4	0.0	0.0
108.06	91	0.15	223	186	6121.8	1944.9	68	1657.2	513.5	4464.6	1431.4	0.0	0.0
109.07	91	0.15	297	175	5154.2	1612.9	68	2115.7	732.7	3038.5	880.2	0.0	0.0
109.09	123	0.15	285	246	4013.0	1719.4	57	2627.3	1126.8	770.3	320.3	-615.4	272.3
109.11	123	0.15	292	205	7014.9	2654.4	62	2822.2	1142.9	2717.8	956.9	1484.9	554.6
107.19	128	0.15	249	215	5910.8	2150.0	64	2412.5	739.8	1670.8	644.1	1827.5	766.1
108.19	128	0.15	309	204	8315.0	2980.8	64	3937.2	1442.2	2764.5	1030.6	1613.3	508.0
109.12	128	0.15	262	227	7831.1	2812.7	64	2717.1	995.3	3294.7	1155.1	1819.3	662.3
109.17	128	0.15	266	213	6255.5	2345.2	62	1621.3	593.9	2451.6	902.0	2182.6	849.3
107.01	129	0.15	270	261	12957.6	4392.2	68	4337.1	1509.9	7286.8	2086.9	2333.1	795.4
Mexican Variety - 1.8x1.8 m Planting, 1991													
102.02	30	0.30	50	38	63.6	15.2	76	27.6	5.0	36.0	10.2	0.0	0.0
103.02	30	0.30	64	42	77.2	17.1	78	22.0	4.0	55.2	13.1	0.0	0.0
104.02	30	0.30	67	52	71.2	19.0	73	22.2	4.9	49.0	14.1	0.0	0.0
102.04	64	0.30	158	141	1947.1	546.7	72	823.4	212.5	1123.7	334.2	0.0	0.0
103.04	64	0.30	172	144	1754.3	486.0	72	816.5	208.5	937.8	277.5	0.0	0.0
105.04	64	0.30	140	158	2232.0	564.3	75	959.9	222.6	1272.1	341.7	0.0	0.0
103.06	91	0.30	247	184	3088.5	951.9	69	1290.6	438.4	1797.9	513.5	0.0	0.0
105.07	91	0.30	140	185	4109.0	1536.1	63	1348.7	523.6	2760.3	1012.5	0.0	0.0
104.06	92	0.30	314	173	3640.1	1269.0	65	1641.2	626.3	1998.9	642.7	0.0	0.0
103.09	121	0.30	267	193	5123.8	2107.6	59	1936.4	876.8	1928.1	733.3	1259.3	497.5
101.10	122	0.30	218	154	4370.4	1779.8	59	1839.6	820.9	1646.6	610.4	884.2	348.5
102.08	122	0.30	240	195	4688.2	2037.5	56	1818.6	856.7	1963.0	791.1	906.6	389.7
102.12	122	0.30	245	173	3429.0	1461.7	57	1256.4	576.4	1212.6	485.6	960.1	399.7
103.12	127	0.30	220	191	4868.8	1986.1	59	2021.5	886.6	1684.9	635.3	1162.4	464.2
104.17	127	0.30	338	218	5814.1	2285.5	61	2483.1	1089.1	2264.1	814.3	1066.9	382.1
102.09	128	0.30	303	163	4143.5	1690.7	59	1849.5	811.2	1327.6	502.1	966.4	377.4
103.01	129	0.30	224	281	14290.0	5051.4	65	4812.4	1856.4	6784.6	2308.4	2693.0	886.6

1990-91 DEA YIELD DATA (continued)

Productivity Data for Mississippi Field Plots, 1990-1991

Index Number	Grow Days	Density #/m2	Plant Ht. cm	Plant Diam. cm	Plant Fresh cm	Plant Dry cm	Plant Water %	Stem Fresh g	Stem Dry g	Yield Fresh g	Yield Dry g	Seed Fresh g	Seed Dry g
Mexican Variety - 0.9x0.9 m Planting, 1991													
97.02	30	1.20	67	39	65.9	17.5	73	23.1	4.9	42.8	12.6	0.0	0.0
98.09	30	1.20	47	35	45.9	11.3	75	15.9	3.1	30.0	8.2	0.0	0.0
99.09	30	1.20	37	24	16.7	4.7	72	5.1	1.3	11.6	3.4	0.0	0.0
90.11	65	1.20	145	106	656.2	180.8	72	308.3	83.5	347.9	97.3	0.0	0.0
95.11	65	1.20	140	100	1131.6	324.0	71	576.5	161.2	555.1	162.8	0.0	0.0
89.11	65	1.20	123	76	430.0	122.2	72	192.5	53.5	237.5	68.7	0.0	0.0
99.11	65	1.20	232	126	1078.3	346.2	68	533.2	173.5	545.1	172.7	0.0	0.0
88.11	65	1.20	160	86	480.1	142.2	70	246.1	71.0	234.0	71.2	0.0	0.0
87.12	91	1.20	180	80	565.6	194.2	66	284.1	102.9	281.5	91.3	0.0	0.0
88.12	91	1.20	125	51	130.4	37.2	72	58.2	16.2	72.2	21.0	0.0	0.0
96.14	91	1.20	207	104	839.9	296.9	65	410.3	161.7	429.6	135.2	0.0	0.0
87.14	91	1.20	186	79	732.8	244.4	67	278.2	98.2	454.6	146.2	0.0	0.0
89.10	91	1.20	170	99	1078.2	321.5	70	290.4	89.8	787.8	231.7	0.0	0.0
96.13	91	1.20	224	133	1498.4	541.2	64	635.8	254.4	862.8	286.8	0.0	0.0
97.14	91	1.20	230	147	2427.6	763.3	69	955.6	326.0	1472.0	437.3	0.0	0.0
97.19	120	1.20	221	83	653.8	261.2	60	334.8	132.4	319.0	128.8	0.0	0.0
95.23	120	1.20	256	99	1079.1	424.5	61	543.0	226.4	536.1	198.1	0.0	0.0
87.19	120	1.20	271	112	1681.0	650.2	61	690.4	267.1	637.8	244.7	352.8	138.4
96.22	120	1.20	221	113	1938.2	767.0	60	868.7	344.0	551.9	214.2	517.6	208.8
87.17	120	1.20	251	95	750.7	287.5	62	305.2	129.7	445.5	157.8	0.0	0.0
97.16	121	1.20	288	129	2144.0	937.1	56	1026.2	468.6	594.9	242.5	522.9	226.0
99.16	121	1.20	221	83	1305.0	555.6	57	560.7	238.9	391.7	162.8	353.2	153.9
100.15	122	1.20	234	130	2123.1	872.3	59	759.3	342.3	835.9	326.2	527.9	203.8
100.17	122	1.20	175	125	1721.8	752.4	56	495.4	193.5	591.7	258.4	634.8	300.5
Colombian Variety - Plot E, 0.91x1.8 m Planting, 1990													
35.00	91	0.60	77	72	159.9	37.8	76	75.4	13.7	84.5	24.1	0.0	0.0
36.00	91	0.60	111	104	341.3	85.0	75	169.3	32.9	172.0	52.1	0.0	0.0
38.00	93	0.60	137	108	752,0	214.1	72	387.9	100.2	364.1	113.9	0.0	0.0
39.00	110	0.60	182	128	1385.5	419.7	70	751.5	227.3	634.0	192.4	0.0	0.0
40.00	147	0.60	200	100	1131.8	389.6	66	533.4	236.1	598.0	153.5	0.0	0.0
41.00	147	0.60	220	140	1697.1	576.5	66	950.0	357.9	747.1	218.5	0.0	0.0
42.00	147	0.60	150	143	2627.9	883.5	66	1496.7	555.7	1131.2	327.8	0.0	0.0
Hybrid Variety - Plot F, 0.91x1.8 m Planting, 1990													
43.00	145	0.60	152	191	2101.2	593.6	72	1137.6	333.5	963.6	260.1	0.0	0.0
44.00	145	0.60	230	210	10477.2	2654.2	75	6716.7	1843.0	3760.5	811.2	0.0	0.0
45.00	91	0.60	67	84	369.7	92.9	75	153.6	33.6	216.1	59.3	0.0	0.0
Jamaican Variety - Plot H, 0.91x1.8 m Planting, 1990													
46.00	91	0.13	102	94	810.7	184.6	77	421.8	78.2	388.9	106.4	0.0	0.0

Correlation Matrix for Marijuana Plant Parameter Relationships, 1990-91

	Growth Days	Density	Plant Ht.	Plant Diam.	Plant Fresh Weight	Plant Dry Weight	Plant Water	Stem Fresh Weight	Stem Dry Weight	Yield Fresh Weight	Yield Dry Weight	Seed Fresh Weight	Seed Dry Weight
Growth Days	1.000												
Plant Density	0.015	1.000											
Plant Height	0.846	0.009	1.000										
Plant Diameter	0.729	-0.315	0.830	1.000									
Plant Fresh Weight	0.628	-0.350	0.687	0.867	1.000								
Plant Dry Weight	0.660	-0.328	0.704	0.870	0.989	1.000							
Plant Water	-0.689	-0.245	-0.664	-0.476	-0.378	-0.470	1.000						
Stem Fresh Weight	0.658	-0.365	0.722	0.844	0.939	0.917	-0.377	1.000					
Stem Dry Weight	0.696	-0.336	0.746	0.853	0.943	0.945	-0.442	0.985	1.000				
Yield Fresh Weight	0.529	-0.334	0.609	0.824	0.962	0.932	-0.280	0.857	0.849	1.000			
Yield Dry Weight	0.562	-0.328	0.630	0.843	0.969	0.958	-0.358	0.853	0.862	0.990	1.000		
Seed Fresh Weight	0.435	-0.155	0.396	0.528	0.660	0.728	-0.490	0.452	0.530	0.565	0.637	1.000	
Seed Dry Weight	0.446	-0.145	0.403	0.523	0.632	0.706	-0.527	0.430	0.511	0.528	0.604	0.994	1.000

CRITICAL VALUE (2-TAIL, P<0.05) = +/- .198; N-98

ATTACHMENT 2
1985-68 YIELD DATA – UNIVERSITY OF MISSISSIPPI

UNIVERSITY OF MISSISSIPPI
1985 YIELD STUDY DATA

Table 1. Statistics for the Production of Marijuana from Plants of Different Age

Week	Plant A	WET WEIGHT (g)			DRY WEIGHT (g)		% of Dry Leaves to Dry WP[1]	% of Dry Leaves to Wet WP	% of Dry stalk/stem to Wet WP	% of Dry plant Wet WP	% of Wet leaves Wet WP	% of Wet stalk/stem to Wet WP	% of Dry leaves to Wet Leaves	Height (cm)
		Whole Plant	Stalk/ Stems	Leaves	Stalk/ Stems	Leaves								
12	1	328	182	146	82	53.5	39	14	25	42	45	56	37	180
13	2	1309.7	702	607.7	380	130.5	26	10	29	39	46	54	29	231
14	3	1055	657	398	282	158.8	36	15	28	42	38	62	40	269
15	4	2163	1197	966	622	372.5	37	17	29	46	45	55	39	286
16	5	2222	1518	704	726	241.0	25	11	33	43	32	68	34	224
17	6	2768	1533	735	823	268.2	25	12	36	48	32	68	36	281
18	7	1972	1331	641	655	221.5	25	12	33	40	33	67	35	300
19	8	1724	1278	446	658	271.4	20	10	39	49	26	74	34	328
20	9	3472	2305	937	1220	388.7	24	11	35	46	27	73	41	259
21	10	2364	1661	503	854	217.6	20	10	39	50	23	77	43	358
Average		1867.77	1259.4	638.37	630.8	222.37	27.7	12.3	32.6	44.8	34.7	65.4	36.3	271.6

[1] Whole Plant

UNIVERSITY OF MISSISSIPPI
1986 YIELD STUDY DATA

Table 2. Statistics for the Production of Marijuana from Mature Plants

Plant g	WET WEIGHT (g) Whole Plant	DRY WEIGHT (g) Stalk/ Stems	Leaves	Stalk/ Stems	Leaves	% of Dry Leaves to Dry WP[1]	% of Dry Leaves to Wet WP	% of Dry Stalk/Stem to Wet WP	% of Dry Plant to Wet WP	% of Wet Leaves to Wet WP	% of Wet Stalk/Stem to Wet WP	% of Dry Leaves to Wet leaves	Height (cm)
1	3869	2635	1261	1456	709	33	18	37	56	32	68	56	249
2	2680	1620	1060	688	351	34	14	26	39	40	61	30	231
3	3712	1200	552	620	181	23	31	36	47	30	70	35	213
4	2333	1292	841	680	289	30	14	32	45	39	61	36	226
5	3730	1218	532	570	171	23	10	33	43	30	70	33	221
6	2344	1334	1038	621	319	34	14	27	40	44	56	35	225
7	2283	1541	742	810	140	15	6	36	43	32	68	19	257
8	2231	1478	813	734	280	28	13	33	46	36	64	34	224
9	1168	808	360	400	130	25	11	34	45	31	69	36	224
10	1336	965	411	540	157	23	11	39	51	30	70	38	244
Average	2155.3	1401.1	754.2	713.9	273.7	26.8	12.2	33.3	45.5	34.5	65.7	35	238

Appendix B

Report of the Domestic Cannabis Eradication and Suppression Program

This report is the work of the notorious narc, Charles Stowell. It is reproduced unedited and uncorrected to show the quality of the work produced by the California Department of Justice, using taxpayers' money.

Stowell was used all around California in hundreds of marijuana cases. His testimony was accepted by the courts until he faced vigorous cross-examination. He mis-identified legal vegetation for marijuana at the Donald Scott Ranch in Ventura County. The subsequent raid resulted in Scott's death.

Stowell was also used as an instructor, and many of his students continue to testify regarding the material covered in his seminars.

The misinformation contained herein is immense and staggering. It gives you an idea of the kind of statements you are likely to face at trial. Material to refute aspects of this report is easily obtained from any number of books available in most bookstores. Titles include:

Closet Cultivator, by Ed Rosenthal*
Domestic Marijuana, Dr. Ralph Weisheit
Marihuana Reconsidered, by Dr. Lester Grinspoon*
Marijuana Botany, by Robert Clarke*
Marijuana Growers Guide, by Mel Frank and Ed Rosenthal*
Marijuana Growers Handbook, by Ed Rosenthal*
Marijuana Medical Papers, by Tod Mikuriya
Marijuana Medicine and the Law, by Robert Randall
Marijuana, the First 12,000 Years, by Abel
Why Marijuana Should Be Legalized, by Ed Rosenthal*

---

* Available from Quick Trading Co.   800-428-7825, ext. 102

ACKNOWLEDGEMENTS

When I was Deputy Incident Commander at C.A.M.P. from 1986 to 1989, Jack Beecham taught me one thing. That was to give credit to those people who work so hard in this program. In the preparation of this report I want to thank:

1. Annie Collins, San Francisco Field Division
2. Sgt. Frances Jones, CA National Guard
3. Sgt. Richard Nicolazzi, CA National Guard
4. Sgt. Cheri Lynn McMillan, CA National Guard
5. Spc/Lauren Oehler, CA National Guard
6. Sgt. Fritz Eberly, CA Highway Patrol

These folks make up the DCE/SP unit at the Sacramento R.O. and to them I say thank you.

PART 1 "THE PROBLEM"

INTRODUCTION AND PREFACE

In 1990 all Federal, State, and local law enforcement in the United States seized 9 tons of heroin, 131 tons of cocaine, and 27 tons of dangerous drugs. Those three drug groups the media so often refer to as "Hard Drugs", equalled 167 tons of drugs seized. In 1990 all Federal, State and local law enforcement in the United States seized 4128 tons of cannabis. In other words, 24 times more cannabis was seized than all other drugs combined.

If we assume that law enforcement seizes ten percent of all the drugs available to the American public that would mean that 90 tons of heron, 1310 tons of cocaine, 270 tons of dangerous drugs and 41,280 tons of Cannabis were available in 1990 to the drug abusers of America.

The Domestic Cannabis Eradication and Suppression Program efforts in California, are centered around the Campaign Against Marijuana Planting (C.A.M.P.). Federal Agencies grant funds and manpower to C.A.M.P. and participate as members and on the C.A.M.P. Policy Board. To date C.A.M.P. and the participating agencies have done an outstanding job in reducing California's cannabis cultivation. Law enforcement collectively, can boast a three-quarters reduction from 800,000 known plants in 1983 to last years' total of 199,000. Cannabis however remains the largest cash crop in California.

The ten highest money producing crops in California are in the following order grapes, cotton, commercial nursery products, hay, flowers and foliage, lettuce, tomatoes, almonds, oranges, and strawberries. In relation to these legimate crops cannabis is far more lucrative in terms of profit. For example, in 1983 the cannabis seized in California was valued at 4.2 billion dollars, while grapes that year's highest value legitimate crop, brought in only 947 million dollars.

HISTORICAL BACKGROUND

Cannabis has for many years been the "Gateway Drug" through which the youth of America travel into the world of drug abuse. In a survey conducted in California in 1988, 95 out of every 100 narcotic arrestee's stated that they had entered the drug subculture through the use of cannabis.

Cannabis provides an education into the world of the drug subculture by teaching our youth how to lie. They learn to lie to themselves, their parents, authority figures such as teachers and the police. They learn how to buy drugs. They learn how to find and patronize drug dealers, they learn not to front their money, they learn the meaning of "rip off", "stash" and "good or bad product", all by buying and using cannabis.

THE PLANT

The term marijuana as defined in the law means..."all parts of the plant. Cannabis Sativa L. (and any of its varieties); whether growing or not; the seeds thereof; the resin extracted from any part of such plant and every compound, salt, derivative, mixture, or preparation of such plants, its seeds or resins."...

That definition would seem to cover just about everything, but as with an insurance policy or the hearsay rule, it's more important to know the exceptions or what isn't covered than what is....such terms do not include the mature stalks, oils or cakes made from the seeds of such plants, or other compounds, manufactured salt derivatives, mixture or preparation of such mature stalks (except the resin extracted therefrom), fiber oil or cake or the sterilized seed of such plant which is incapable of germination....

Why doesn't the definition really cover the whole plant? Why are there exceptions? Cannabis is without a doubt one of the oldest and most widely cultivated plants in the world. As a matter of fact cannabis appears in world literature for the past five thousand years. While its mind altering effects are the primary reason for its cultivation, there are a claimed variety of legitimate commercial uses, namely, its fiber for rope, the rapidly drying oils from the seeds for plants, and the seeds themselves for birdseed. (However, no legitimate use exists in any form.)

The definition of marijuana under the Controlled Substances Act is consistent with the definition under the Singles Convention, under which cultivation of Cannabis is illegal or legally restricted in almost every country and on almost every continent. The fact is, a country may allow cultivation under legal restrictions, this was the case here in the United States during World War II when supplies of fiber for rope were effectively cut off.

The majority of botanists classify Cannabis Sativa L. as a single botanical species. (Under Federal and State law Cannabis Sativa L. is illegal no matter the variety and is legally considered a single species.) But some, most notably Richard Schultz maintains there are at least three species: (1)

Cannabis Sativa L., (2) Cannabis Indica, (3) Cannabis Ruderalis. This disagreement between botanists has lead to some interesting debates and on occasion a criminal defense predicated on the premise that the defendant was cultivating a distinct species and as such was wrongly charged, since the law covers only Cannabis Sativa L.

The traditional way of defining separate species is that offspring resulting from a cross between two species cannot reproduce successfully. All Cannabis plants can cross freely, resulting in fully fertile hybrids. Without going into any further discussion as to the relative merits of proper botanical classification, suffice to say the higher courts have consistently held that Cannabis Sativa L is the single species.

What we can say with some finality is that all varieties of Cannabis can be broken into two distinct types of categories. The fibrous type and the resinous or drug type.

CANNABIS, CHEMICAL COMPOSITION

The Cannabis plant is quite complex in its chemical composition. There are in excess of 460 distinct chemical compounds which comprise the plant, over 60 of which are cannabinoids. The primary psychoactive ingredient is delta 9THC (Tetrahydrocannabinol). The percentage of THC in the plant material is used as the means of measuring the relative potency or psychoactive strength of the plant. The fibrous type, which is often referred to as ditch weed, has an extremely low THC content and is virtually worthless in the illicit market. The drug type naturally has a high THC content and commands premium prices. Another group of chemicals worth mentioning are the over 100 Terpenes which give Cannabis its distinctive aroma.

Cannabis is a dioecious plant, which means that the male and female flowers develop on separate plants. However, on occasion in the absence of a male plant both sexes have been found to develop on the female plant. These plants are referred to as hermaphrodites or more properly, monoecious.

Cannabis can be propagated either sexually or asexually. Seeds are the result of sexual propagation. Since sexual propagation involves the recombination of genetic material from two plants, variation of the genetic material will result in some offspring differing from the characteristics of the parent plant. These offspring are called hybrids.

Asexual propagation or what is popularly known as cloning is no more than taking cuttings from one plant, which allows for the exact replication of the characteristics of the single parent plant. ie Sex, bio-mass, and the THC content.

The reason that sexual difference is important is that through selective breeding, the underground horticulturists are able to produce hybrids that have a higher THC content, while at the same time having the potential for reducing or altering the detectable profile, (color and size) of the plant. Think of it, a perfect Cannabis plant, only 5 feet tall, vs 18 feet, earth tone color rather than the distinctive green

and 14% THC. To an extent that is exactly what has transpired. In the mid-1970's, law enforcement began hearing about a new super grass called SINSEMILLA (meaning literally without seeds). Chemical analysis of sinsemilla colas or flowering tops of the female plant, showed a THC content of from 3 to 4 times that of the marijuana which was being imported from Mexico during the early 1970's.

For centuries folklore has speculated that the female Cannabis is more potent than the male. There is little scientific evidence to support this contention. Scientific analysis shows the THC content of the leaves of the mal and female plant to be roughly equal. What is known is that the top most portions of both plants have the highest THC concentrations.

The sinsemilla horitculuturists, through selective breeding of plants of the resinous type have developed hybrids of extremely high potency. They also remove all of the staminal or male plants before pollination. The pistillate or female in trying to attract the male pollen, produces massive clusters of unfertilized flowers or colas. How this ultimately affects the chemical production within the plant is a mystery. The theory is that when a plant is fertilized, the energy of the plant is directed into seed production and the THC level drops dramatically.

This would seem to have some creditably in that after the male plant releases its pollen it is effectively at the end of its life cycle and the THC content decreases as the plant dies. Remember that up until this point the new growth or top of both plants have nearly equal THC content.

Weeks are added to the female plants life cycle by removing the pollen source. In addition more THC is allowed to accumulate, resulting in massive coals of quality plant material, known on the street as "BUDS".

The sinsemilla grower harvests only the colas trimming away any extraneous leaves. These extraneous sun leaves or shakes as they are called are considered waste material. Conversely the Mexican or Colombian growers harvest sun leaves, stems and seeds increasing the weight of plants by up to 50% through the inclusion of virtually worthless plant material which contains little if any THC.

Since colas of the female plant are the only concern to the sinsemilla grower, it is critical to be able to sex the plant at an early age. To do this, we must know something about the normal life cycle of the cannabis plant (we will see later that the normal cycle can be altered especially under indoor conditions).

LIFE CYCLE

In the normal lifecycle of the cannabis plant, the seeds are planted in the spring and usually germinate in 5 to 7 days. Shortly thereafter, the first true serrated leaves appear. These leaves will normally start with one leaflet then 3 leaflets, up to 11 leaflets, almost without exception in an odd number, until the start of flowering, at which point the process reverses itself.

For the first two to three months the growth of the plant responds to the increasing day length with vigorous growth of up to two to three inches per day. With the summer solstice (June 21 the longest day of the year), the photo period reverses, with the shorter days and longer nights, thus ending the vegetative stage.

The extended period of darkness tells the plants that it's time to complete its life cycle. Given 10 hours of light per day, a plant may take 10 days or so to flower, where if exposed to 16 hours of light it could take up to 90 days. By controlling the photo periods or length of daylight, as in an indoor growing operation the grower can force flowering and thus shorten the normal life cycle of the plant. Thus we can also see the effect of latitude on marijuana production. Those areas located closer to the equator experience two growing seasons per year, while areas in the extreme northern latitudes can expect at most one short season.

The male plants will flower from one to four weeks prior to the females. The first sign of flowering in the plant is the appearance of prefloral nodes along the main stem behind the leaf spur. The females are more easily recognized at a young age than the males, due to the appearance of two long white, yellow or pink hairs or pistils protruding from the nodes, where as the male develops a curved claw shape node. For practical purposes the cultivator waits until the actual flowers form on the male plants.

The male flowers consist of five petals, which may be yellow, white or green in color. As the flowers hang down and open five stamen or pollen sacs emerge. The female never develops what lay persons would consider a true flower.

CULTIVATORS

The sinsimella grower will germinate multiple seeds and transplant them in large containers or cultivation sties since they cannot differentiate male or female at that point. One male may be retained for breeding purposes by covering the male flowering tops with paper bags to collect the pollen. The male flowering tops may also be harvested prior to the opening of the pollen sacs. The colas, and hence the yield will be considerably smaller than the female plants but the relative potency quite high.

With the removal of the male plants the female plant will continue to flower for four to five weeks, extruding vast amounts of resin in an effort to propagate. The amount of resin visible on the exterior of the colas is thought of erroneously by some growers as indicative of THC content thus announcing harvest time. This is not the case as the exterior resin has nothing to do with the THC content. As the photo period begins to shorten to the area of 10 hours of sunlight per day, the sun leaves begin to turn brown, signaling the approaching end of the plants life and the shutdown of internal chemical producing apparatus of the plant.

The harvest at this point involves no more than the cutting of the coals, trimming away the sun leaves and hanging them to dry. The growers will hang the colas upside down in the belief that the THC will continue to be forced to the tops. The drying process involves awaiting the evaporation of approximately 90% of the water in the plant so that it is dry enough to burn.

The knowledgeable grower and ultimate consumer will also exercise more than a casual concern as to temperature and lighting conditions under which they store the final product. THC will over a period of time degenerate. The higher the temperature the faster the degeneration. As an expert witness I often testify as to the decline of THC within the plants. Studies at the NIDA Cannabis Research Project at the University of Mississippi have shown that even under ideal storage conditions, (68 to 72 degrees with no light), cannabis loses 1/2 of its stored THC in the first six months. After twenty-four months all THC is virtually gone from the harvested plants.

LAW ENFORCEMENT

From 1978 until 1988 law enforcement efforts in the State of California concentrated on the eradication of outdoor marijuana cultivation sites. Having done an outstanding job law enforcement realized a new menace which was becoming apparent in our state. Indoor cultivations were created to fill the void caused by aggressive law enforcement outdoors. To quote an article appearing in the September issue of the "Chief's of Police Magazine" by Larry M. Hahn, Supervisory Special Agent/Program Coordinator Operation Green Merchant, Drug Enforcement Administration, Washington, D.C..

INDOOR CANNABIS CULTIVATION:
AN ARTICLE BY DEA STAFF COORDINATOR
LARRY M. HAHN

Cannabis Sativa L, commonly know as marijuana, continues to be the most abused drug in this country. Since the 60's it has been the drug of choice among abusers. According to a recent National Household survey approximately 10 million Americans use marijuana. However, instead of the foreign grown variety sought after in the 60's and 70's, the drug abuser of today prefers the homegrown, highly potent, indoor sinsemilla variety of cannabis. Unfortunately, as the popularity of sinsemilla increases, so does the number and sophistication of illegal entrepreneurs who domestically cultivate it. Motivated by huge profits and the demand for the drug, indoor cannabis growers will continue to flourish.

Sinsimilla is a Spanish world that means "without seeds". This form of cannabis is obtained from the female plant. The flowering top of the unfertilized female plant, called the colas or "bud," produces the strongest concentration of THC. THC is an abbreviation for delta-9-tetrahydro-cannabinol, the chemical which causes the psychoactive effects desired by the abuser. Indoor cultivation provides a controlled environment to minimize pollination, allowing the sinsemilla to reach its maximum potency. Unlike traditional harvest methods, only the sinsemilla portion (colas or buds) of the plant is retained for sale. The stems, stalks and leaves, referred to as "shake," is usually discarded. The "shake" contains a much lower THC content than the colas.

In the sinsemilla process, male plants are weeded out during the early growing stage to prevent pollination. Lives have been lost in outdoor growing situations where a marijuana cultivator carelessly failed to eliminate the male plants in his patch. The male plants ultimately pollinated his neighbors meticulously tended female plants, therefore destroying the sinsemilla crop and the profits. Growing marijuana indoors not only creates a controlled growing environment, but allows cannabis to be grown year round regardless of outside climate or season. Because of improved agronomy, three to four growing cycles are possible per year utilizing indoor cultivation techniques.

The three essential ingredients needed to grow cannabis are light, water, and nutrients. All of these are employed in the most popular indoor growing method - the hydroponic method. Hydroponic growing does not require soil. Water instead, is utilized to deliver the necessary life supporting nutrients in an artificial growing media. The cannabis root system is shallow and effectively supported in non-soil, porous growing material such as lava rock or rockwool. Water and fertilizer pass freely to the roots through the growing medium. The light necessary to complete the plants photosynthesis (the life sustaining activity of all plants) is provided by fluorescent, metal halide or sodium vapor lights. Advanced cultivators utilize a combination of these lights in the growing cycle to produce the ultimate sinsemilla quality plants. Special fertilizers, plant hormones and steroids, carbon dioxide and advanced horticulture techniques are all used by the informed illegal grower to "push" the plant into producing the highest grade, most potent sinsemilla. Information on indoor hydroponic growing techniques is easily obtained from counter-culture, open source, pro-marijuana periodicals and publications.

There are legitimate applications of hydroponics to grow legal plants, such as flowers, vegetables and fruits. However, hundreds of hydroponic supply companies have sprung up throughout the United States to cater almost exclusively to indoor cannabis growers. The lights, fertilizers and various other growing equipment sold by these stores are legal to possess or sell. In the past several years many of these hydroponic supply stores have been seized and the owners arrested by Federal, State and local law enforcement agencies. Investigations proved the stores employees knew the merchandise sold would be used to grow marijuana. Some of these stores also provided advice on how to grow marijuana and provided seeds or seedling plants to start the customers indoor grow. Law enforcement success in investigating these stores has resulted in an acute

exchange of investigative techniques through underground pipelines in the drug culture.

"The demand for the potent, sinsemilla variety of marijuana, the lucrative profits involved and the decrease in foreign source cannabis will all contribute to a steady expansion of indoor cultivation in the future", according to John T. Peoples, Chief of DEA's Cannabis Investigation Section. Last year over 1600 reported indoor growing operations were seized by Federal, State and local agencies. This represents a 20% increase over the previous year and the trend is expected to continue. Every state reported indoor grows in 1991. For the past ten years domestically produced marijuana has been the most popular among abusers. This popularity parallels the decrease in foreign produced cannabis. It is currently estimated that approximately 25% of cannabis consumed in the United States is produced domestically. By 1995 it is estimated that 50% of the marijuana consumed in this country will be grown here.

Indoor grows, range from several plants grown in closets to thousands of plants grown in subterranean, specially constructed sites capable of producing sinsemilla worth millions. A healthy indoor-grown marijuana plant can produce up to a pound of sinsemilla within a four-month growing cycle. Sinsemilla presently averages $2,500 - $3,500 per pound at a wholesale level. An investment of several thousand dollars in hydroponic equipment can grow 100 plants to maturity in four months producing a potential $250,000.00 crop of sinsemilla. Hundreds of plants can easily be grown inside the average residence. As horticulture techniques improve this drug increases at an alarming rate. The marijuana of the 60's and 70's contained .5-2% THC. The indoor grown variety of today averages 8-10% THC. The record THC content of sinsemilla to date is 19.74% which was seized at a sophisticated indoor grow operation in Arizona in October, 1990.

The harmful effects of this new potent marijuana is currently under scientific study. It is well documented that cannabis contains known toxins and cancer-inducing chemicals which are stored in fat cells for long periods of time. Cannabis use results in long-term impairment effects on the brain, the respiratory system, the immune system and the reproductive process. THC and marijuana smoke have been directly linked to miscarriage, in utero fetal death, stillbirth and infant death just after birth, along with behavioral and biological abnormalities of offspring.

For the last several years DEA has conducted a special enforcement program - Operation Green Merchant - which target the domestic indoor cannabis cultivation industry. Through intelligence gathering processes indoor growers are identified.

Traditional and innovative investigation techniques are then applied against the suspect and illegal operation. DEA along with State and local law enforcement agencies have had significant success under this program. Over 700 grow sites have been seized. Hundreds of violators have been arrested and millions of dollars in drug assets seized. This program continues to expand and is an excellent catalyst for multi-agency cooperation efforts against this expanding drug phenomena.

Many factors indicate that indoor cultivation of cannabis will continue to increase in the future. Continued efforts by the law enforcement and prosecution communities in pursuit of indoor cannabis will significantly reduce the availability of cannabis in the United States.

ENVIRONMENTAL DAMAGE CAUSED BY CANNABIS CULTIVATION

Substantial quantities of high nitrogen fertilizers are used by growers to enhance the production of cannabis. These chemicals are usually in liquid or pellet form and are hand applied or injected into drip systems using electronic metering systems. Most cultivation sites are located on slopes which are near water sources, usually streams. While there is some danger of these chemicals leaking into streams, the biggest hazard occurs after the plants have been harvested and the sites abandoned. We have found that, in nearly every case, the fertilizer not used during the growing operation was left at the site and exposed to the elements. In some cases, there have been several hundred pounds of fertilizer dumped and left.

During winter rains these abandoned chemicals are most likely to leak into streams. This can result in a chemical imbalance of the stream and adverse effects of aquatic life.

Another hazard is the indiscriminate use of rodenticide by the cannabis grower. Typically, growers spread large quantities of rat killer type poisons in and around cultivation sites to protect plants from being eaten by rodents. The Forest Service has found large numbers of dead rats and squirrels, as well as a few larger animals such as foxes in the vicinity of cultivation sites where rodenticide have been used. This not only has an adverse effect on the small animal population but also can effect larger animals up the food chain.

As in the case of the previously mentioned fertilizers, substantial quantities of rodenticide are left after sites have been abandoned. Since the active ingredient in these rodenticide is usually strychnine, it's (sic) introduction into streams during winter rains is of particular concern.

Another adverse environmental impact caused by cannabis cultivation activity is the intentional killing of deer by growers in the vicinity of cultivation sites. Some growers, in the belief that deer will forage on young cannabis plants will methodically kill deer which are in or near the sites. Bear and mountain lion are sometimes killed and their carcasses hung at sites to discourage deer approaching.

The Forest Service considers the potential environmental hazards created by this criminal activity to be a significant threat to forest ecosystems, but statistics are hard to come by. The Chief of the Forest Service, Dale Robertson,

however, testified in 1988 before the House Committee on Agriculture that :

On about 80 percent of the cultivation sites we have located, we have found poison designed to kill wildlife which eat cannabis plants. These pesticides and poisons are of such high concentration that they are dangerous. After harvesting the growers leave these poisons in the forest where they may eventually find their way into the water and into the forest environmental as a whole.

"Review of the Drug Law Enforcement Activities of the Forest Service and the Omnibus Public Lands Act of 1987," Hearing before the Subcoma. on Forest, Family Farms, and Energy of the House Com. on Agriculture, t Cong., d sess., P. 38 (July 12,1988) (copy enclosed). See similarly "Going to Pot: Marijuana Cultivation on Public Lands and Federal Response," 27th Report by the Com. on Government Operations, H.Rep. 100-454, 100th Cong., 1st sess. (Nov 1987), pp. 19-20 (copy attached); "Drug Safety Issues," supra.

"Going to Pot" relies heavily upon reports prepared by the General Accounting Office (GAO), including "Additional Actions Taken to Control Marijuana Cultivation and other Crimes on Federal Lands," GAO/RCED-85-18 (Nov.1984) and "Illegal and Unauthorized Activities on Public Lands - A Problem with Serious Implications," GAO/CED-82-48 (March 10,1982) (copies attached). GAO reported numerous incidents of resource damage. "These incidents involve marijuana growers suspected of causing wild land fires, cutting timber and shrubs for growing sites, using unauthorized poisons and pesticides, shooting and poaching wildlife, and littering the land with structures and growing equipment."

Much of the information cites in these published reports derived from the Forest Service. That agency may posses more recent figures or statistics than those cited in the above reports. You may therefore also wish to consider consulting them.

NATURE AND EXTENT OF THE PROBLEM

The rapidly escalating problem of illicit cannabis cultivation poses a new challenge to narcotics law enforcement in the United States. The seriousness of this problem can be judged in terms of the quality and quantity of marijuana produced domestically. From the standpoint of quality, the production sinsemilla has increased substantially in the United States. Through the process that produces sinsemilla, a single plant can yield approximately one pound of product that has on the average a higher THC (Delta-9-Tetrahydrocannabinoid) content than standard marijuana. In terms of its potential health hazards, i.e., the higher the THC content, the more serious the health consequences associated with its use.

In terms of quantity, the estimated size of the cannabis crop grown in the U.S. has considerably increased in recent years. The estimated amount of marijuana produced from the domestic crop for 1981 as reported by the National Narcotics Intelligence Consumer Committee (NNICC) was 1200 metric tons. Although this estimate was based on the best information available at the time it was considered conservative. A primary goal of the 1982 Domestic Eradication/Suppression Program was to develop an intelligence data base concerning domestic cannabis cultivation. The data collected indicated that our previous estimates may have been considerably lower than the actual amounts under cultivation.

It should be noted, however, that these estimates and the methods used to calculate the amount of marketable marijuana produced remain imprecise. Major efforts are underway to develop accurate estimates. Samples of plants from sites throughout the country will be submitted for analysis to the contractor for the National Institute on Drug Abuse. Despite possible variations in total weight estimates, we recognize that there is a substantially greater amount of marijuana being produced in the Untied(X) States than ever before.

The prosecution of individual cannabis growers is also a new challenge for many prosecutors. Given terrain and security measures that often make a pre-raid surveillance impossible, it is difficult to establish an association between growers and specific cannabis plots. Ground access to mountain top of other remote sites is often limited to one road. Under such conditions, one lookout or cooperative resident some miles from growing site can warn the growers of intruders by CB radio. DEA, in cooperation with several U.S. Attorneys, is currently developing seminars for prosecutors to educate them in techniques to offset these problems.

Another problem is prosecutors are often reluctant to indict and judges and juries are likewise hesitant to convict and adequately sentence growers. Further, local budget restrictions which have resulted in layoffs of deputies have prevented some sheriffs from applying the manpower to the program which they otherwise would be able to commit.

Finding a site and the means to safely destroy thousands of pounds of wet, bulky cannabis plants is a challenge for any law enforcement officer. The DEA office of Science and Technology is currently attempting to find solutions to these problems. For U.S. Forest Service and Bureau of Land Management (BLM) employees, personal and resource safety have become a major concern as growers retaliate for the destruction of their cannabis crops. U.S. Forest Service and BLM officials know of many occasions where their employees have been threatened and their personnel and agency equipment damaged or destroyed by angry growers. Forest officials have told us they suspect that many forest fires have been set by individuals seeking to retaliate for enforcement actions.

DEA'S MARIJUANA SUPPRESSION/ERADICATION PROGRAM

Prior to 1981, DEA's cooperative eradication programs were limited to Hawaii and California. This was expanded during 1981 to include Oregon, Florida, Missouri and Kentucky. Since that time, the program has expanded rapidly to include 25 states in 1982 to all 50 in 1990. While some states are more significant than others with regard to the amount of marijuana production discovered thus far, all of the participant states are experiencing some illicit growth for financial profit.

DEA's strategy has been to provide a varying level of support, depending upon the perceived volume of cultivation, but in every case sufficient to support an aggressive search program in each State. DEA's role in this cooperative venture has been to encourage state and local efforts and to contribute training, equipment, funding, investigative and aircraft resources to support their efforts. The planning process for the current Suppression/Eradication Program has been highly coordinated at the Federal level by all related agencies. Regular strategy and policy guidance sessions are conducted by the White House Drug Abuse Policy Office and frequent contact is maintained with the U.S. Forest Service and the Bureau of Land Management.

Our Headquarters Program Coordinators have held meetings with DEA field division Special Agents in Charge (SAC) and their Division Coordinators. Those planning sessions are being repeated by the DEA Division Coordinators with their respective State and local counterparts. Together they are developing an operational plan for each participating state. The plans will be the basis for the allocation of resources by DEA and other Federal agencies.

In 1990 DEA-sponsored training schools were held from coast to coast within the United States. The DEA sponsored schools were three phase in 1990. Training was given in thermal imaging, indoor cultivations and aerial observation. These schools are designed to train State and local law enforcement officers in aerial observation techniques, the legal requirements to obtain search warrants in their states, methods to conduct raids to destroy the cannabis crop, and procedures to arrest and prosecute those individuals identified with the cultivation. Participants include not only State and local officers, but Agents of the U.S. Forest Service and Bureau of Land Management who play an active role. We are also planning to sponsor a number of seminars for State and Federal prosecutors to enhance their awareness of the cultivation problem and to address legal questions regarding warrants, asset seizures, appellate review, defense tactics and the cross certification of State Federal prosecutors.

The DEA and The California National Guard, as well as, the Civil Air Patrol provide aircraft to the California Cannabis Program. In addition to their critical role in locating plots, aircraft are required to move enforcement personnel into the often remote growing areas and to remove the plants once the eradication takes place.

Our office of Science and Technology, in cooperation with the U.S. Department of Agriculture, is developing methods to assist states prepare for the use of herbicides which will occur where deemed appropriate during the 1992 Federal Strategy for prevention of Drug Abuse and Drug Trafficking and in close coordination with appropriate Federal Agencies.

The marijuana program depends on the efforts of many agencies. In addition to the u.s. Forest Service and Bureau of land management activities described earlier, the Department of Defense Liaison Office is advising State national guard commanders of the logistical assistance they can provide law enforcement elements. In addition, agents of the Bureau of Alcohol, Tobacco and Firearms (ATF) have participated in raid teams throughout the country, and have been instrumental in reducing the threat of injury to raid teams by identifying and neutralizing dangerous concealed traps, some of which are potentially deadly.

The involvement of multi-state intelligence networks in the program has been at the discretion of the states; however, the Western States Intelligence Network (WSIN) will play a major role on the cooperative operation currently being planned for California.

There are a number of variables in this program. First, the type and level of State and local resources available for eradication vary from state to state. Secondly, there has been a gradual increase in the number of state agencies, such as State Forest Services, Offices of Emergency Services, etc., which have begun to make equipment and expertise available to the state enforcement elements. In addition, the states are attempting to identify and use alternate labor sources to cut down cannabis plants. The process of manual eradication is highly labor intensive. As noted, the plot sites are often remote, and in states such as California, Oregon and Washington, are in steep rugged terrain. Law enforcement officers must secure the area, arrest growers, check for concealed traps, perform a plant count, take photographs and process samples in response to search warrants and evidentiary requirements.

Only then can they begin the task of cutting cannabis plants which can reach 12-15 feet in height and, in some circumstances, grow in groves a thick as bamboo thatches. The plants must be bundles and tied and then carried some distance to the nearest trail or road to be loaded on trucks. Irrigation hoses, which often run for considerable distances and have been buried to avoid detection must then be trucked to a suitable suit for burning. This represents an extensive use of law enforcement manpower.

In an attempt to offset this problem, some states are looking to possible alternate labor sources. Law enforcement personnel would still control the raid teams and conduct all of the appropriate legal tasks, however, once the site is secure, non-law enforcement personnel could con-

duct the actual cutting, bundling and hauling under law enforcement supervision at a greatly reduced cost. There are obviously a number of problems related to the use of non-law enforcement personnel, but we are encouraging the states to consider alternate labor as a means to reduce costs and spare law enforcement personnel for more critical tasks.

Future funding costs for DEA will be offset by the continued coordinated efforts with the Forest Service and bureau of Land Management. DEA coordinated funding to county sheriffs who have U.S. Forests within their jurisdiction with the U.S. Forest service to ensure there is no duplication. Often, the Forest Service will fund the program in one county, while DEA supports an adjacent county that has no U.S. Forest within its limits. In some areas, the Forest Service and Bureau of Land Management are able to provide forest camp housing and feeding facilities for raid team personnel.

CONCLUSION

If we are to make serious inroads in the marijuana production problem in the Unites States, there are challenges that all of us in government must face. Members of Congress and other Government leaders should lend their voices and help make the public more aware of the threat that illegal cultivation of cannabis represents to both the health of the nation and the rights of the citizens to move freely and safely through the parklands and national forests of this country. The military should be encouraged to incorporate marijuana production detection as a regular part if their ongoing air training activities and State governors should be encourages(X) to consider using National Guard and other state Agencies for the detection and suppression of marijuana production. In addition, the states should be encouraged to support the use of herbicides when appropriate in order to effectively and efficiently eradicate large cannabis plots and to reduce the prohibitive labor costs of manual eradication programs. This would have added benefit of sending a signal of encouragement to foreign governments faced with even greater marijuana production problems than our own.

HEALTH EFFECTS
MARIJUANA SMOKING: FACTORS THAT INFLUENCE THE BIOAVAILABILITY OF TETRAHYDROCANNABINOL

As taken from the Pharmacological Reviews dated 1986 by the American Society for Pharmacology and the Health Aspects of Cannabis by Leo E. Holister and Dr. P. Mann of the Veterans Administration Medical Center and Stanford University School of Medicine Palo Alto, CA. Also, the NIDA, National Institute on Drug Abuse Research Monograph Series by U.S. Department of Health and Human Services dated 1990.

INTRODUCTION

Marijuana smoking is the most commonly used method for the self-administration of delta-9-tetrahydrocannabinol (THC), the active principal of marijuana. The inhalation of marijuana smoke induces subjective effects ("high") that are rapidly perceived by the smokers. The perception of these effects allows smokers the capacity to achieve, within certain limits, their desired level of high by changing the puff volume, the interval between puffs, and the number of puffs taken. Therefore, the manner in which marijuana cigarettes are smoked (smoking dynamics) is probably the most important factor in determining the bioavailability of THC However, the following factors are also important: (1) the potency of the marijuana smoked; (2) the amount of unchanged THC present in the smoke inhaled (i.e., the amount of THC not destroyed by pyrolysis); (3) the amount of THC lost in side-stream smoke; (4) the method of smoking (cigarettes vs. pipe smoking); and (5) the amount of THC trapped in the mucosa of the upper respiratory tract. A review of the experiments conducted permitting(X) evaluation of the relative importance of these factors is presented in this chapter.

METHODS COMMON TO ALL CLINICAL STUDIES

SUBJECTS

Male and female, healthy, paid volunteers who use marijuana no more than two times per week participated in the studies. They were thoroughly informed about the experimental procedures, the purpose of the investigation, and the potential risk. All signed an informed consent approved by the Committee on the Protection of the Rights of Human Subjects of the University of North Carolina at Chapel Hill.

EXPERIMENTAL VARIABLES

Subjective Ratings of Intoxication. The major psychological effect of marijuana as a temporary euphoric effect with diversely perceived sensory, somatic, affective, and cognitive changes that are commonly described as a high. To measure this effect, we asked the subjects to rate their degree of high at frequent intervals during the experiment on a graph form provided for them. For this rating, the subjects were asked to estimate their level of high on a scale of 0 to 100; zero represented no effect and 100 repre-

sented the highest they had ever been after smoking marijuana. Every time a rating was to be made, subjects were given their previous rating to use for comparison. This technique allowed the subjects to rate themselves as experiencing relatively more, less, or the same effects as those rate in the previous time interval.

Physiologic Effects. Since the most consistent physiologic effect of marijuana in humans is cardiac acceleration, the an EKG was continuously recorded on a polygraph before the beginning of smoking (baseline) and throughout the duration of the experiment. The results are reported as the percentage of heart rate acceleration over baseline values.

Determination of the THC Plasma Concentration. Blood samples were drawn through an indwelling needle before the initiation of smoking and at frequent intervals thereafter. The plasma obtained was analyzed by standard radioimmunoassay procedures (Owens et al. 1982; Cook et al. 1982).

STATISTICAL ANALYSES

For comparison, the means of the data plus or minus the standard errors of the mean (SEM) were calculated and are reported as such throughout the text. Areas under the curve (AUG's) were analyzed statistically by means of regression analysis and t test for either dependent paired data or independent non-paired data as appropriate.

MARIJUANA POTENCY

To investigate the influence that marijuana potency per se has on the peak THC plasma concentration produced, a regression analysis was done on the results on experiments in which National Institute on Drug Abuse (NIDA) marijuana cigarettes of eight different potencies (range 1 percent to 6.24 percent THC) were smoked. The marijuana potencies investigated, the number of subjects tested, the mean peak THC plasma concentrations, and the range of individual peak THC plasma concentrations are illustrated in figure

1. The results indicate the presence of a statistically significant correlation between the potency of the marijuana smoked and the peak THC plasma concentrations. However, as shown in this figure, wide individual variations in peak THC plasma concentrations occurred consistently across all of the marijuana potencies investigated. This variability in THC plasma concentrations indicates that factors other than the potency of the marijuana smoked, particularly the smoking dynamics, influence the magnitude of the resulting THC plasma concentrations.

PYROLYTIC DESTRUCTION

When marijuana is smoked, a portion of its THC content is destroyed by pyrolysis before reaching the mouth of the smoker, Information regarding the amount of THC destroyed by pyrolysis is derived from both cigarettes and water-pipe smoking.

HEALTH EFFECTS OF MARIJUANA

For many years, it has been a widely held view, especially among the younger generation, that marijuana differs from heroin, cocaine, LSD, and other "hard drugs" in that the former is relatively harmless. As a result of this wide spread attitude, marijuana cultivators and traffickers have been treated substantially more leniently in the state and federal courts than have other dealers in "hard drugs."

In recent years, scientific evidence has accumulated that the health consequences of marijuana are not only real, but that they are dramatic and profound, and may well affect persons now unborn as well as the actual users. The degree of harm inflicted by illegal conduct is certainly a relevant consideration in determining what punishment is appropriate. The United States offers the present memorandum to bring before the court some of the accumulating evidence of marijuana's harmful effects.

Marijuana contains a total of 421 known chemicals, which include a variety of toxins and cancer-inducing chemicals. The primary psycho-active agent in delta-9-tetrahydrocannabinol ("THC"). While THC is primarily responsible for the mind-altering effects of marijuana, the adverse health effects of the drug result not only from the THC, but also from the other chemicals which marijuana includes.

From the standpoint of their biological effects, the significant characteristics of THC and related compounds contained in marijuana (called cannabinoids) is that they are "lipophilic," or fat soluble. Because of this fat-soluble characteristic, once ingested into the body, they gravitate to and accumulate in internal organs with a heavy concentration of fat cells, which include the brain, sexual organs as testes and ovaries, the adrenal glands, liver, kidneys, and the heart. This fat solubility means that THC and other cannabinoids tend to remain in the body long after the mind-altering effects of the drug have ceased. It is not unusual, for example, for a urine test to show positive two to four days after a joint is smoked. (1) In this respect, marijuana differs substantially from alcohol and other drugs which are water soluble and which are flushed from the body within a few hours after they are consumed. The human body's waste removal system is water based, and consequently is not that well equipped to manage removal of fat-soluble substances. Mann, pp.97-8.

Scientific research done within the last fifteen years has demonstrated that use of marijuana has substantial adverse health effects not previously suspected. They include impairing effects on the brain tissue and psychological functioning, and damage to the reproductive, immunological, respiratory and cardiovascular systems.

A. Effects on the Brain

It has long been recognized that marijuana has distinctive behavioral and psychological consequences in addition to the pleasurable effects which motivate its use. As long ago as 1971, studies of young marijuana users had disclosed a spate of symptoms including:

> Very poor social judgement, poor attention span, poor concentration, confusion, anxiety, depression, apathy, passivity, indifference, and often, slowed and slurred speech. An alteration of consciousness which included a split between an observing and an experiencing portion of the ego, an inability to bring thoughts together, a paranoid suspiciousness of others, and a regression to a mote infantile state were all very common...
>
> In some individuals, instead of apathy, hyperactivity, aggressiveness, and a type of agitation were common. In no instance were these symptoms in evidence prior to the use of marijuana. (2)

In their more extreme form, the adverse effects of marijuana use can include suicidal tendencies, withdraw, feelings of depersonalization, flashbacks and schizophrenia. (3) In some respects the effects of marijuana use can mirror the onset of senility and old age. (4) In adolescents, it is severely disruptive of the maturation process, causing regression in pushing young users back toward infantilism by self absorption and the desire for instant gratification. (5)

Perhaps the most distressing consequence of marijuana use are its implications for the inability of large number of adolescents and young adults to assume responsible positions in society. Closely related but less well known are the physiological effects of marijuana on the brain. Research done in the last 15 years makes clear that marijuana's a long-term impact on the brain's make-up and functioning goes far beyond the short-term pleasurable sensations which it creates.

Starting in the late 1960's, Dr. Robert Heath, then chairman of the Department of Psychiatry and Neurology at Tulane Medical School, did research aimed at identifying the physiological effects of marijuana use on the brain. In his human patients who used marijuana, Dr Heath observed symptoms including an amotivational syndrome, abnormal irritability and hostility, abrupt mood swings and impaired short term memory. (6)

In order to determine to what extent these symptoms observed in humans might be physical in nature, Dr. Heath undertook a series of experiments using Rhesus monkeys. He focused on the limbic area of the brain, which is the center of pleasure, hostility, hunger, and other emotional expressions related to chronic marijuana use. He implanted electrodes into various areas known to be associated with emotional expression. They study revealed in the THC-exposed monkeys abnormal electroenphalogram (EEG) brain wave patterns from the areas of the brain directly reacted to the most common symptoms evidences by chronic marijuana users. These studies suggest that those sites identified as integral components within pathways for expression of emotion and feelings are the most profoundly affected. Dr. Heath concluded that his findings in the patients, as well as in Rhesus monkeys, suggest that marijuana asserts a more localized effect as the species moves up phylogenetically. (7)

Following the termination of the EEG study, the test monkeys were sacrificed to perform pathologic analysis of their respective brain cells. Specialists in cell biology studied the actual appearance and structure of the brain cells of the monkeys involved in the test. Monkeys receiving THC, both intravenously and through smoke, displayed disproportionate numbers of substantially altered brain cells. The greatest damaged appeared in the sections of the brain associated with the pleasurable experiences of marijuana. Among the types of abnormalities observed were inclusion bodies within the nuclei of the brain cells, which have been associated with old age, but which were found in monkeys who used marijuana in the studies. Other abnormalities included widening of the space between nerve connections (synoptic clefts) and abnormal opaque deposits resulting from the clumping together of synoptic vesicles. (8) Both the synoptic clefts and vesicles chemically transmit nerve messages, all being necessary for human thinking, feeling, and doing. These physiological changes would therefore directly impair the normal function of neurotransmission.

In another study aimed at detecting long term physical effects of marijuana use, Dr. John P. McGahn performed CAT scans on the brains of the monkeys in Dr. Ethel Sassenrath's experiments. (see Section B, infra) A year after the last use of marijuana, he found significant brain atrophy in the monkeys given daily THC doses for three to five years, as compared to those who received either short term doses or none at all. (9)

In considering the aforesaid damage to the brain found in these studies, it is well to remember that such physiological changes can be permanent and long-lasting. Unlike other body cells which periodically die and are replaced, brain cells that die or are severely damaged are not replaced. Obviously, at birth a person starts with billions of brain cells, many potentially "in reserve" for future use in the even others die. But the bottom line is that the total number of brain cells is finite, and if enough damage is done, substitution and takeover may not be completely successful.

A good sum-up of the subject of marijuana effect on the brain is the following comment by Dr. Heath of the Tulane study:

> People might drink rather heavily for twenty to thirty years and never get into serious trouble so far as alterations in their brains are concerned. But with marijuana it seems as though you have to use it only for a relatively short time in moderate to heavy use before persistent behavioral effects, along with other evidence of brain damage, begin to develop. Animal data confirms what many of us have suspected from clinical experience with marijuana users; namely, that this drug produces distinctive changes in the brain.
>
> As quoted in Mann, p.91.

B. Effects on the Reproductive Process

Marijuana use in women has shown to alter the level of several sex hormones, with corresponding consequences for sexual functioning. The 1977 study by Drs. Bauman and Kolodny discovered that defective menstrual cycles appeared in a small group of marijuana users approximately three times as frequently as in non-users. The same study also disclosed in the same women consistently high levels of testosterone, a male hormone, and significantly lower levels of prolactin, a pituitary hormone involved in the production of milk in a nursing mother, than in the non-marijuana using group. These hormonal consequences are known to have a significant adverse effect on individual development, especially during adolescence. Although Dr. Bauman did not view these results as conclusive, for several reasons including the small size of the test group, she noted the similarities of these results to those reached in animal tests, and called for urgent further research on the possible effects of marijuana on the human female endocrine system. (10)

Perhaps of greater concern than the reproductive consequences of marijuana use for the user are its effects on offspring. These effects begin at the time of conception, since THC is passed not only through mother's milk but also through the placenta. (11)

Between 1974- 1978, a long-term study was conducted by Dr. Ethel Sassenrath at the University of California at Davis using Rhesus monkeys. The results of this study demonstrated a substantially higher incidence of reproductive loss— that is death of the offspring prior to or during the birth process in monkeys receiving a THC does equivalent to one joint a day. Instead of the 10-12 per cent reproductive loss found to be normal among Rhesus monkeys. Dr. Sassenrath's THC-exposed group experienced a rate of fetal loss of 42%. These included instances of early spontaneous abortion, in utero fetal death, still birth and infant death just after birth. In addition, the pregnant THC mother had a significantly lower body weight gain than the control mothers, and the male offspring of the THC mothers not exposed to THC. Low birth rates contribute to a higher incidence of infant mortality within one month of birth. Further, when the THC fetuses and dead babies were examined they found to have a range of subtle abnormalities including water on the brain and degenerative changes in cardiovascular structures.

In Dr. Sassenrath's study, substantial behavioral differences were noticed between the THC-treated mothers and offspring and those in the control group. The mothers exposed to THC seemed far less interested in their offspring. The THC babies displayed higher levels of irritability, screamed longer and louder than others and tended to be avoided by others. (12)

A study by Psychologist Peter Fried at Carlton University in Canada has shown significant behavioral abnormalities in the human offspring of women using large quantities of marijuana during pregnancies. After examining the offspring of 420 women (60 of whom used marijuana) at birth, 4 days, 9 days, 30 days and periodically thereafter, Fried found that the children of heavy users responded abnormally slowly to visual stimuli and exhibited exaggerated tremors and startles interpreted as symptomatic of nervous system immaturity. While these symptoms began to disappear at approximately one month of age, Fried himself concluded that there was no way of knowing whether or not subject abnormalities remained. (13)

An expansive study conducted between 1977 and 1979 at the Boston City Hospital focused on more than 2,500 newborn babies and was directed primarily at examining the effects of maternal alcohol consumption on the offspring. In the process, the researchers collected data concerning marijuana smoking and the delivery of infants with features compatible with the fetal alcohol syndrome. Among other conclusions, this study showed a direct correlation between marijuana use and both pre-pregnancy illness in the mother and the tendency to deliver low birth weight babies. (14) The significance of low birth weight related directly to infant mortality. Low weight infants are substantially more likely to die within a month of birth than infants of normal weight. (15)

There is also evidence that marijuana use inhibits sexual development and function in males. A study by Dr. Wylie Hembree of Columbia University in which 16 subjects were tested during periods of marijuana use and non-use revealed, during the marijuana smoking period, a 40% decrease in the number of sperm and a 20% decrease in sperm mortality. (16) In addition to sperm number and mortality, morphology is critical to conception. In 1979 using Rhesus monkeys, Dr. Carol Smith demonstrated that even one does of THC profoundly inhibits the production in males of testosterone and other hormones which stimulate the sex organs. (17) Testosterone is not only critical to the development of sperm, but also to the maturation process in adolescent males.

A research report by Dr. Susan Dalterio at the University of Texas has shown that the consequences of marijuana use may be felt in the male offspring of female mice exposed to THC, well after they are born. In addition to its reported ability to suppress hormone production by the testes and the pituitary, marijuana can suppress male copulatory behavior. In her experiment, mothers were exposed to THC on only one occasion prior to birth, and on the first six days following birth. Following the limited exposure, the ale offspring were observed to exhibit abnormal behavior — a lack of interest in the female mice, and a gross overweight condition. Dr. Dalterio also observed a striking parallel between this behavior and the behavior of castrated mice.(18) Other work by Dr. Dalterio has revealed substantial reductions in both testerone and normal sexual development in males, resulting from THC exposure either during fetal development or after birth. (19)

Further research by Dr. Dalterio has uncovered chromosomal damage in the testes of the THC-exposed mail mice, as well as in the testes of some of their offspring, who had not themselves been exposed to marijuana. Over 25% of the sons of THC-using fathers were never able to produce normal pregnancy, displaying instead an abnormally high rate of infertility, pre-natal and post-natal death, and several birth defects. (20)

There appears to be good reason to believe that marijuana use has a significant adverse effects on the reproductive process in human males as well. Research by Dr. Marietta Issudirides in Athens, Greece, using an electron microscope to study and compare the sperm of hashish user and non-users, revealed a significant decrease in sperm count and mortality among the users and also distinct morphological abnormalities in a majority of the sperm of all of the hash-smoking subjects. (21)

C. Effects on the Immune System and Other Cellular Effects

Research by the same Dr. Issidorides on the effects of long-term hashish use on the blood revealed that well over half of the long-term male users displayed a cell trait that is common in women but extremely rare in men. (22) In further studying the chemical make-up of the aberrational blood cells, Dr. Issidorides discovered that those cells displayed a substantial reduction in the amount of arginine which they contained. Arginine is one of the number of amino acids necessary for the manufacturing of protein for growth or replacement due to again. (23)

From these and other observations she developed a hypothesis which appears to explain many of the other correlations with regular marijuana use which have otherwise been observed. According to this hypothesis, the biological effects observed in chronic cannabis users may be explained by arginine depletion which, in itself, can cause chromosomal aberrations, decreased sperm maturity and mortality, defective ovulation, growth retardation, immunosuppression, and the reaction of latent viral infections and central nervous system effects such as anorexia, motor incoordination, and lethargy. (24) Dr. Issidorides is presently pursuing further research to prove or disprove the validity of several aspects of her arginine depletion hypothesis. As applied to the immune system, however, a number of studies by others already confirm the substantial effects of marijuana use.

A study by Dr. Bruce Petersen and Dr. Louis Lemberger in 1974 show that human phagocyte, whose function is to engulf, neutralize and digest foreign substances such as asbestos, were significantly reduced among pot smokers as compared with non-smokers. (25) In a 1978 study ont he immunosuppressant effects of the THC mice injected with herpes virus, Dr. Albert Munson found that the injection of THC reduced the resistance of the mice to the virus approximately 96-fold. When compared with the immunosuppressant effects of well known drugs used in organ transplant surgery, the researchers found that THC fell between the widely use immunosuppressant drugs flumenthazone, which resulted in only a 10-fold decrease in resistance, and cyclophosphamide, which decreased resistance to herpes by 260 times. (26)

In a 1983 study, Dr. Arthur Zimmerman of the University of Toronto discovered that a small does of THC in mice significantly impairs the ability of immune system cells to remember and recognize a previous exposure to the specific foreign body, thus significantly suppressing and slowing the formation and deployment of appropriate antibodies. (27)

While not all human studies have shown that the immune system is affected by marijuana, those studies which have produced a negative finding have used subjects which were neither long term nor heavy users. The studies supporting the conclusion of a depressive effect on the immune system are supported by empirical observations that marijuana using young people tend to be ill more frequently than non-users. (28)

Apart from studies relating to the immunological system, several researchers have demonstrated a connection between marijuana use and an abnormally high rate of chromosome damage. Dr. Akira Morishima, studying adult male regular marijuana users, has found a direct correlation between the frequency of use and the number of cells with an abnormally small number of chromosomes. Looking at T-lymphocytes, he found that marijuana, more than any other illegal drug he has studied, is closely correlated with a high rate of chromosome destruction or damage. (29) His conclusion has been confirmed and supported by the work of others. (30)

D. Effects on the Respiratory System

Marijuana smoke contains many of the same chemicals contained in tobacco smoke.(31) Marijuana cigarettes are, however, generally smoked more intensely, inhaled for a longer period, unfiltered, and smoked to the very end so the heaviest concentration of the most damaging chemicals is consumed by the smoker. Numerous studies which have been done on human, lung cell tissue, rats and other laboratory animals have indicated that the adverse effects of marijuana smoke in various contexts equal or surpass the similar effects of tobacco smoke. (32)

E. Effects on the Cardiovascular System

Although little research has been done on the long term consequences of marijuana on the heart, studies do demonstrate that it substantially elevates the rate of heartbeat and the blood pressure during the period that psychological effects are felt. Also, for the same period marijuana decreases the force with which the heart can pump the blood decreases the volume capacity of the heart, and thus decreases the amount of blood that can be pumped every minute. (33) For persons suffering from angina pectoris, it has been shown that the use of marijuana has approximately twice the effect of tobacco in reducing the level of activity at which chest pain is experienced. (34) While scientific data does not yet exist to demonstrate it, the great similarities between tobacco smoke and marijuana smoke suggest that the long term consequences of the two for heart function is similar. It is now widely known that heart disease is the greatest adverse health effect of cigarette smoking. (35)

CONCLUSION

An overwhelming amount of recent scientific research has been done which underscores the harmful effects of marijuana, specifically, the impairing effects on the brain, the respiratory system, the immune system, and the reproductive process, as well as the adverse effects on babies born to animals and humans exposed to THC and marijuana smoke. Although some of the results relating to the hazardous effects of marijuana are reports from short-term animal studies or studies involving small numbers of subjects, the clear message of this research, when viewed in the aggregate, is that there is much reason for great concern about the health effects on human users. Marijuana is simply not the safe nor harmless drug that most people would like to believe. Primarily because its active drug ingredients are fat soluble and remain in the body longer than any of the so-called "hard drugs," the health consequences for permanent physiological damage of marijuana is just as great or even more substantial.

Accordingly, there is good scientific reason supporting congress' actions in grouping marijuana with other very serious and harmful drugs for purposes of the penalties which are imposed. The efforts of marijuana advocates to deny its harmful consequences has been relatively success-ful for far too long, and has mislead thousands of young people to experiment freely and thus expose themselves and their children to a wide-range of short term and long term harms. The United States asks the Court to take due account of the severe impact of marijuana utilization on human health and well-being. Since defendants herein profited in their marijuana trade, their respective punish-ments must adequately reflect the actual damage and poten-tial future harm to society that they have wrought.

SUMMARY

I am optimistic that, with your support and the support of Federal State and local law enforcement through out California we will reorganize, revitalize, and reunify the domestic Cannabis Eradication and Suppression Program in California. Significant progress has been made and will continue to be made in our effort to suppress the illicit pro-duction of marijuana in California. In Part II of this report I ask you to consider a three phase program rather then sole-ly the single phase manual eradication program now uti-lized. Thank you for this opportunity to discuss our activi-ties and for your assistance and support.

Charles A. Stowell
Senior Special Agent DEA Sacramento
California Statewide Domestic Cannabis Eradication and
Suppression Program Coordinator

REFERENCES

1. United States Department of Justice, Main Justice Statistics 1-800-732-3277
2. National Institute of Drug Abuse (NIDA), 1-80—662-4357
3. National Clearinghouse for Alcohol and Drug Information, 1-301-468-2600
4. Drugs and Crime Data Center and Clearinghouse, 1-800-666-3332
5. Drug Enforcement Administration, Statistical Information Office, 1-202-307-1000
6. Partnership for a Drug Free America, 1-212-922-1560
7. Drug Enforcement Administration, Cannabis Investigations Section, 1-202-307-8333
8. Drug Enforcement Administration, California Statewide DCESP Coordinator, 1-916-978-4225
9. United States Immigration and Naturalization Service, United States Customs, United States Coast Guard
10. The California Department of Agriculture
11. Camp Final Report 1990
12. Review of the Drug Law Enforcement Activities of the Forest Service and the Omnibus Publis Lands Act of 1987
13. Marijuana Cultivation on Public Lands and Federal Response by the 100 Cong. 1st sess. November 1987
14. Testimony before Congress on DEA Operations by for-mer DEA Administrator John Law dated 1982
15. Testimony before Congress on USFS Operations by Chief of the Forest Service Dale Robertson dated 1988
16. GAO/CED-82-48 Reported dated March 10, 1982, GAO/RCED-85-18 Reported dated November 1984
17. National Institute on Drug Abuse (NIDA)
18. The University of Texas
19. Psychiatry Letter, Clinical Diagnosis and Treatment of Post
20. Drug Impairment Syndrome (PDIS) dated 1988 Health Aspects of Cannabis, Pharmacological Review dated 1986
21. Veterans Administration Medical Center and Stanford University School of Medicine, Palo Alto, California Re: Acute and chronic effects of cannabis in humans dated 1986
22. Supplemental Sentencing Memorandum of the United States of America, RE: Health Effects of Marijuana dated 2/9/87 at the District of Hawaii.
23. The O.N.D.C.P. "A Comprehensive National Strategy" May 1988
24. IPAC Counternarcotics Series, Marijuana Cultivation, State of Hawaii March 1991

FOOTNOTE, DURING THE PREPARATION OF THIS REPORT, NUMEROUS DIRECT PASSAGES WERE TAKEN ALL OR IN PART FROM THE ABOVE LISTED REFERENCE DOCUMENTS.

U.S. DRUG SEIZURES
1990
(IN TON QUANTITIES)

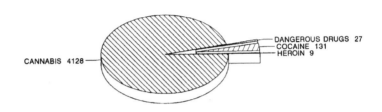

CANNABIS 4128

DANGEROUS DRUGS 27
COCAINE 131
HEROIN 9

GROSS $$ VALUES
CANNABIS VS AGRI-CROPS

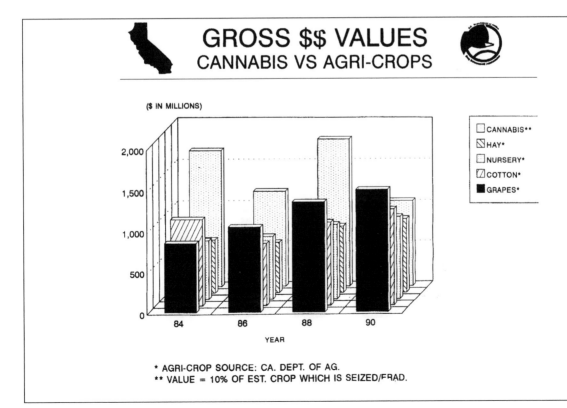

($ IN MILLIONS)

☐ CANNABIS**
◺ HAY*
☐ NURSERY*
▨ COTTON*
■ GRAPES*

YEAR

* AGRI-CROP SOURCE: CA. DEPT. OF AG.
** VALUE = 10% OF EST. CROP WHICH IS SEIZED/ERAD.

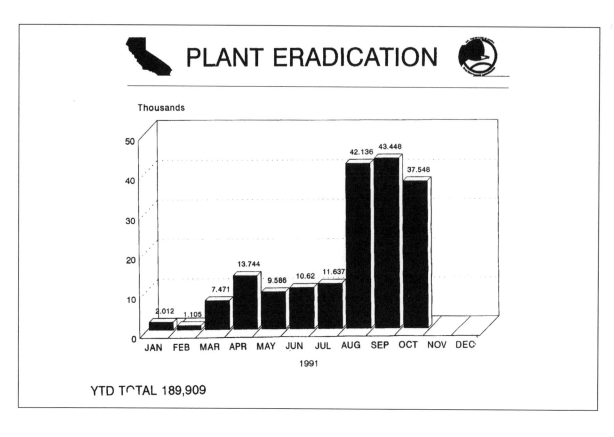

PLANT ERADICATION

Thousands

YTD TOTAL 189,909

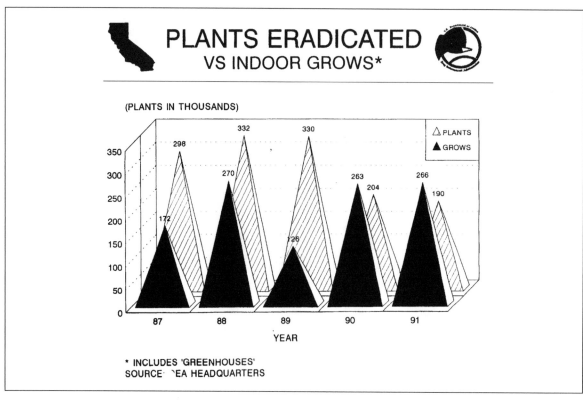

PLANTS ERADICATED
VS INDOOR GROWS*

(PLANTS IN THOUSANDS)

△ PLANTS
▲ GROWS

YEAR

* INCLUDES 'GREENHOUSES'
SOURCE: DEA HEADQUARTERS

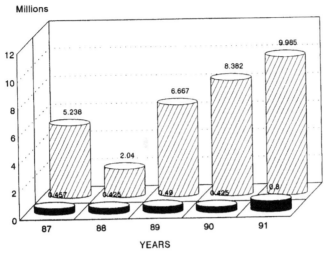

CANNABIS ASSET SEIZURES
VS DEA FUNDING LEVELS*

Millions

ASSETS
FUNDING

9.985
8.382
6.667
5.238
2.04

0.457 0.425 0.49 0.425 0.8

87   88   89   90   91

YEARS

* DIRECT FUNDS TO STATE & LOCAL

1991 DOMESTIC CANNABIS ERADICATION/SUPPRESSION PROGRAM STATISTICS

States	Eradicated Plots Outdoor	Cultivated Plants Outdoor	Sinsemilla* Plants Outdoor	Ditchweed Eradicated	Indoor Grows Seized	Indoor Plants	Total Plants Eradicated	Bulk-Processed Marijuana	Number of Arrests	Weapons Seizures	Arrests Seized (Value)
Alabama	2,284	163,294	40,884	0	20	1,600	164,894	5	122	13	$234,699
Alaska	0	21	21	0	98	6,583	6,604	39	71	21	$2,721,902
Arizona	50	4,839	1,554	8	11	1,544	6,391	3,847	67	40	$117,522
Arkansas	1,733	106,405	56,314	0	44	4,138	110,543	379	192	128	$1,134,484
California	1,089	181,829	151,529	80	303	45,562	197,141	2,651	966	687	$6,833,463
Colorado	58	13,211	11,811	17,022	53	9,888	40,121	107	105	16	$1,883,080
Connecticut	60	2,404	2,075	0	4	787	3,191	100	9	13	$88,430
Delaware	100	13,365	0	0	27	26	13,391	0	3	0	$500
Florida	2,023	92,190	10,140	0	156	12,147	104,337	474	661	99	$2,912,734
Georgia	1,411	300,583	238,186	0	12	1,763	302,346	3	153	60	$965,287
Hawaii	3,351	528,755	348,978	0	9	3,235	531,990	0	501	34	$1,675,707
Idaho	26	1,675	1,210	0	30	3,039	4,714	0	39	16	$195,042
Illinois	1,141	337,730	27,749	9,080,937	49	2,900	9,421,567	990	239	35	$1,118,830
Indiana	2,313	206,494	13,052	69,930,512	86	19,025	70,156,031	2,891	474	96	$1,339,668
Iowa	55	62,917	0	627,080	7	799	690,796	136	35	12	$42,080
Kansas	509	21,751	7,217	10,774,960	21	3,795	10,800,506	1,183	109	54	$1,361,269
Kentucky	8,380	809,366	728,339	8,000	58	6,722	824,088	0	439	141	$1,496,039
Louisiana	466	79,009	70	0	38	11,877	90,886	34	195	25	$377,267
Maine	382	20,794	2,388	0	65	3,648	24,442	49	163	82	$404,404
Maryland	608	11,210	2,631	0	13	803	12,013	15,696	108	74	$997,950
Mass.	313	9,185	9,088	296	122	3,336	12,817	0	305	143	$1,807,870
Michigan	2,131	50,871	8,646	2,325	62	3,053	56,249	396	125	99	$565,795
Minnesota	74	191,790	18,020	2,221,450	58	7,664	2,420,904	982	159	92	$1,170,900
Mississippi	683	72,947	7,290	0	8	846	73,793	112	77	23	$340,350

1991 DOMESTIC CANNABIS ERADICATION/SUPPRESSION PROGRAM STATISTICS (continued)

Missouri	1,163	1`04,693	49,074	13,012,323	34	2,003	13,119,019	4,814	436	126	$1,271,074
Montana	6	710	0	100	23	1,469	2,279	71	188	26	$1,431,782
Nebraska	11	2,960	10	9,299,298	47	2,130	9,304,388	219	142	12	$23,102
Nevada	10	365	365	0	20	2,159	2,524	106	44	28	$1,029,060
New Hamp.	94	2,418	322	1,101	24	623	4,142	0	67	29	$370,434
New Jersey	54	1,411	230	0	11	605	2,016	338	45	56	$256,000
New Mexico	50	4,208	1,660	0	39	1,132	5,340	41	93	78	$102,406
New York	201	11,693	7,316	0	41	3,314	15,007	247	114	85	$3,018,966
N. Carolina	4,048	198,470	20,294	0	26	18,188	216,658	0	244	64	$139,000
N. Dakota	4	23,020	0	3,480,000	6	324	3,503,344	0	10	1	$100
Ohio	961	56,684	16.972	0	156	7,355	64,039	153	271	296	$1,902,183
Oklahoma	1,464	790,623	13,985	4,845,429	41	2,175	5,638,227	117	143	63	$368,374
Oregon	609	16,311	12,714	0	415	36,227	52,538	267	648	1,225	$2,807,280
Pennsylvania	427	12,703	1,533	35	35	895	13,633	20	38	13	$132,550
Rhode Is.	26	1,113	0	0	7	448	1,561	0	13	9	$2,250
S. Carolina	961	22,801	0	0	32	1,600	24,401	300	162	23	$1,523,204
S. Dakota	99	56,508	85	3,676,431	9	270	3,733,209	50	22	1	$226,706
Tennessee	1,357	508,816	366,208	0	70	2,539	511,355	117	325	103	$1,198,775
Texas	96	22,997	13,540	608,559	17	2,738	634,294	59	25	26	$334,268
Utah	17	1,434	851	19	6	280	1,733	201	27	8	$41,420
Vermont	119	6,422	6,422	6,741	11	3,187	16,350	106	74	55	$86,880
Virginia	687	27,610	525	0	51	1,856	29,466	113	127	69	$63,315
Washington	120	5,751	5,751	0	262	30,104	35,855	266	416	290	$5,043,716
W. Virginia	398	47,229	41,244	227,352	12	2,078	276,659	563	96	29	$417,248
Wisconsin	464	78,076	5,442	5,964,331	100	3,446	6,045,853	759	266	112	$1,011,089
Wyoming	4	125	0	1,700	8	983	2,808	40	11	18	$244,021

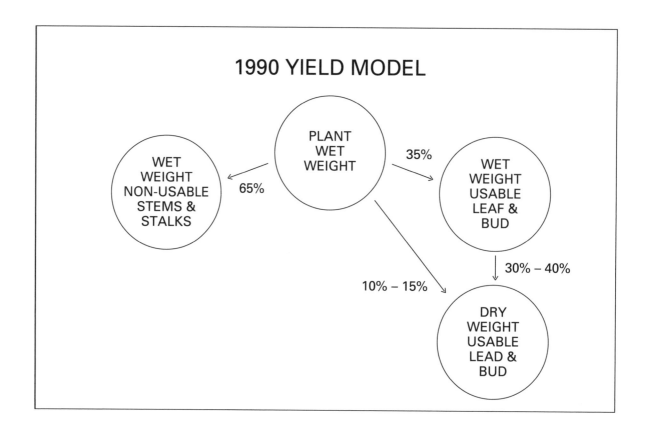

1990 YIELD MODEL

PLANT WET WEIGHT

WET WEIGHT NON-USABLE STEMS & STALKS — 65%

35% — WET WEIGHT USABLE LEAF & BUD

30% – 40% — DRY WEIGHT USABLE LEAD & BUD

10% – 15%

PRESENTLY

- Plant yield is 1.0 pound/plant
- Plant water is 50–60% of the fresh weight
- Planting density is 3x3 feet or 4840 plant/acre
- Smokeable leaf yield is 13% of the plant fresh weight, leaf material is air dry
- Upon drying the plant loses 90% of its water
- In 1989: 5.6 million plants weighing 2548 MT were eradicated, mean plant weight = 454.6 g

UNITS OF MEASURE

Weight:
    kilogram   = 2.2046 pounds
    pound   = 453.5924 grams
    ounce   = 28.349527 grams
    metric ton = 1000 kg
Distance:
    foot   = 0.3048 meter
    meter   = 3.281 feet
                = 39.34 inches

Area:
    acre   = 43560 square feet
    hectare   = 0.4047 acre

SOME CRITICAL POINTS

- Plant's composition of stems, leaves, flower buds and seed changes over the annual growth cycle
- Stems comprise 40% of the plant after 60 days
- Seeds comprise 24% of the plant at 126 days
- Plant yield is about 36% of the plant at 126 days
- A yield of pound/plant is not always a good estimate because of planting densities and plant age
- Plant weight varies inversely with planting density

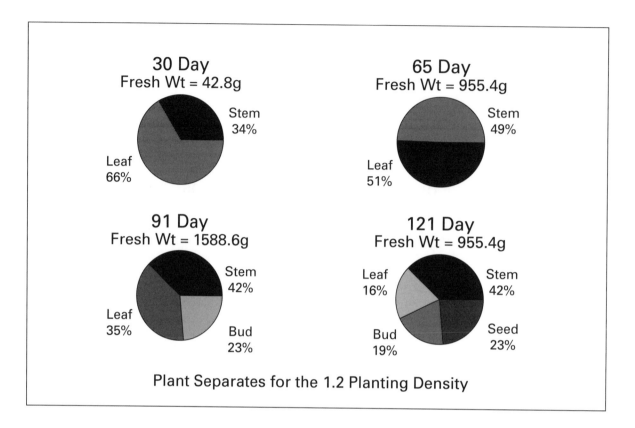

Plant Separates for the 1.2 Planting Density

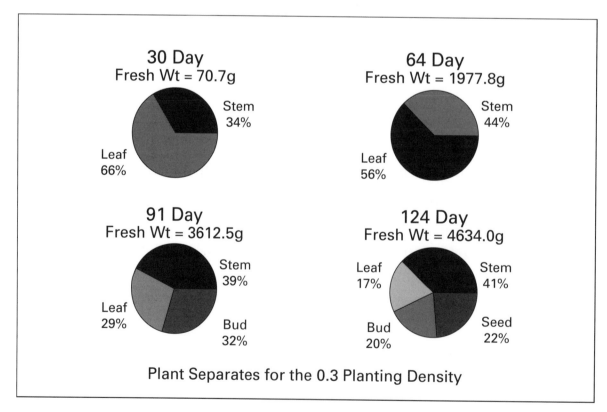

Plant Separates for the 0.3 Planting Density

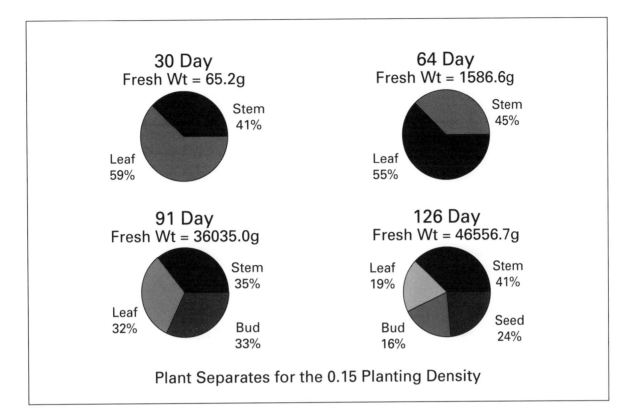

30 Day
Fresh Wt = 65.2g

Stem
41%

Leaf
59%

64 Day
Fresh Wt = 1586.6g

Stem
45%

Leaf
55%

91 Day
Fresh Wt = 36035.0g

Stem
35%

Leaf
32%

Bud
33%

126 Day
Fresh Wt = 46556.7g

Leaf
19%

Stem
41%

Bud
16%

Seed
24%

Plant Separates for the 0.15 Planting Density

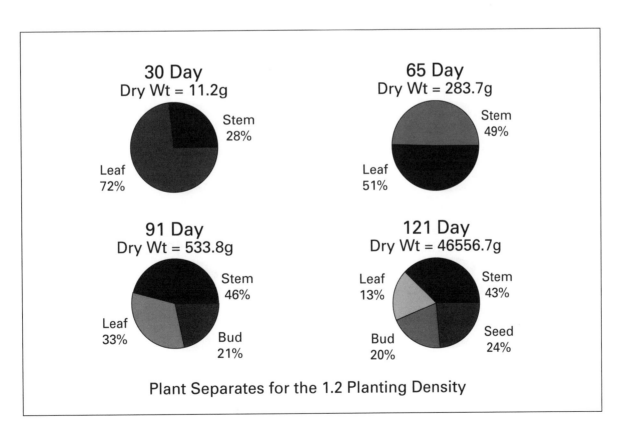

30 Day
Dry Wt = 11.2g

Stem
28%

Leaf
72%

65 Day
Dry Wt = 283.7g

Stem
49%

Leaf
51%

91 Day
Dry Wt = 533.8g

Stem
46%

Leaf
33%

Bud
21%

121 Day
Dry Wt = 46556.7g

Leaf
13%

Stem
43%

Bud
20%

Seed
24%

Plant Separates for the 1.2 Planting Density

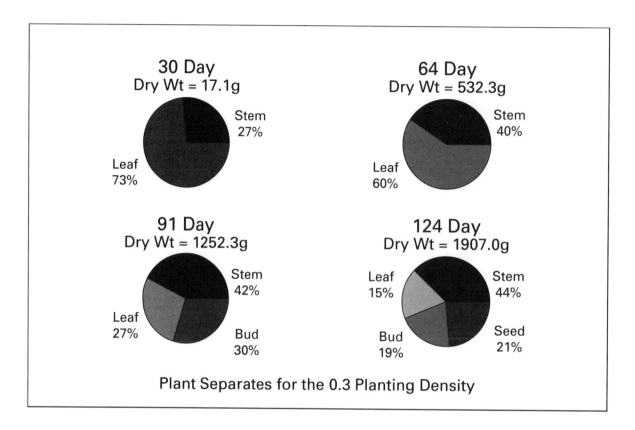

30 Day
Dry Wt = 17.1g
Stem 27%
Leaf 73%

64 Day
Dry Wt = 532.3g
Stem 40%
Leaf 60%

91 Day
Dry Wt = 1252.3g
Stem 42%
Leaf 27%
Bud 30%

124 Day
Dry Wt = 1907.0g
Leaf 15%
Stem 44%
Bud 19%
Seed 21%

Plant Separates for the 0.3 Planting Density

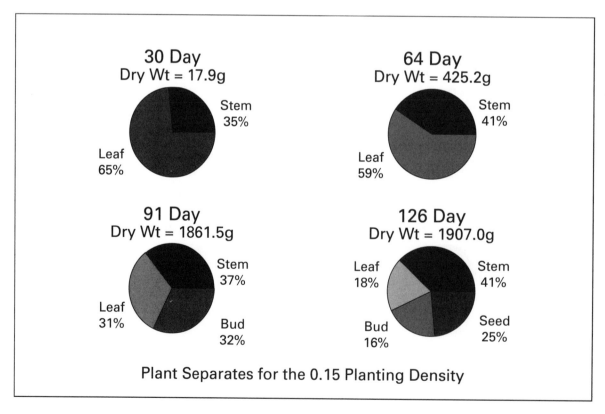

30 Day
Dry Wt = 17.9g
Stem 35%
Leaf 65%

64 Day
Dry Wt = 425.2g
Stem 41%
Leaf 59%

91 Day
Dry Wt = 1861.5g
Stem 37%
Leaf 31%
Bud 32%

126 Day
Dry Wt = 1907.0g
Leaf 18%
Stem 41%
Bud 16%
Seed 25%

Plant Separates for the 0.15 Planting Density

PROBLEM 1

Problem: Under what conditions would plant yield be one pound per plant?

Given: • Plant growth and the proportion of the plant separates vary over the annual growth cycle (Figures 17 and 18)

• 453.6 grams equal 1.0 pound

• Yield is the marketable leaves and flower buds

Assumptions:

• The plant yield is 63% of plant's dry weight (oven dry)

• Plant growth rate is a straight line average between two consecutive growth stages.

Solution:

Plant Dry Weight = 453.6g x (1/.63) = 720 grams

Growth Rate = $\frac{(\text{Plant OD Wt @ Day 2}) - (\text{Plant OD Wt @ Day 1})}{(\text{Growth Day 2}) - (\text{Growth Day 1})}$ = A g/day

Plant Age = Day 1 + $\frac{(720 - \text{Plant OD Wt Day 1})}{\text{Growth Rate g/day}}$

Plant age when yield is 435.6 g/plant for three planting densities.

Planting Density	Growth Rate (day 64-91)		Plant Age when yield = 453.6 g	
	O.D. g/day	A.D. g/day	O.D. days	A.D. days
1.20	9.6	10.6	NA	NA
0.30	26.7	29.3	75	70
0.15	53.2	58.5	70	69

NA—plant yield at 121 growth days is less than 453.6 g

* Plant age when yield is 435.6 g/plant will be younger if plant yield is calculated on an air dry basis.

Summary:

Plants will be those at moderate planting density and be at least 70 to 75 days old. Older plants will have h igher yields. Dense plantings will have lower yields per plant and will not achieve 453.6 g/plant before harvest.

ESTIMATED PLANT PRODUCTIVITIES
FOR THREE PLANTING DENSITIES

Density	Plants per Hectare	Plant Fresh Weight kg	Plant Dry Weight kg	**Field Production**	
				Fresh Weight kg/ha	Dry Weight kg/ha
1.20	11960	2.072	0.847	24782	10138
0.03	2990	5.675	2.429	16969	7264
0.15	1495	8.236	3.091	12313	4622

- Assumed 140 growth days; Regressions from Figures 15&16
- All weights require adjustment for seed and stem separates
- Plants/hectare x 2.471 = plants/acre
- Kg/hectare x 5.447 = pounds/acre

PREDICTIVE MODEL MAJOR INPUTS
I. Ancillary Data

A. Seizure Date: day, month, year

B. Location: country, state; latitude, longitude

C. Planting Pattern: scattered, rows, rectangle, etc.

D. Planting Density:

E. Plant Fresh Weight:

F. Plant Size: height, diameter

G. Photoperiod

PREDICTIVE MODEL: YIELD COMPUTATIONS
II. Yield Parameter Relationships

A. Growth Days: siezed records, height, diameter

B. Plant Fresh Weight: direct, height, diameter

C. Plant Dry Weight = 33.5% of Fresh Weight

D. Yield:

   Fresh Weight = % of Plant Fresh Weight
   = Plant Fresh Wt - Stem Fresh Wt

   Dry Weight = % of Plant Dry Weight
   = Plant Dry Wt - Stem Dry Wt

E. Yield Estimates

   Plants x Yield/Plant

   Plot Area x Plant/Subplot x Yield/Plant

OUTDOOR CANNABIS YIELD SURVEY

Your Name:_____

Your FTS Number: _____

State for which you are reporting:_____

1. Indicate the percent of outdoor cultivated plants eraticated in your state in September 1991 for each category. The categories are divided into 13 groups based upon plant diameter. The sum of the percentages for the 13 groups must equal 100%. Plant diamtere is defined as the broadest distance across the plant's canopy. Remember answer only for plants as they were observed during the month of September.

a. seedlings	_____	%
b. less than 6 inch diameter	_____	%
c. 6 inch to less than 1 foot diameter	_____	%
d. 1 foot to less than 2 feet diameter	_____	%
e. 2 feet to less than 3 feet diameter	_____	%
f. 3 feet to less than 4 feet diameter	_____	%
g. 4 feet to less than 5 feet diameter	_____	%
h. 5 feet to less than 6 feet diameter	_____	%
i. 6 feet to less than 7 feet diameter	_____	%
j. 7 feet to less than 8 feet diameter	_____	%
k. 8 feet to less than 9 feet diameter	_____	%
l. 9 feet to less than 10 feet diameter	_____	%
m. 10 feet diameter or greater	_____	%
Total =	_____	%

2. When are seeds or starter plants normally planted outdoors?
Indicate the month and day. _____

3. When does harvest usually begin?
Indicate the month and day _____

4. When is the harvest season usually completed?

_____
Indicate the month and day _____

TERMINOLOGY

- Plant Composition: Stems, leaves, flowers, seeds
- Plant Material: Assumed to be leaves and flower buds; no seeds or stems
- Dried Material: Air Dried contains 10% water
                   Oven Dried contains 0% water
- Yield: Total saleable material from the plant, i.e., leaves & flower buds; no seeds or stems
- Plant Weight: The weight of the entire plant either fresh (green) or dry (oven dry or air dry)

STUDY OBJECTIVE

Combined Data Sets – 1990 & 1991

Characterize plant parameter relationships for making productivity estimates

Develop a PC based, first generation model for making estimating plant yields from scant or robust data inputs

Notes

ENDNOTES FOR INTRODUCTION

1. U.S. v Michael L. Wyman and Nancy C. Hadley. U.S. District Court, District of Kansas, Topeka. Case # 94-40038-01/02-RDR.

ENDNOTES FOR CHAPTER 9

1. These are actual statements I've heard PEs make on the stand.
2. California v. James MacPhee, Orange County Superior Court, Case #C-82830 PC-1000 (diversion hearing).
3. California v. Todd Johnson, Woodlake Municipal Court, #4429, September 1988.
4. California v. Larry Foose, El Dorado Municipal Court, testimony of PE Officer Oscar Betts, December 17, 1991.
5. Ibid.
6. U.S. v. Rod and Cynthia Klein, District of South Dakota, CR 87-40005.

ENDNOTES FOR CHAPTER 10

1. For a comprehensive discussion of State Constitutional Law as it applies to these issues see the monthly column in The Champion, by John Henry Hingson. Hingson's scholarly and useful comprehensive monograph on the subject is available through the National Association of Criminal Defense Lawyers.
2. The Exclusionary Rule is the court-created rule of law that evidence which is gained through violation of an individual's rights is excluded from any judicial proceeding against that individual. In recent years judicially created exceptions to the rule — such as the "good faith" exception — have substantially reduced its effectiveness.
3. Dash, Criminal Justice in Crisis, (Special Committee on Criminal Justice in a Free Society of the American Bar Association Criminal Justice Section, November 1988).
4. For those who aren't lawyers, but want to read some of the original source material, the following outline will get you easily to the cases I have discussed. Reported decisions are identified by "citations", for example, "United States v. Mendonsa, 989 F.2d 366, (9th Cir. 3/30/93), No. 91-30413", as above, reveals the following information:

    "United States v. Mendonsa" is the title of the case. The first party listed is the "plaintiff", or the "petitioner", the party who initiated the case. Where the title starts out "U.S. v.", or "State/people" v., it's usually a criminal case.

    " X F.2d Y ."Is the "citation" or "cite." That tells you where in the library, or computer system, the case can be found. X is the volume number and Y is the page number. "F.2d" or whatever appears in the space between the two numbers is the Reporter name. The Reporter is the series of books, usually beginning with

volume 1, in which the written decisions of a particular court are reported in chronological order. "F.2d" is the abbreviation for "Federal Reporter, Second Series", the Reporter in which decisions of all United States Courts of Appeals are reported.

"(9th Cir." 1993)" is the court which decided the case, and the year in which it was decided.

Where the decision is too recent to be in a published book, the citation is left blank, except for the case number, for example, "No. 91-30413."

5. McDonald v. United States, 335 U.S. 451, 455-56, (1948).
6. Aguilar v. Texas, 378 U.S. 108 (1964), and Spinelli v. United States, 393 U.S. 410 (1969).
7. See, e.g., State v. Jones, 706 P.2d 317 (Alaska 1985) (relying on article 1, 14 of the state constitution); State v. Jackson, 688 P.2d 136 (Wash. 1984) (article 1, 9); State v. Horwedel, 674 P.2d 623 (Or.App. 1984) (Or. Rev. Stat. 133.545(3); Or. Const. article 1, 9); State v. Kanda, 620 P.2d 623 (Haw. 1980) (article 1, 7).
8. "The affiant" is the person, usually a police officer, who swears out the affidavit.
9. See, e.g., State v. Northness, 20 Wn.App. 551 (1978), (defining categories of informants).
10. State v. Bantum, 1 P.2d 861 (Wash. 1931).
11. State v. Chatmon, 515 P.2d 530 (Wash. 1973).
12. State v. Rodriguez, 769 P.2d 309 (Wash.App. 1989).
13. LaFave SEARCH AND SEIZURE (1987,) at 728. (Emphasis supplied).
14. 61 Wn. App. 699.
15. Jones v. United States, 266 F.2d 924, 928 (D.C. Cir. 1959).
16. Trott, The Successful Use of Snitches, Informants, Co-Conspirators, and Accomplices as Witnesses for the Prosecution in a Criminal Case 2, (United Sates Justice Department 1984).
17. United States v. Bernal-Obeso, 989 F.2d 331 (9th Cir. 3/29/93).
18. See also, Zeese, How Prosecutors Use Informants, 1 DRUG L. REP 130-31 (Sept.-Oct. 1984).
19. State v. Fisher, 639 P.2d 743 (Wash. 1982), but see, dissent.
20. State v. Casto, 692 P.2d 890 (Wash.App. 1984); State v. Steenerson, 688 P.2d 544 (Wash.App. 1984).
21. A statement against penal interest, State v. O'Connor, 692 P.2d 208 (Wash.App. 1984).
22. 1 W. LaFave, SEARCH AND SEIZURE, at 644.
23. State v. Bean, 572 P.2d 1102 (Wash. 1978); State v. Estorga, 893 P.2d 813 (Wash. 1991).
24. *State v. Sieler, 621 P.2d 1272 (Wash. 1980).*
25. Don't overlook this legitimate tactic, even in the face of strenuous opposition. Although many courts seem reluctant to allow this, common law in most states makes the search warrant process open to the public unless affidavits are specifically sealed. See, e.g.,

Cowles Publishing Co. v Murphy, 637 P.2d 966 (1981):

Although the informed public concept is generally associated with the legislative and executive branches, it is equally true of those involved in the judicial process. Access to search warrants and affidavits of probable cause can reveal how the judicial process is conducted. The procedures employed by the prosecutor and law enforcement can be evaluated. Access may also disclose whether the judge is acting as a neutral magistrate.

26. State v. Jackson, 102 Wn.2d 432, 439, 688 P.2d 136 (1984).

27. United States v. Canieso, 470 F.2d 1224, 1231 (2d Cir. 1972); Rebell, The Undisclosed Informant and the Fourth Amendment: A Search for Meaningful Standards, 81 Yale L.J. 703, 716 (1972).

28. See, e.g., United States v. Montgomery, 554 F.2d: 754, 757-58 (5th Cir. 1977); Spinelli, at 414; 1 W. LaFave SS 3.3(f); Rebell, at 715-20; Kamisar, Gates, "Probable Cause," "Good Faith," and Beyond, 69 Iowa L. Rev. 551, 558-66 (1984).

29. The Informer's Tip as Probable Cause for Search or Arrest, 54 Cornell L. Rev. 958, 967 (1969); Kamisar, at 567.

30. See, e.g., State v. McPherson, 698 P.2d 563 (Wash.App. 1984). Compare, State v. Donahue, 762 P.2d 1022 (Or.App. 1988).

31. Wash.Rev.Code 42.17.314 (codifying In re Rosier, 717 P.2d 1353 (Wash. 1986); State v. Maxwell, 791 P.2d 332 (Wash. 1990), (applying the statutory protection to the search warrant process, while refusing to rule on the constitutional issue) State v. Butterworth, 737 P.2d 1297 (Wash. 1987) (specifically declining to rule on the Constitutional issue).

32. See, Hearst Corp. v. Hoppe, 580 P.2d 246 (Wash. 1978).

33. 580 P.2d at 253, quoting, Restatement (Second) of Torts, 652 D at 383 (1977).

34. Affirmed on other grounds, 984 F.2d 1053, (9th Cir. 1993).

35. A copy of the opinion is available at the home office of the NACDL.

36. The Washington Supreme Court has now addressed this subject, ruling that the use of the device does constitute a search, and must be preceded by judicial approval. *State v. Young, 123 Wn.2d 173 (1994)*. The court's ruling is delightful:

The infrared device invaded the home in the sense the device was able to gather information about the interior of the defendant's home that could not be obtained by naked eye observations. Without the infrared device, the only way the police could have acquired the same information was to go inside the home. Just because technology now allows this information to be gained without stepping inside the physi-

cal structure, it does not mean the home has not been invaded for the purposes of Const. art.1, SS 7.

Merely because it is generally known that the technology exists to enable police to view private activities from an otherwise nonintrusive vantage point, it does not follow that these activities are without protection.

Interestingly, the court based its decision on state constitutional law, but went on to rule that the use of the device also violates the Fourth Amendment.

37. Karo, 82 L.Ed.2d 540.

38. Karo, 82 L.Ed.2d 541-43.

39. Ciraolo, 476 U.S. at 217.

40. Katz v. United States 389 U.S. 347, 361-362, 19 L.Ed.2d 576, 88 S.Ct 507

41. Ciraolo, 90 L.Ed.2d at 218, n. 3.

42. Steele, Lisa J., Waste Heat and Garbage: The legalization of Warrantless Infrared Searches, 29 Criminal Law Bulletin 19 (1992).

43. 1 LaFave, SEARCH AND SEIZURE, at 342-343.

44. State v. Compton, 538 P.2d 861 (Wash. App. 1975).

45. State v. Remboldt, 64 Wn.App. 505, ___ P.2d ___ (1992), review denied ___ Wn.2d ___.

46. Oliver v. United States, 466 U.S. 170, 80 L.Ed.2d 214, 104 S.Ct. 1735 (1984).

47. Oliver, 466 US at 177, 80 L.Ed.2d at 222/223 (emphasis added).

48. Oliver, 466 US at 178, 80 L.Ed.2d at 224 (emphasis added).

49. 480 US at 301, 94 L.Ed.2d 335.

50. United States v. Magana, 512 F.2d 1169 (9th Cir. 1975) cited in 1 LaFave, SEARCH AND SEIZURE, at 416.

51. LaFave, supra, at 416 (footnotes omitted).

52. 931 F.2d 1481, n.2.

53. Boyd v. United States, 116 US 616, 630, 6 S.Ct. 524, 532, 29 L.Ed. 746 (1886); United States v. Shaibu, 895 F.2d 1291, 1293 (9th Cir. 1990); United States v. Winsor, 846 F.2d 1569, 1574 (9th Cir. 1988).

54. Kaiser Aetna v. United States, 444 U.S. 164, 179-80, 62 L.Ed. 2d 332, 100 S.Ct. 383 (1979).

55. State v. Dixon, 766 P.2d 1015 (Or. 1988).

56. State v. Barnett, 703 P.2d 680 (Hawaii 1985).

57. State v. Myrick, 688 P.2d 151 (Wash. 1984).

58. State v. Perry, 25 Wn.App. 621, 612 P.2d 4 (1980); State v. Seagull, 95 Wn.2d 898, 632 P.2d 44 (1981).

59. See, e.g., State v. Crandall, 697 P.2d 250 (Wash.App. 1985) (because hunters regularly frequented the property); State v. Hansen, 714 P.2d (Wash.App. 1986) (fields were "clearly visible to both [the defendant's] neighbors, and to any passerby."

60. State v. Seagull, 632 P.2d 44 (Wash. 1981).

61. Wheeler v. State, 659 S.W.2d 381, 390-91 (Tex. Crim. App. 1983).

62. McCabe & Schlim, Concept and Applicability of "Knock and Talk".

63. Schneckloth v. Bustamonte.

64. LaFave, SEARCH AND SEIZURE, Sec. 8.2 (a)-(k). No one factor is determinative of the issue.

65. State v. Smith, 789, 801 P.2d 975 (Wash. 1990).

66. 713 F.Supp at 1156 n.8.

67. 514 F.2d at 559-561.

68. Talkington, 843 F.2d at 1049.

69. Bumper v. North Carolina, supra. State v. Browning, 67 Wn.App. 93, ___ P.2d ____ (1992).

70. United States v. Shaibu, 895 F.2d 1291, 1293 (9th Cir. 1990).

71. Cf., Los Angeles Police Department v. Yates, 907 F.2d 879 (9th Cir. 1990):

   Nowhere is the protective force of the Fourth Amendment more powerful than it is when the sanctity of the home is involved.... The sanctity of a person's home, perhaps our last real retreat in this technological age, lies at the very core of the rights which animate the amendment.

72. Shaibu, at 895 F.2d 1294.

73. California v. Greenwood, 486 US 35, 100 L.Ed.2d 30, 108 S.Ct. 1625 (1988).

74. See also, United States v. Upton, 763 F.Supp 232 (1991).

75. Italics provided. This commendable rule has not survived. Even an intentional lie will not result in suppression if it is not necessary to probable cause.

76. Grano, A Dilemma for Defense Counsel: Spinelli-Harris Search Warrants and the Possibility of Police Perjury, 1971 U. Ill. L.F.

77. 1 LaFave SEARCH AND SEIZURE at 704.

78. Dash, Criminal Justice in Crisis, (Special Committee on Criminal Justice in a Free Society of the American Bar Association Criminal Justice Section, November 1988).

79. Id., 98 S.Ct. at 2676-77.

80. United States v. Martin, 615 F.2d 318 (5th Cir. 1980); United States v. Park, 531 F.2d 754, 758-59 (5th Cir. 1976).

81. Cord, at 103 Wn.2d 368.

82. State v. Thetford, 109 Wn.2d 392, 745 P.2d 496, (1987).

83. United States v. DeLeon, 979 F.2d 761, (9th Cir. 1992).

84. United States v. Colkley, 899 F.2d 297, (4th Cir. 1990).

85. Franks, at 438 U.S. 155-56, 171.

86. See Franks v. Delaware, 438 U.S. 154, 156, 57 L.Ed.2d 667, 98 S.Ct. 2674 (1978).

87. LaFave, SEARCH AND SEIZURE (1987), at p. 45-46 of 1993 pocket part.

88. Note here that at the hearing, the government may present evidence to counter the defendant's evidence, and this presentation may include facts not contained in the affidavit but which support the conclusion that the facts ailed in the affidavit are true. This is not contrary to the rule that a facially insufficient affidavit may not be supplemented by facts not presented to the magistrate. See 2 LA FAVE at 202.

89. State v. Cord, at 103 Wn.2d 372. See, also, United States v. Namer, 680 F.2d 1088, 1094 (5th Cir. 1982).

90. United States v. Williams, 737 F.2d 594 (7th Cir. 1984).

91. United States v. Davis, 617 F.2d 677 (D.C. Cir. 1979), cert. denied, 445 U.S. 967 (1980).

92. State v. O'Connor, 39 Wn.App. 113, 118, 692 P.2d 208 (1984).

93. State v. Jackson, 102 Wn.2d 432, 688 P.2d 136 (1984).

94. Franks v. Delaware, 438 U.S. 154, 156, 57 L.Ed.2d 667, 98 S.Ct. 2674 (1978)

95. See United States v. Reivich, 793 F.2d 957 (8th Cir. 1986).

96. Reivich, at 962. See, Colkley, at 301

97. 118 Wn.2d at 875.

98. United States v. DeLeon, an otherwise wonderful case, without discussion or citation, appears to embrace the following standard:

   We find that if the omitted information had been included in the application for the search warrant, *no reasonable person could have found probable cause to issue the warrant.* 979 F.2d at 764. (Emphasis supplied).

99. State v. Buccini, 810 P.2d 178 (Arizona Supreme Court, En Banc, 1991).

100. 810 P.2d at 183

101. See, 2 LA FAVE, SEARCH AND SEIZURE 4.4 at 199 (2d ed. 1987) (quoting United States v. Ventresca, 380 U.S. 102, 85 S.Ct. 741, 13 L.Ed.2d 684 (1965)).

102. See Franks, 438 U.S. at 168-169.

103. 810 P.2d at 186.

104. 2 LA FAVE, SEARCH & SEIZURE (2d ed. 1987) at 187.

105. 2 LA FAVE at 188.

106. United States v. DeLeon, at 979 F.2d 763.

107. State v. Toney, 60 Wn.App. 804, 810 P.2d 929, *review denied* 117 Wn.2d 1003 (1991).

108. State v. Estorga, 60 Wn.App. 298, 304 n. 3, 803 P.2d 813, *review denied* 116 Wn.2d 1027 (1991).

109. In fact such an invitation was extended in Cord:

   Acceptance of appellant's argument would require us to incorporate the California test into Const. art. 1, 7. Appellant has not offered any argument in support of this nor did he appear to recognize it as an issue. Therefore, we do not consider it here.

   Cord, at 103 Wn.2d 368-369.

110. Wong Sun v. United States, 371 U.S. 471, 484-85, 9 L.Ed.2d 441, 83 S.Ct. 407 (1963); Silverthorne Lumber Co. v. United States, 251 U.S. 385, 392, 64 L.Ed. 319, 40 S.Ct. 182 (1920); State v. Maxwell, 114 Wn.2d 761, 769, 791 P.2d 223 (1990).

111. See State v. Petty, 48 Wn.App. 615 (1987).

112. Chief Justice Williams, dissenting in State v. Cord, at 103 Wn.2d 88 - 89.

ENDNOTES TO CHAPTER 13

1. Examples include a prosecutor, law enforcement officer, county or municipal employee, or private person acting in concert with one of these individuals.

2. 403 U.S. 388 (1971).

3. For purposes of discussion, Section 1983 actions and Bivens actions shall be referred to collectively as "1983/Bivens" actions except where distinctions are made.

4. 185 Ga. App. 774, 365 S.E. 2d 889 (1988); see note 51 infra.

5. See Reeves v. Udolf, No. C85-116G (N.D. Ga. 1987) (unpublished opinion)

6. See Reeves v. Udolf, No. 88-8232 (11th Cir. 1988) (appeal withdrawn)

7. See Kelleher v. Udolf, No. C85-122G (N.D. Ga. 1988).

8. See Kelleher v. State, 185 Ga. App. 774, 365 S.E. 2d 889 (1988).

9. See G. Beaver, Police Brutality: A Call to Arms, The Champion, at 18 (July 1991).

10. See Northeast Georgia Radiological Assoc. P.C. v. Tidwell, 670 F.2d 507 (5th Firc. 1982) (Unit B).

11. 403 U.S. 388 (1971).

12. A state itself or individuals named in their official capacity as state officials (as opposed to their individual capacity) cannot be named as parties in a 1983 action except when injunctive relief is sought. See Will v. Michigan Dept. of State Police, 491 U.S. 58 (1989).

13. See Brouer v. County of Inyo, _____ U.S. _____, 109 S. Ct. 1378 (1989).

14. See Graham v. Connor, 490 U.S. 386 (1989).

15. See Goodwin v. Metts, 885 F.2d 157 (4th Cir. 1989).

16. See Paul v. Davis, 424 U.S. 693 (1976).

17. See Kelleher v. Udolf, No. C85-122G (N.D. Ga. 1895).

18. See U.S. Const. Amend VII; Stack v. Boyle, 342 U.S. 1 (1951); Reeves v. Udolf, N. C85-116G (N.D. Ga. 1987) (unpublished opinion).

24. Because of the doctrine of absolute immunity from state common law claims, pendent claims generally are not actionable against federal actors who act within the scope of their authority. See Westfall v. Erwin, _____ U.S. _____, 108 S. Ct. 580 (1988); Barr v. Matteo, 360 U.S. 564 (1959).

19. See Zinerman v. Burch, _____ U.S. _____, 110 S. Ct. 975 (1990) Hudson v. Palmer, 468 U.S. 327 (1984) Parratt v. Taylor, 451 U.S. 527 (1981).

20. See Byrd v. Stewart, 803 F.2d 1168 (11th Cir. 1986).

22. See Davidson v. Cannon, 474 U.S. 344 (1986); Daniels v. Williams, 474 U.S. 327 (1986).

23. See Chrisco v. Shafran, 507 F. Supp. 1312 (D. Del. 1981).

24. See Briscoe v. LaHue, 460 U.S. 325 (1983); Strength v. Hubert, 854 F.2d 421 (11th Cir. 1988).

25. See Smith v. Wade, 461 U.S. 30 (1983).

26. See 42 U.S.C. 1988 (1982).

27. See Wilson v. Garcia, 471 U.S. 261 (1985).

28. See Patsy v. Board of Regents, 457 U.S. 496 (1982).

29. See Carlson v. Green, 446 U.S. 14 (1980); see also McCarthy v. Madison, _____ U.S. _____, 112 S. Ct. 1081 (A92) Schweiker v. Chucky, _____ U.S. _____,

108 S. Ct. 2460 (1988). In addition to Bivens action, an action under the Federal Tort Claims Act may be available against federal actors. See 28 U.S.C. 2680(h) (1991). In a FTCA action, notice must be given to the Government six months before suit is filed. Id. 2675. Additionally, punitive damages are not available in an FTCA action, nor is the right to a jury trial. Id. 2402, 2674. The statute of limitations for such an action is two years. Id. 2401(b).

30. See Haring v. Prosise, 462 U.S. 306 (1983); Allen v. McCurry, 449 U.S. 90 (1980).

31. See Fred R. Civ. P. 11:28 U.S.C. 1927 (1991); Pavelic & Leflore v. Marvel Entertainment Group, _____ U.S. _____, 110 S. Ct. 458 (1989).

32. 914 F.2d 505 (4th Cir. 1990).

33. See Stump v. Sparkman, 435 U.S. 349 (1978).

34. See Burns v. Reed, _____ U.S. _____, 111 S. Ct. 1934 (1991); Imbler v. Pachtman, 424 U.S. 409 (1976).

35. See Harlow v. Fitzgerald, 457 U.S. 800 (1982); see also G. Beaver, note 9 supra, at 19-20.

36. See Jeff v. Dallas Indep. School Dist., _____ U.S. _____, 109 S. Ct. 2702 (1989); Monell v. Dept. of Social Services, 436 U.S. 658 (1978).

37. See e.g. O.C.G.A. 15-16-24 (Michie 1990) (sheriff is vicariously liable for actions of jailers).

38. Rule 26 provides for the discovery of "any matter, not privileged, which is relevant to the subject matter involved in the pending action." Rule 26 also provides that any information is discoverable if it "appears reasonably calculated to lead to the discovery of admissible evidence."

39. See Landis v. North American Co., 299 U.S. 248 (1936); Campbell v. Eastland, 307 F.2d 478 (5th Cir. 1962).

40. See Webling v. Columbia Broadcasting System, 608 F.2d 1084 (5th Cir. 1979); Campbell v. Gerrans, 592 F.2d 1054 (9th Cir. 1979).

41. See Baster v. Palmigiano, 427 U.S. 308 (1976).

42. 127 F.R.D. 466 (W.D.N.C. 1989).

43. See N.C. Gen. Stat. 8-56 (Michie 1988).

44. See F.R.E. 501.

45. See Walker, 127 F.R.D. at 468-70.

46. Id.

47. See Frankenhouser v. Rizzo, 59 F.R.D. 339 (E.D. Pa. 1973).

48. See Ganger v. Payton, 370 F.2d 709 (4th Cir. 1967); Sinclair v. State, 278 Md. 243, 363 A.2d 468 (1976); Scott v. State, 53 Ga. App. 61, 185 S.E. 131 (1936); Nichols v. State, 17 Ga. App. 593, 87 S.E. 817 (1915); of. Penney v. State, 157 Ga. App. 737, 278 S.E. 2d 460 (1981) (mere filing of a lawsuit against a judge does not disqualify him from handling the civil plaintiff's criminal case).

49. A prosecutor may, however, predicate the dismissal of a criminal action upon a release of other from civil liability. See Town of Newton v. Rumery, _____ U.S. — —, 107 S. Ct. 1187 (1987).

50. See note 48 supra.

51. Counsel in Kelleher and Reeves were Bobby Lee Cook, Sr., James Wyatt, Norman Johnson, Billy Spruell and Howard Machel.

ENDNOTES FOR CHAPTER 14

1. Reference is to the Federal Rule of Evidence since many state rules parallel the Federal Rules. See e.g. Durflinger v. Artiles, 727 F.2d 888 (10th Cir. 1984).

2. Slakan v. Porter, 737 F.2d 368 (4th Cir. 1984) (court, in affirming judgment for the inmate against a prison guard, found no error in admission of video tapes showing a hose spraying water. Tape demonstrated injury prisoner could have suffered from water hose.)

3. Sprynczynatyx v. General Motors, 771 F.2d 1112 (8th Cir. 1985) (court cautioned that a tape admitted without a limiting instruction might be hearsay if offered to prove the truth of the matter asserted). Compare, United States v. Weisz, 718 F.2d 413 (D.C. Cir. 1983), cert. denied 104 S.Ct. 1285 (1984) (video tape made contemporaneously with the events is not a reenactment and is admissible without a limiting instruction).

4. See e.g. United States v. Strissel (C.A. 4, No. 89-5534 12/17/90) (48 CrL. 1282).

5. Hale v. Firestone Tire, 756 F.2d 1322 (8th Cir. 1985).

6. If you have pinned down the cop in a preliminary or bail hearing, use that transcript.

7. Grimes v. Employer's Mutual Liability Insurance Company, 73 F.R.D. 607 (D.C. Alaska 1977).

8. See e.g., United States v. Mojica, 746 F.2d 242 (5th Cir. 1984).

9. See also, Louis Vuitton v. Spencer Handbags, 765 F.2d 966 (2d Cir. 1985); People v. Heading, 39 Mich. App. 126, 197 N.W. 2d 325, 328-29 (1972).

10. See, Federal Rules of Evidence 803(6) which allows the records as an exception to the hearsay rule.

11. See e.g., United States v. Hathaway, 798 F.2d 902 (6th Cir. 1986).

12. See, Anderson v. United States, 417 U.S. 211 (1974).

13. See, Federal Rule of Evidence 901(1).

14. See Federal Rule of Evidence 902(2).

For Further Research

1. Melvin Belli's, *Demonstrative Evidence*, 10 Wy. L.J. 15

2. Dombroff's *Innovative Developments In Demonstrative Evidence*, Arizona Law Journal, 1979

3. *Jones on Evidence*, 6th Ed.

4. *McCormick On Evidence*, Lawyers 3rd Ed., Title 8, Chapter 21.

5. *Ivey v. State*, 3 A.L.R. 4th, 367 (Alabama) (courtroom re-enactments of the crime).

6. *Lawson v. Belt*, R.C.O. 339 N.E. 2d 381 (Illinois) (Charts, drawings and diagrams are allowed if they help illustrate or explain testimony or help the jury better apply testimony).

7. *State v. Campbell*, 22 A.L.R. 3rd 824 (Montana) (Photographs are allowed in criminal cases to explain or help the jury apply testimony).

8. *Zelber v. Winters*, 712 P. 2d 525 (Idaho) (video re-enactments are admissible to accompany the testimony of an expert who is recreating the event).

ENDNOTES FOR CHAPTER 15

1. For those who have difficulty locating counsel familiar with this complex area, one excellent resource is F.E.A.R. A non profit organization whose initials stand for Forfeiture Endangers American Rights, this group maintains a list of attorneys who understand forfeiture laws. F.E.A.R. can be contacted at F.E.A.R. Foundation, 265 Miller Avenue, Mill Valley, CA 94941 (415) 388-8128.

2. I realize that my repeated urgings to "get a lawyer" may seem self-serving. That's not my purpose here. As unpopular as we have become in today's media, we are essential to the protection of citizen's rights in this difficult area. If you don't have knowledgeable counsel the government will mindlessly roll over you without even noticing the bump.

3. U.S. v Oaks, 872 F. UP 817 – E.D. Wash. 1994.